Becoming the 0.1%

Gareth Timmins is a former Royal Marines Commando who has spent time in Iraq, Somalia, Egypt and Afghanistan. Since leaving Afghanistan, he has worked for several ultra-high net-worth individuals in London, whilst providing a physical security and business development consultancy to blue-chip companies in the City of London.

Gareth completed his studies in Psychology after six years gaining a Diploma of Higher Education in Psychology and a BSc (Hons) in Forensic Psychology.

In more recent years, he founded Nought Point One (Projects) – a quintessentially British fitness and adventure brand specialising in distinctive outerwear and essential tools, and inspired by the Royal Marines' high standard of excellence and performance.

Becoming the 0.1%

34 Lessons from the Diary of a
Royal Marines Commando Recruit

GARETH TIMMINS

HODDER

First published in Great Britain in 2021 by Hodder & Stoughton
An Hachette UK company

This paperback edition published in 2022

1

A CIP catalogue record for this title is available from the British Library

Paperback ISBN 9781529363531
Hardback ISBN 9781529363500
eBook ISBN 9781529363517

Typeset in Sabon MT by Palimpsest Book Production Limited,
Falkirk, Stirlingshire

Printed and bound in Great Britain by Clays Ltd, Elcograf S.p.A.

Hodder & Stoughton policy is to use papers that are natural, renewable
and recyclable products and made from wood grown in sustainable forests.
The logging and manufacturing processes are expected to conform to
the environmental regulations of the country of origin.

Hodder & Stoughton Ltd
Carmelite House
50 Victoria Embankment
London EC4Y 0DZ

www.hodder.co.uk

*Dedicated to and in loving memory of
Tom Curry, Ben Whatley, and Ben Reddy.*

*By perseverance, study, and eternal desire,
any man [& woman] can become great*
– General George S. Patton

CONTENTS

INTRODUCTION

For the creation of this diary, I have to thank my mum. Shortly before the train doors closed ready for my departure to Commando Training Centre Royal Marines (CTC/CTCRM), she handed me a diary that she had purchased at the station shop, and her departing words were, 'Write things down, anything. I want to read what you've been doing, and when times get hard, it will hopefully help you cope.' For the next nine months, I wrote in the diary often two or three times every day, until I was finally handed my Green Beret and became a Royal Marines Commando.

After that, I put the diary away, but as the years passed by, it became increasingly apparent that I had an underlying duty to finish what I started in 2005 – to bring the diary and its contents to life; allowing others to read exactly what it took, and still takes, to achieve the coveted Green Beret.

I knew I needed a strong title for this book that not only documented a journey towards something significant, but one that also linked to Royal Marines training. After weeks of deliberation, I recalled arguably the best Royal Marines advert ever: '99.9% Need Not Apply'. That was an actual statistic back in 2003, representing the odds of success from walking into a recruiting office to reaching the end of training and getting a Green Beret – only 0.1% (1/1000) made it through the process from start to finish. Hence the title: *Becoming the 0.1%*.

I discovered that most, if not all, previous literature about Commando training had in some way embellished the accounts, based loosely on faulty memories or by constructing events based on others' recollections, making both depictions somewhat inaccurate. Moreover, contemporary television documentaries about life as a Royal Marines recruit have consistently failed to portray the true existence and incredible hardship that recruits endure while residing at Commando Training Centre Royal Marines (CTCRM), Lympstone. Therefore, I felt a responsibility to get my first-hand account out there.

I wanted to offer not only the raw and intricate insights into life at Lympstone, but a fundamental recipe manual for success, which can be used by the reader to achieve any of life's challenges.

I have recently completed a period of study in Forensic Psychology, a fascination and line of enquiry that was sparked by a need to understand my younger self; why I was attracted to the Royal Marines, and why I was so willing and eager to experience war.

Although my studies transcended to a more general under-standing of psychology as I matured throughout the six years of university, I am still fascinated by our (human beings') inability to live in relative harmony and our almost irresistible, arguably predisposed urge to commit unimaginable acts of violence on one another. I hope to merge my experience in the military and security risk management sectors with behav-ioural/cognitive science research and theory to explore and deconstruct human behaviour and decision-making.

In doing so, I plan to investigate the effects of social isola-tion on cultural groups living on the fringes of Western societies and how, in extreme cases, such inequalities lead to radicalisation and terrorism – thus exploring various new methods of counter-radicalisation. I also intend to explore behavioural change in relation to climate attitudes, public engagement, and global sustainability.

I believe that my personal experiences will allow me to bring new approaches and dimensions to contemporary research.

I struggled at school and required assistance at reading in specially funded and dedicated reading units. I almost certainly had undiagnosed ADHD, which severely hampered my ability to focus and absorb academic material. Consequently, I left high school with only one GCSE – in Religious Education (RE), of all things – the irony being that I am a complete atheist. The point is that my journey towards writing this book has been littered with adversity – a journey fuelled by a nagging urge to get better, to reach a point of satisfaction and in some respects, peace. I am no different to anyone else, nor have I found what I am searching for. The fundamental question is . . . do we ever?

By reading and exploring this account, I sincerely hope this book will both provide you with the inspiration to make positive changes, and enable you to find the tools that will create the opportunities and future you desire. I want to demonstrate how much can be achieved when faced with significant, life-changing disappointment, stark realisation and uncertainty, coupled with a desperate need to establish one's identity and purpose.

All these insights and lessons require constant investment, practice, and application – much like the dedication required to maintain and enhance a competition-level state of strength and conditioning. The mind is no different, and despite my emerging understanding of psychology over the past seven years, I continue to struggle with my own mental health.

This is an account for all, and one that I hope makes an enduring, positive impression on your journey through adversity, growth, and transformation.

Gareth Timmins, 2021

1

MY EARLY YEARS

I grew up surrounded by rugby league. My dad was an ex-professional player and by the time I was born, he was the strength and conditioning coach at Castleford Tigers RLFC – a top-flight team who competed in a league equivalent to football's English Premiership. My mum and I would attend all the home games, and over the years I found myself surrounded by dedicated, full-time athletes, some of whom had achieved everything possible in the game.

It was an environment that encapsulated the alpha male, and the rugby players often cultivated their stereotypical image with extreme language, vulgarity, and at times ridiculous, foolish behaviour. Yet such a bond off the field allowed them to maintain the integrity of professionalism on the field.

I believe exposure to such an intense, professional environment embedded a belief system within me that forged an internal drive and a relentless desire to be successful, coupled with a striving to win my father's admiration. My dad was a difficult man to please and my attempts were often met with criticism. He always spoke to me as if I was an adult, in a raw and very direct fashion, the same way that he and the other players spoke to one another.

Although my parents served in the military – my dad was a Royal Navy Physical Training Instructor (PTI) and diver, and my mum a Royal Navy Wren, I never gave the military a single thought.

Rugby was my calling. When I played my first game at eight years old, I visualised being an elite athlete every day without fail and would constantly strive for that elusive edge of perfection as I matured with age. Soon I had developed an obsessive relationship with rugby that was arguably underpinned by OCD. I played and trained hard to master the game and become the absolute best in my position. This personal campaign eventually got me selected for Wakefield District and Yorkshire Under 16s.

Being selected gave me a new drive. I would undertake extra training on the field with my dad to become better than my adversaries, and I would not leave the street or go in the house until I had hit the lamp-post on the opposite side of the road ten consecutive times with both left and right lateral passes. Once I found acknowledgement in rugby league, I was focused, determined, and unrelenting in my need to succeed.

After my time with Yorkshire, I went to play for Hunslet Hawks – a professional first division club in South Leeds. It was here I played my best rugby and had the time of my life. By this stage, my skills were outstanding and I couldn't get enough of training. At the age of sixteen, I would do the academy training session, stay back and train with the Under 21s, then try to get something in with the first team – if I was allowed by the coaching staff.

Although I loved it at Hunslet, it wasn't enough; I wanted to be the best and have my name on the back of a shirt in the Super League. So I went for a trial at Bradford Bulls, who were then an unstoppable force; but my experience at Bradford did not go to plan and I was handed my first significant taste of rejection in life. I felt like a burden there, rather than an asset, and I left the club due to a lack of a strong physical presence and, with all honesty, the killer speed required to play at Super League level.

My final shot came at Leeds Rhinos, probably the best club in rugby league during that era, with an academy and youth development system that was arguably the best in the world. Our academy team had the likes of Danny McGuire, Ryan Bailey and Chev Walker, and had won the Championship for five consecutive years. It was an academy of future Super League greats.

I played in the academy under David Plange, who had come to Leeds as the academy head coach from Hunslet Hawks. Dave was a tough man and a very strict authoritarian, and I went from idolising him at Hunslet to not liking him one bit at Leeds. He was too harsh with us young lads and often singled out people for a good roasting, which was awful – the classic Alex Ferguson 'hairdryer' treatment.

At Leeds I really learnt my trade, training and playing among the future best players in the world, which was an absolute privilege. Yet something was not right; by the age of eighteen, I was training with the first team during pre-season, but I never felt part of the general set-up. I was offered a contract over four years, shortly before my nineteenth birthday, but the cash on offer was a complete joke and I would not accept it, despite fierce objection from my father.

During my early playing years as an amateur, my dad was always brutally honest about my performances, and such criticism and lack of belief from him were often extremely difficult to accept. However, once I started hitting the mark around the age of sixteen and beyond, I won him over, and after that he supported me like no other. He would take me to every session at Hunslet, Bradford, and Leeds, regardless of the often 'fresh' early morning timings, then pick me up after lunch and take me back in the evening.

But in truth and retrospect, rugby league brought me nothing but misery, disappointment, and rejection once I was on the verge of becoming a full-time professional. Throughout my time playing at the very top level, I never felt wanted or valued as a player, apart from at Hunslet Hawks; but Hunslet wasn't good enough for me – I wanted the big time – to be an elite athlete and sit at the top table.

Now my passion for rugby was deteriorating fast, and disillusionment began to creep in. The pro scene was not what I had expected: there was far too much pressure applied to performance, which prevented me from fully enjoying the game to which I had dedicated my life.

I left Leeds for two reasons. Firstly, over a contract dispute, but secondly, because the Under 21s coach was giving opportunities to a player who didn't possess the same ability that I did, but whose dad was a friend of the coach. This was the final straw; I left the coach a voicemail, saying, 'Thanks for the contract offer, but no thanks,' and that was it – I was no longer a rugby league player.

As a result, I slipped into no-man's-land. This was not in the script at all: I had brushed off school thinking that rugby was my calling – literally everything I had done for the last ten years had gone into turning pro. I had no plan B, because for me that had equated to self-doubt, and there was no place for that in my psychology.

Without the daily commitment of training, or weekend matches to worry about, I started going out. Weekends were now consumed by drinking excessive amounts of alcohol and experimenting in recreational drugs, along with the occasional overnight stay in a local police station.

My purpose had been taken away; I didn't have a clue what I was going to do with my life, or even what interested me. I still craved the physical contact, however, and that is where the fighting came in. Drunken, drug-fuelled brawls became the norm most weekends – I was so completely lost without a purpose and desperately needed a mentor, as a prison sentence seemed almost inevitable.

In fact, shortly before my eighteenth birthday, I was involved in an horrific fight outside a pub in Hemsworth and was arrested and charged with ABH and Affray and almost sent straight to prison. My only saving grace was that it was my first offence, although the CCTV footage looked terrible.

One thing was for certain, when I wasn't pissed or creating social problems, I still had a ferocious desire to be highly successful; I loved money, nice clothes, and expensive cars. I just didn't know how to bridge the gap between my thirst for success and how to find the correct avenue to get me there – and crucially, something that stimulated me.

I am not writing this to demonstrate my level of perceived masculinity, or how macho I was. My aim here is merely to emphasise the personality traits, experiences, and behaviour patterns that drew me towards the Royal Marines. I didn't know who I was, basically, and I needed questions answering.

Thankfully, as I write this today, some sixteen years on, I know exactly who I am and understand my capabilities and limitations. I am a different person today, someone who thankfully no longer possesses such aggressive tendencies and displays a lack of empathy for others. Don't get me wrong, I still love watching contact sports, especially the UFC, and taking part in all things physically demanding, but my days of seeking out conflict have long gone, since having my son and maturing naturally with age.

They say that timing is key. Indeed, it is.

I started working for local employment agencies doing whatever job they threw at me – one was making garage doors, another was sweeping a woodwork factory in Featherstone – but they typically lasted for all of forty-eight hours, because of my attitude. Later, I got a longer appointment through my dad as a pool lifeguard at Lightwaves Leisure Centre in Wakefield, West Yorkshire.

This period made me realise one thing – I was not the type of bloke who was happy plodding along. The normal and mundane 9–5 job did not excite me. I had to do something that was self-rewarding and fulfilling, a job that made me feel proud every day, which maximised the limits of my mental and physical self. I wanted to feel like I was heading somewhere positive – on a journey, you could say – every time I woke up.

I knew during this time that I was different to most, if not all of my mates in the village. I wasn't happy, in fact deeply depressed, earning a few quid and living for weekends, only to spend them getting wasted on booze and drugs. I knew I had the internal conviction to be who I wanted to be. Put another way, I wanted to reach levels of achievement that not everyone could attain. After a period of anarchy, I once again became hell-bent on success.

Without realising it, I was about to embark on the greatest adventure of my life . . . the Royal Marines Commando course.

One morning, still awake and heavily intoxicated from the night before, my best friend, Chris Snowden, and I were flicking through the TV channels when we stumbled across Sky News. They were showing coverage of British Royal Marines Commandos driving round Iraq during 2004, looking to capture or kill Uday and Qusay Hussein . . . the sons of Saddam Hussein.

THAT WAS IT!

The footage resonated with me, filling my young mind with

intrigue, fascination and excitement, like nothing had in a very long time. Finally, I knew my direction of travel, although I was fully aware of how difficult this road would be, if not impossible.

To be honest, I knew I was a robust and mentally tough lad from my years of playing rugby, so I thought, *OK, let's see how I would fare in the Royal Marines.* It is a rite of passage that is thirty-two weeks long – the longest and most gruelling basic military course in the world, and the absolute pinnacle of physical and mental fortitude and endurance.

I assumed it would be easier to join the Army, Navy, or RAF, but that was not good enough – not everyone could be a Royal Marines Commando. That was a whole different level of sheer greatness and total respect. My granddad had always said, 'You need to go in them Royal Marines,' but when I was younger, I never gave it a second thought. Now, at nineteen, approaching twenty, it was the only thing on my mind.

Filled with mixed feelings of excitement and trepidation, I went from Fitzwilliam, West Yorkshire, via train to the Armed Forces Careers Office in Leeds, only a few days after watching the Royal Marines cutting around Iraq.

Once inside I was confronted by three desks: Army, RAF, and Navy/Royal Marines. A Royal Marines Commando in there caught my eye immediately and I was awestruck by him. Embroidered onto the right shoulder of his uniform, I could see his Royal Marines Commando Flash and Parachute (Para) Wings situated just below and I thought, *what kind of a bloke could possibly achieve such a feat?*

He talked to me in-depth about the joining process, and about his own experiences of training, and it sounded horrendous. He had actually just broken his leg while completing the 30-miler – the final Commando Test – and was talking to me in a cast while brandishing crutches. He asked me why I wanted to join, and I told him that I wanted to get my Green Beret and walk around with 'Royal Marines Commando' on my shirt sleeve, go to war as soon as possible, kill the enemy, and get a medal. That was it – the most absolutely outrageous career requirements, looking back.

My first step was to do the Royal Navy's Psychometric Test. This was a four-part, multiple-choice paper consisting of thirty questions in each section, and I had to score a minimum of 50 per cent correct answers in each of the four sections to be assured of a good pass. If I failed to meet this grade for the Royal Marines, I could have explored viable opportunities in the Navy, but that filled me with little to no excitement.

The test sections were: Reasoning, nine mins; Literacy, nine mins; Numeracy, sixteen mins; Mechanical Comprehension, ten mins. I failed my first test on the mathematics section – it wasn't particularly hard, but you had to work fast. This failure meant I had to wait six to twelve months before I could undertake the resit.

I was absolutely gutted. In all fairness to myself, I didn't revise – something I had never done – and for the next twelve months, I was back in no-man's-land again with the thought of being a fully trained Royal Marines Commando burning ferociously inside me.

During this period, I asked my boss and friend at the time, Steve Wood, who was a qualified maths teacher, to help me become sharper, and to mentor me with the type of questions that I had encountered. I started practising daily and it became an obsession. I would not be happy until I got 100 per cent every time, like when I was hitting the lamp-post with my rugby ball.

I reapplied, but by this point the mental strength I'd developed playing rugby had slightly wavered, and doubt began to creep in. As a result, I chose to join the Royal Navy first, then if successful on the test resit, my plan was to transfer to Royal Marines at a later stage. However, it wasn't what I really wanted, I was simply scared of failure.

One night I was sat at home with my dad watching TV, when we got talking about my future. I told him about my plan and route to the Marines.

He said, 'Gareth, never in your life will you be as ready to go for the Marines as you are now.'

His endorsement and confidence in me changed everything that evening and altered the trajectory of my life. I immediately called my recruiting officer and told him of my intention.

He said, 'To be honest with you, Gareth, out of the many people we've had come through here, you seem to have all the qualities to go for the Royal Marines. I've thought this from day one, so I have no problem in transferring you over.'

This was rare, because once you've put your name down for one force, that's it. It's all based on numbers and the recruitment officers need to hit their own recruitment targets.

Now it was game on and over the next six months I dedicated my life 100 per cent to joining the Royal Marines. My friend Craig Jones, my best friend Chris, and my dad were the only three people who took my new quest seriously and believed I had what it took to give the course a respectable shot, if not complete it. Literally everyone else thought I was a total joke and laughed at the notion of me even trying to become a Royal Marine.

Craig introduced me to Dave Evans at a gym in Upton, West Yorkshire; he was an ex-Royal Marines Commando Physical Training Instructor (PTI) and physically represented my idea of what a Royal Marines Commando would look like.

Dave became a mentor, calling me frequently, and would often massage my anxieties. John Riddle, another local lad who was serving at the time, was also fundamental along with Craig in supporting me during this pre-joining period. This phase would lay the foundation – preparing my mind and body for what would turn out to be the most harrowing challenge of my life.

My conditioning regime consisted of high-intensity circuits two to three times a week at a sports centre in Wakefield. The sessions, which lasted one hour, included sprints of an indoor five-a-side football court, pad and bag work, and other all-bodyweight or lightweight exercise stations, such as burpees, press-ups, mountain climbers, squat thrusts and core stability stations. I also went running three times a week: 3-mile run best effort, 10k in around 60 minutes, and 8–10 miles steady state.

In addition, I went to Roundhay Park in Leeds, or Pontefract Racecourse, and would do up to seven hill-sprints up humongous hills at both locations. This was also part of the Leeds Rhinos pre-season training, done at 07:00 every Saturday morning to condition the legs against Lactic Acid build-up – thus training the body to withstand the onset of fatigue.

Mondays, Wednesdays and Fridays were days where I would do double sessions; upper-body weights focusing on specific muscle groups, for example, chest (press-up strength), back (pull-up strength), and shoulders followed by a run or cardio in the evening. I also went to Minsthorpe Swimming Pool every Saturday and swam for forty-five minutes, alternating between one length breaststroke and one length front crawl. Finally, I would go to Minsthorpe School Gymnasium to train in jiu-jitsu, wrestling and boxing taken by Ian Jones – local professional MMA fighter and Craig's brother. My routine was strict, disciplined and unwavering.

The first step was to run three miles in under 22.30 minutes on a treadmill supervised by a personal trainer at Fitness First in Leeds. I came in at 18.40 minutes, which left the instructor completely astonished.

Next was the medical assessment, which had me slightly worried; I had ruptured the Anterior Cruciate Ligament (ACL) in my left knee playing rugby for a team in Pontefract, meaning on the odd occasion it would dislocate through exercise, or by something as simple as losing my footing on a wet tiled floor.

I needed an ACL reconstruction, but the NHS doctor said that sometimes it was possible to avoid having the major operation – if the other supporting ligaments were strong around the injured knee, and by doing quality leg strength work, to help stabilise the knee. So, this is what I decided to do, as an operation would have held me back a further twelve months and the Marines would not look at anyone post-operation.

During an arthroscopy, the surgeon confirmed that my knee was strong from playing rugby and I could avoid the operation, but I was embarking on the hardest and longest military training course in the world; I also had asthma and eczema. All three of which were complete showstoppers and the end to my dream, if the medical inspector should detect them.

In preparation for my medical, my thinking was that I would get into extreme physical condition so that when I took my clothes off for my full body examination, the doc would think, *Bloody hell, this kid is in shape,* and would pass me with minimal evaluation. My rationale worked. When I stripped off, he took one look at my body and said, 'Oof, my boy, I don't think you have a problem physically!'

He carried on with his examination and I lied and bluffed my way through it – passing eventually with great relief. My

ACL left knee rupture, however, was still a massive concern to me and I remained fully aware that if discovered in future, the game would be over. I had set myself up for the possibility that it would dislocate in training and I would be sent to Hunter Company – the Marines' rehabilitation troop. Yes, I would be pulled from regular training, but not thrown out completely, so I had to keep it secret.[1]

By this time, I hoped that the Marines would have seen my potential and would stick with me while my ACL was reconstructed, but I knew this was a massive gamble. The Royal Marines' policy back then was that if an injury was sustained before Week 10, and full recovery was estimated to take around twelve or more months, then the Marines would discharge recruits from training. Anything under twelve months' rehabilitation and you stood a chance of staying. This evaluation was based on several factors, like one's attitude and aptitude to complete training, for example.

I knew my ACL was a major injury and the operation plus rehabilitation potentially required would have taken around twelve months, if not more, so this gamble was playing on my mind immensely.

The next and by far most important phase of the recruitment process was the Potential Royal Marines Course (PRMC), which was a three-day pass or fail selection course in order to join and start training.

The three-day selection course run at the Commando Training Centre Royal Marines (CTCRM), Lympstone (replaced in 2020 by the Recruit Orientation Phase, or ROP), put all budding Commando wannabes through a gruelling

---

1 *TO NOTE: THIS IS NOT ADVISABLE, AS ANYONE FOUND TO HAVE LIED OR OMITTED INFORMATION ON THEIR APPLICATION COULD FACE DISMISSAL.*

series of tests that punished the mind and body. It was a physically and mentally demanding course, involving gymnasium tests, endurance and obstacle courses, and mind games designed to weed out all the misplaced individuals who possessed no fundamental aptitude. This culminated in an interview with a training course Corporal or Officer to assess one's aptitude for training.

I received my train tickets to head down to CTCRM, and by this stage, I had undertaken six months of quality strength and conditioning training, while also abstaining from alcohol. I was given a joining pack from the Leeds careers office, which included tests and a basic programme of how to train for the PRMC, plus the standards required in order to pass the PRMC and instructions on how to get there and what to take.

It took around five hours to reach CTCRM from Wakefield Westgate train station. Believe it or not, CTCRM has its own station called Lympstone Commando, which stops right outside the camp – at the base of the dreaded Bottom Field, an intense battlefield assault course that I would come to know very well over the next three days.

On arrival, I felt like a deer caught in the headlights: CTCRM is a harrowing and intimidating place – dark, depressing, and overwhelming. Around a dozen lads and I were met on the platform by a Royal Marine Drill Instructor, who herded us up like cattle and escorted us to the PRMC block, where we joined around forty-five other lads. The PRMC instructors then stood us all in three ranks (lines) outside the block and all seemed fairly relaxed, apart from a number of recruits, already in their training, who started hurling abuse down at us from their accommodation blocks.

'Go home, lads, it's wank!'

'This will break you – look at that rat's cunt!'

Once in the block, our weight and height were taken, and straightaway one lad was told not to bother unpacking but to go home, because he was underweight at 68kg – the bottom limit was 69kg. That night we were fed and then it was time to get our heads down and rest, ready to start Day One.

I remember feeling a huge sense of accomplishment, even though at that stage I had absolutely no idea about the perilous mountain I had to climb for the next ten to twelve months. But I was also filled with a weird and unnerving sense of both shock and disbelief. Then and even now, I felt this was a make or break moment for me – a fork in the road, and the pressure to prove my doubters wrong was overwhelming.

2

POTENTIAL ROYAL MARINES COURSE

PRMC Day One

Reality struck hard the following morning – the contrast in how we were treated the night before and now was both stark and frightening. On our arrival, we were treated well and now it seemed this was intentional, to lure us into a false sense of security; the shock of capture gripped us all.

At 05:00 on Day One, a Physical Training Instructor – PTI – nicknamed Scary McNairy, booted open the doors to each of the dormitory rooms. This bloke was a scary beast of a man with ginger hair and muscles in his ears. He screamed with pure rage.

'Get up! Get out your fucking beds, you cunts – five minutes, get outside with boots on – 5, 4, 3, 2, 1! Get the fuck outside!'

He was physically ripping lads clean out of their beds and roughing us all up, while another Royal Marine Commando kicked open a locker, releasing a shit-load of old, battered boots.

The sense of panic was unbelievable. We were still half-asleep, scrambling around for our issued combats and numbered rugby shirts to put on.

'Get those fucking boots on!'

We were so frightened and shell-shocked that we ended up with odd boots on. I recall having a size eight on one foot and a ten on the other; it was pure carnage – not ideal when the first test was a three-mile run for time in under twenty-three minutes.

We all failed to get out on time (obviously), so we received a physical roasting consisting of press-ups, squats, burpees, and stress positions for around forty minutes. This was our first taste of the hostility at CTCRM, and what was in store for us over the coming days. For some of the lads, the mistake of taking on this challenge was already apparent.

At 06:00, after our forty-minute thrashing, we started the three-mile run at the base of 'Heartbreak Lane'.

Split into two parts, this consisted of a 1.5 mile run out to a checkpoint as a squad in under 12.5 minutes, followed by 1.5 miles back as an individual best effort in under 10.5 minutes. This first assessment was absolutely horrid and the safety wagon – a minibus following closely behind the pack of runners – was an enduring demonstration of failure, filling up fast with broken hopefuls who had quit, or been pulled off the assessment for running too slow. My boots were killing me and the size eight boot was stopping the circulation to my entire foot. However, I completed the run back to camp in 8.20 minutes and felt so relieved.

After stuffing my face with lunch, it was on to Gym Test 1.

The first assessment was the VO2 Max bleep test: to gain maximum points we had to reach level thirteen, but the pass mark was level eleven. This is arguably straightforward in isolation, but after our early morning thrashing and the three-mile run, we had another hammering gym warm-up prior to the start of the bleep test, which meant we were massively fatigued and under maximum pressure.

Second, was the Press-up Max Test, which immediately followed, where we had to achieve a minimum of sixty press-ups to an audio beep in under two minutes. The press-ups had to be executed in the strictest of form – arms fully locked out and shoulder-width apart – while a partner would lay on his chest putting his extended arm out with his fist on the floor facing away, counting one repetition for every time my chest touched his fist.

Royal Marine PTIs observed, making sure the assessment was carried out flawlessly, jumping on any poor form and screaming at lads who were struggling, not locking their arms out or making 'fucking girly noises', as they called them; it was such an intimidating and uncomfortable environment. Once your knee touched the floor, the assessment was over and those who hadn't reached the target were told they were the worst human beings ever to be born.

The Sit-up Max Test followed, again to an audio beep. We had to achieve eighty in under two minutes, but another round of stress positions interrupted the start of the assessment. Once again my partner secured my feet to the floor. Our elbows had to touch the top of our knees (and stay there) and then the shoulders and elbows had to touch/slap the floor like wings when our backs fully hit the mat for a repetition to count. Knees had to remain together, or else reps were deducted under a hail of abuse and aggression.

After that was the Pull-up Max Test. A minimum of three were required to stay on the course, but we were told to aim for eight good pull-ups (full extension) and only do more if they were good form, i.e., eight good ones were better than ten poor ones. These were carried out to an audio beep again, which seemed to take ages, and they were executed by adopting an over-grasp – a hook-like grip on an old-school wooden beam – which, as you can imagine, was slippery with sweat after the first round of lads went through.

We had to pull ourselves up and hold the position until the

beep sounded, then extend back to hanging, and pull back up on another beep. Our chins had to pass over the top of the bar for one to count and on the way down our bodies had to be straight and 'motionless' until we were fully straight – hanging down from the beam. What's more, our legs couldn't cross. Chins that didn't satisfactorily pass above the bar, or those who couldn't keep up to the beep, were told to drop off or were physically removed.

What wasn't stated in the Gym Test 1 programme was that you got an absolute thrashing by the PTIs beforehand and by the time you hit the bleep test, everyone was in a bad way; some lads had even put up their hand to withdraw voluntarily from the course, and others were throwing up or retching.

At the press-up test, you were asked by the PTIs to remove your T-shirt so they could see your chest hitting your partner's fist. On my back, I have *RM* tattooed in memory of my grandad, Roger Monks, and I knew immediately that someone would think it was a Royal Marines tattoo. I was cringing, looking down like a child hoping nobody would see me, but it didn't work, and the next fifteen minutes became absolute hell for me.

Straightaway, two PTIs rushed over.

'Who the fuck do you think you are? Having that tattooed on your back?'

'You think you're a Royal Marine already, do ya?'

I tried to explain, but they were having none of it, and I was hammered within an inch of my life, while they shouted at me, 'We will guarantee you won't fucking pass this course!' After my special attention (and now subconsciously thinking they were going to fail me), we had two minutes to grab our water bottles and fall into three ranks outside the gymnasium, ready for our swimming assessment.

Once changed, again under extreme time pressure, we were led into the pool area. On the PTIs' instruction, we had to jump off the diving board one by one, then swim the perimeter of the pool breaststroke unaided and exit without using the ladders. On our arrival back at the PRMC block, I felt a massive sense of accomplishment and my confidence was soaring as a result. I was, however, aware that I needed to remain realistic and grounded.

What surprised me was how some of the lads displaying confidence the previous evening – saying how they would join the Special Boat Service (SBS) on completion of training – were now packing their bags and preparing to travel home, having failed or voluntarily withdrawn. I drew strength from this and quietly observed the behaviour of those who remained with intrigue and fascination.

PRMC Day Two

The second day was a test of mental strength, physical endurance, stamina and determination, which took place on the Bottom Field. Both physical assessments were done wearing a combat jacket, combat trousers, a rugby shirt, and boots – which again didn't fit correctly.

The first assessment of the day was the 'death slide' on the high obstacle course – also known as the Tarzan Assault course (the 3rd Commando Test). After all had been down, or in some cases refused and been withdrawn, we were gathered and herded down to the Bottom Field Assault Course, where we received a physical battering of shuttles, high knees, press-ups, fireman's carries, and leopard crawling.

This provided an exit for even more of the lads, due to the

sheer intensity and reinforcing instruction of the PTIs: 'Lads, we can do this all day; we've got nowhere to go – you'll be here all fucking day until you start putting the required effort in.'

For the ones that quit at this point, the unknown ending to this beasting and the fatigue from Day One became too much to bear.

After the beasting, we had to demonstrate confidence at height by completing the high-ropes obstacles, before being shown and practising how to complete obstacles on the Bottom Field Assault Course – two or three obstacles at a time. After an orientation, we were timed around the obstacle course and had to complete it in our best-effort attempt – i.e., as fast as physically possible – under a five-minute cut-off.

Throughout that morning, the expression, 'You're only as strong as your weakest man', was the theme and it influenced the outcome of each segment of the assessments. This meant there were consequences for the entire squad if a few candidates did not do as they were told, or lacked the discipline to take control of their bodies and emotions, which was all the time on the PRMC. What's more, if someone fell behind for any reason and the rest of the group failed to get them back in line, we were all punished.

After a gruelling morning and subsequently stuffing our faces with massive portions of military food, again under time pressure, the afternoon was spent in the gymnasium for Gym Test 2: press-ups and tuck jumps, sprints, fireman's carries. It was by far the hardest hour of the course and the aim was clearly to get rid of all the hangers-on, leaving only the lads they wanted to start training.

True grit, determination and an unrelenting desire to succeed were the ingredients required, whilst battling fatigue in order to get through this session of the course. Although individually assessed, this was very much a team effort. The PTIs were constantly scoring our performance, and if you were seen not to be a team player (or considered 'jack' – jack-the-lad as you're called at Lympstone), or you were not pulling your weight, you were told to withdraw, pack and go home, in not the most loving of manners to say the least.

Come the end of day, I was still in the game and confident I had done enough to pass; although the negative attention my tattoo received was playing on my mind and I did wonder if they would fail me as promised, despite me achieving the required points to start training. By this stage of the PRMC, just over two-thirds of the potential Royal Marines had returned home.

PRMC Day Three

Reveille was called at 05:00, where we were given a bit of grace to pack our personal kit. Afterwards, we had to start cleaning the accommodation blocks at around 05:45 – followed closely by returning our issued clothing to the camp storeroom. Once all that mundane stuff was out the way, we gathered in a lecture room, where we were told whether we had been successful on the course.

I passed the PRMC and was issued with a certificate and a pair of boots and socks ready to begin training. It was a totally unbelievable feeling.

Throughout the course, you had no idea how you were doing. The PTIs were screaming at you, 'Number nine, you're failing this!' or 'You're wasting your fucking time here!' Other times, they shouted, 'Hey, you haven't got enough points to pass, just go and pack your stuff!'

It was a horrible environment to be in and a real test of mental strength to repel their mind games. My rugby days definitely paid off here, and if I took anything from the PRMC, it was that I would never quit, never – at no stage was it a part of my mental processing, it simply wasn't an option.

Out of around sixty lads, only sixteen passed the PRMC course and I was one of them. I was over the moon, so proud of myself and happy, but I'd had a taste of the training (or at least I thought I did) and now knew it was going to be a monster year ahead.

I was to join the 32-week Commando training course only three weeks after completing the PRMC. The speed at which the Royal Marines contacted me caught me off guard, as I was told at Lympstone it would be around a six-week waiting time.

The Start of Training

For those who don't yet fully understand . . .

The Royal Marines Commando Green Beret stands alone within the military arena. It is a rare jewel, a symbol of dedication, professionalism, and competence; a marker of identification for the men who have pushed themselves beyond the levels of their perceived limits of human physical and mental endurance. It offers those who have 'earned' it, the respect of excellence amongst all international military forces and the fear of all enemies.

The following chapters are based on the actual diary entries that I wrote while on the Commando Course. I entered them in my diary several times a day – when I woke, after lectures or during training exercises, and before I went to bed.

Due to the intense nature of training – especially the time spent in the field – at times I had to write brief notes or key words on my hands and arms, and then transfer the contents to the diary, sometimes hours, or even days later. The motivation to keep updating the entries, which often formed pages of activity, highlighting emotions and self-reflection, was extremely difficult to maintain: especially when I was cold, often wet, and debilitated with fatigue.

The original diary entries have been edited for this book, but strong language is used throughout. At various stages, I have included insight, broader explanation, or reflection. These sections are in *italics*, so you can differentiate between the original diary material written in 2005/6 and the sections that have been added when writing this book.

3

COMPARTMENTALISATION

*Breaking training down and other large
undertakings in life*

HOLDING WEEK 1

*Upon arrival at Lympstone, it was decided by the Training
Team that 899 Troop (my troop) didn't have enough recruits
to start training, so we were held for two weeks until 900
Troop joined, at which point we were amalgamated and
became 900 Troop.*

Day 1 – Monday 16 May 2005

Travelling down to Lympstone Commando (CTCRM) from
Wakefield Westgate train station to start Royal Marines
training this morning with mixed emotions. I'm feeling
anxious but excited about what to expect, but also tired and
pissed off – because in 5 hrs I lose all my freedom. This journey
feels like I'm sat on the Pepsi Max (*rollercoaster*). There's a
part of me that's screaming to get off!

Arrived at Lympstone with the same harrowing feeling I
left the PRMC with. It doesn't seem two minutes since I was
last here. I didn't want to come back so soon; I don't feel
ready mentally, but I know I had to start this sooner or later.

Having been met on the station by the Drill Instructor, we

were escorted up through the camp to the Foundation Block – this really is an intimidating place. The camp is very hostile and unwelcoming: all around are recruit troops of lads at various stages of training being instructed by their Royal Marines training team, which generally involves a lot of shouting and verbal abuse.

This place instils fear and naturally causes you to withdraw from any form of social interaction with any 'trained' Royal Marine – they are to be avoided at all costs, as engaging with them reduces you to a small child – a submissive disposition like getting told off by a school teacher. However, avoiding such interaction is impossible to achieve, which gives me anxiety.

Walked into Foundation Block – 60 beds and lockers in rows, side by side, just like in the film 'Full Metal Jacket'. The foundation block is completely stripped of anything that reminds you remotely of home. It's like a prison, an old and tired institutional set-up.

Day 2 – Tuesday 17 May

Up and out of bed at 05:30.

It has been pure hell today. We had swimming (PT) with the physical training instructors (PTIs) and then had to collect and sort all our kit out before going for injections and detailed medical check-ups. Finally, we had Gym Assessment, which was the same as Gym Test 1 on the PRMC. Absolutely horrible and so hard! Very tired today. It has not been a good day for me – felt angry and worried when reflecting on the magnitude of the task ahead. The 99.9% Need Not Apply is an actual statistic – from the moment someone walks in the careers office to when they pass out as a Royal Marines Commando, only 0.1% make it.

Been doing my admin – washing, cleaning, and ironing – all evening until 00:00 and the Corporal says we are up and out of bed at 05:00 tomorrow.

Day 3 – Wednesday 18 May

Alarm screaming at 05:00 and up to a cold shower. Looking forward to today, it's our first day wearing combats, boots, and a Royal Marines 'black' beret. Breakfast at 06:15. The showers and the Foundation Block are freezing on a morning! Had an awful day today, we had an English test for 3 hours then had 40 mins of hell getting thrashed by 9 PTIs all screaming at us. It's 23:30 now and we have a maths exam in the morning. Been up now since 5 and it's been non-stop! The Troop Commanding Officer, Cpt W, gave us a good inspiring talk.

Day 4 – Thursday 19 May

A recruit in Week 11 came into the Foundation Block this morning selling his kit, he's just dropped out of training. It brings it home how tough these next 32 weeks are going to be. Feeling fed up today – got another 3 weeks of this foundation shit as we don't have enough lads to take through training, so we have to wait for another bunch of lads to join us in a week's time. Usually you do only 2 weeks in foundation, but we must do 4!

There are some weird ways of talking down here. Getting used to the slang is hard and hilarious:

Phys – Physical exercise
Scran – Food
Hoofing – Great

Prof – Profited: if you've had an extra hour in bed, you have proffed

Dipped – Lost out: if you get less sleep than the rest, you have dipped

Spinning a Dit – Telling a story

Oggin – Water: the PTIs often say, 'Get in the fucking oggin'

Nutty – Sweets and chocolate

Dobied – Washed either yourself or an item

Wrapped your tits in – Given up or quit

Honking – Disgusting: that fitness session was honking, or he is honking – dirty, smelly or ugly

Rat's cunt – Ugly fucker

Day 5 – Friday 20 May

It's 05:30, making my bed and preparing for our first locker inspection. Mine looks good, although I haven't dobied my PT clothes, underpants, and socks. Hope the Corporal doesn't notice! We are having a talk next week with the Colonel commanding the camp. He's done SBS and SAS and is meant to be absolutely nails but inspiring, so I'm looking forward to listening to him. We have PT this morning, 1½ mile run and swimming. Our troop PTI looks like a right hard bastard, but he seems really young. He's been everywhere with the Corps; Iraq, Sierra Leone, the lot.

The run ended up being 3 miles today in under 22 mins, which I found OK, but the swimming was much harder. I feel so good at night-time – relaxed and excited, but then shit on a morning. Just generally not in control, anxious, and a bit down.

Day 6 – Saturday 21 May

We are due to get hammered in the gymnasium this morning: two camp circuits, 800m each best effort, rope climbs, and IMF – Hell.

I got mud on my trainer on the way over and the PTI saw it when we turned up at the gym. He made me tell the mud off for being on my trainer. He said the mud dare not touch him, because he has a Green Beret and he could walk on water. He also gave us a warning that if we don't put 100% in during the sessions, he would put his hand down our throats and rip our souls out and leave us limp on the floor!

PT was an 80-minute nightmare, then swimming. However, we have been given 6 hours leave and I haven't seen a television or read a paper for a week. Going for our civilian clothes inspection now, and if I pass, I can go into Exeter to watch the FA Cup Final.

During training, before any recruit is allowed to leave camp for a specified segment of leave/downtime (based on their stage of training – the recruits in early weeks of training get smaller leave blocks), all must parade to the duty corporal in the guard room to get their civilian clothes inspected. During this tense period – if you're wearing 'gash' (shit) civilian clothing as perceived by the inspector, or when told to tell a joke and you don't make them laugh, then you are told you can't go ashore, or have to rejoin the queue with either a better joke or a better item of clothing on.

Day 7 – Sunday 22 May

This morning we had to go to church. The King's Squad were there and they pass out of training next Friday – lucky bastards.

I stared at them with such admiration and a sense of awe at what they've achieved; they made it, completed the toughest course in the world. Also, two Royal Marines' children were getting baptised. Starting to feel a sense of enjoyment down here now and feeling proud, but still weary as I know I'll have to dig really deep to reach my goal of becoming a Commando and getting the Green Beret.

LESSON 1

Managing your emotions by utilising the methods of compartmentalisation, and mentally strategising to ensure long-term success, is essential to reduce anxiety, self-doubt, and the overwhelming effects on emotions.

On arrival at Lympstone, I was met with the news that training was not going to commence as expected on 16 May 2005. With such a disappointment, it would have been easy to fall into a state of mental negativity.

The delay was due to a lack of numbers (to take through training), which meant an extension to the Foundation Phase by an extra two weeks until 900 Troop arrived. The first two (holding) weeks of training were bearable, but freedom as we knew it had gone; the 'Trained Ranks' at Lympstone now had complete control over our lives. The culture shock was a raw and unnerving experience.

Knowing that training had not even got underway during those initial weeks was a bitter pill to swallow. Staring down the barrel of thirty-three weeks from that point was arguably detrimental to anyone's success on the road to achieving their

Green Beret, and consequently some left during this period without officially even starting week one of training.

Two forms of visualisation

At the base of a major, risk-laden undertaking, and during one's endeavour to achieve the Green Beret, it is important to acknowledge two forms of visualisation to prepare the mind for success:

1. *Do* visualise what achieving the Green Beret or other large undertaking will do for you. Write down the positives: reinforce them mentally and reflect/visualise on how achieving that goal will transform your life – the opportunities and life chances it will afford. During moments of fatigue and disillusionment, which will surely come, this process of positive reinforcement will provide an anchor of stability, ultimately safeguarding the integrity of achieving the end goal.

Reflection: Positives could include things like global travel, facilitating personal growth through greater social and cultural awareness; fulfilment through pride, self-confidence and self-worth; greater earning potential (post-service) and job opportunities; and so on.

2. *Do not* visualise the process: the time, commitment and discomfort you will have to endure to achieve the end goal. I believe doing so could be extremely detrimental to your success in achieving your endeavour. However, do accurately acknowledge the personal sacrifice required. This will inform your preparation and perhaps highlight a need to invest in it more thoroughly. Also, as you progress

through the weeks, keep a constant appreciation of how far you are travelling – building, progressing, and getting closer to your end goal. It is essential to create and implement a mental strategy to break training and other goals down to ensure success.

The week method

To manage the enormity of the task ahead, in my mind, I worked on breaking training down into small segments. I gave myself a good talking to and said, right: 'Strike off one day at a time, just survive and use each week as a key marker. For now, Gareth, forget about the main prize, let each week be a victory.'

After two weeks, I made the diary entry 'WEEK 1 of 32' at the start of the third week. The simple process of writing that down had a positive mental impact. I can remember how it made me feel to this day, knowing the countdown had begun.

Breaking the weeks down into manageable chunks reduced any tendency to become overwhelmed, anxious, and disheartened. In my experience, adopting such strategies to long-term goals is essential. I utilised the exact same strategy throughout my six-year study of psychology, and it worked well: I broke down the six-year course into years, then into three three-month blocks (nine months of term time).

The day method

Even during times of severe sleep deprivation, I broke training down into a single day and focused solely on the most challenging point to overcome, which was almost always PT. In doing so, physical training became a very doable undertaking. Do not get me wrong, it was by no means easy, not in the slightest. However, doing one or two hours of hard physical and mental output in a day, whilst blocking out what was to come the following day, kept despair and stress at bay.

Over time, experience gained whilst utilising this method of deconstruction taught me that biting down with grit and determination to get through a day – to survive and stay on course, then eventually retreat to bed for a much-needed sleep – afforded the mental comfort of a better day the next morning; a chance to recharge, reset and go again.

The unforeseen value

An awareness of the day method to achieving a long-term goal is crucial to success. The seemingly negligible achievement of completing each day – the unnoticed, subtle, and slight progression of acquiring your goal – is what often discourages 99.9 per cent of those who try and fail at any large endeavour to change their lives.

People want quick results and therefore lack the patience that the 'mundane' requires. Success on the Royal Marines Commando course requires an understanding that small, productive actions repeated daily and with 'consistency' over a long and sustained period, will lead you to the Green Beret, or any other goals you may have.

Therefore, during moments of disillusionment, ask yourself where you would rather be: on course to achieving something of tangible significance, or sat in a pub? I went back to my local pub after fourteen years of joining the Royal Marines. Nothing there had changed, the context of the conversations remained the same . . . but I had!

Key Points:

- Looking too far ahead on large undertakings can be detrimental to success. Therefore, break down long-term goals into manageable stages.
- Visualise what achieving the end goal will do in transforming your life for the better, but don't visualise the process.
- Highlight key markers of victory along the way to achieving something special. Acknowledge and celebrate them before moving on.
- Breaking down long-term goal acquisition into a single day at times of fatigue and stress, and then focusing on the hardest point to overcome, alleviates the overwhelming burden of the overall challenge.
- Each day under the belt is a valuable building block – its significance should not be underestimated.
- If your rationale takes a momentary hit, write down why you chose to do it, reinforce the positives and reset ready for continuation.

4

MENTAL RESILIENCE

One's fundamental need to adapt

HOLDING WEEK 2

Day 8 – Monday 23 May 2005

It's 06:45 and on our way to Portsmouth today to see the Royal Marines museum, then to see HMS *Victory*, which should be good – looking forward to it.

Just arrived back at camp, it took four hours to get home and it was shit, a complete waste of time! Didn't even see HMS *Victory*.

Now 18:30 and waiting to go to Barnstable now for three days Adventure Training (AT). This doesn't normally happen, but we have to wait for the other troop to join us to start training, so this is a 'stocking filler' apparently. I'm tired today, can't be bothered at all.

Day 9 – Tuesday 24 May

Woke up in a tent this morning next to the sea, it was absolutely freezing, raining, and blowing a gale all night – hardly had any sleep at all. Sergeant just came into the tent and told us that we're going mountain climbing today, but it's absolutely freezing – the weather is shocking, and we have to wear shorts and shitty waterproof clothing.

Although it was wet and freezing, climbing was brilliant. We had to hang 200ft high off the cliff face – scary as hell! The Royal Marines or Special Boat Service (SBS) were on exercise on the water near our tent, we could hear helicopters and gunfire – unbelievable experience – so exciting, they were also flying down the river on the side of the ridge raiders and hovercrafts. Quality, I so want to be one of them boys!

Day 10 – Wednesday 25 May

Last night was better and I managed to sleep OK. I'm going bodyboarding – don't fancy it at all, the weather is terrible again! Corporal PTI B is taking us, he's crazy, but I have a lot of respect for him. Cut away all the bullshit and I think he'll be a good man and one of the lads.

Just arrived back, it was a good laugh – PTI B was surfing and we all went for a pint after, but we can't tell the rest of the Training Team.

Day 11 – Thursday 26 May

I'm pissed off because our Troop Commander let us watch the Champions League Cup Final last night, but said we had to walk there and back to the recreation room. Some of the lads went on bikes and got caught, so we ended up getting pulled out the football and sent back to our tents. Some of the lads down here are clowns, they have no idea how serious this is at all – we're in the Marines, for fuck's sake. I think we're going to get a right beasting sooner or later.

We ended up going kayaking in Ilfracombe harbour, it was absolutely quality. It's 19:30 and we're heading back to Lympstone now.

Day 12 – Friday 27 May

Up at 05:30 and feeling really fatigued. We have PT and I can't think of anything worse. Also dreading swimming after!

Just came back from PT, it was so hard, I think part of it is because I'm tired and drained. It was thirty mins of pain and we had to do 2 × full rope climbs. Just before we got to the ropes, Brad told a PTI he was going to be sick. The PTI said, 'Fuck off and stand there, if you're going to be sick, pull your collar out and do it in and down your shirt.'

Our T-shirts must be tucked in our shorts. He ended up being sick inside his T-shirt and was then dragged outside by the scruff of his neck! Mentally, it was difficult to watch because I know at some point that will be me.

Day 13 – Saturday 28 May

We are heading to the Millennium Stadium this morning to escort the football team flags out on the pitch for the promotion play-off games to Division 2.

Just arrived back to camp, we helped out with the pre-match presentations then watched Lincoln City and Southend battle it out for promotion. Southend won 2–0. The game was shit!

I'm starting to feel pretty down about all this. We are meant to be having tomorrow off, but we have to go back to the Millennium Stadium to do the same for another two teams. We're there Monday as well. I'm going to be absolutely shattered on Tuesday and we've been warned that training hasn't even started yet.

P.S. Two of the lads had their lockers trashed this evening by the Training Team and everything was thrown out the window.

Day 14 – Sunday 29 May

We were there again today for Hartlepool vs Sheffield Wednesday. The weather was red hot and there were loads of girls around, which is a rare thing now being stuck on camp. We did some pre-match presentations in front of 60,000 people – it was brilliant, a right buzz!

On our way back to the bus, all the public were being dick-heads, calling us pussies and shit – some bloke pulled Ben Whatley's bag off his shoulder and the lad's mate grabbed him and said, 'Mate, they will fucking paste us.' Ha ha ha, I love that.

Recruit Griffin is leaving, decided it's not for him. One down!

LESSON 2

The fundamental need to adapt to change quickly, in order to remain effective and assure long-term success.

My experiences over the past twenty-plus years have taught me many things in terms of the make-up of mental resilience, but nothing is more fundamental for 'sustained' personal growth, productivity and effectiveness than one's ability to adapt to change quickly.

Cultural change
Let us look at two types of uncontrollable change we encounter at various stages of our lives. Firstly, cultural change as a result

of international travel requires the individual to adapt to differing social and cultural norms and expectations.

For example, going from the UK to the Middle East, and vice versa. Such vastly different continents require adaptions in communication, cultural alignment and differing ways of living, to name but a few – all of which are underpinned by social intelligence and cultural awareness. Therefore, to establish emotional stability and assure immediate to long-term success, it is vital to adapt to new surroundings instantly, and nothing requires this understanding more than venturing inside the confines of Commando Training Centre Royal Marines, to start training.

Societal change

We experience societal shifts too. Technological advancements are continuously altering and shaping the way we must navigate our lives. Thus, our propensity to adapt with speed and efficiency to such changes, and crucially not 'resist' them, ultimately predicts how well we will thrive successfully in ever-changing environments. For example, adapting to the inception of the internet, the mobile phone evolution, and other technological devices is vital, as technology is constantly changing the world, and how we must negotiate our lives. Change in life is inevitable, nothing ever stays the same, and as a result we must acknowledge our role to engage in the continual efforts of personal development.

Some years ago, I visited the San Francisco 49ers – the American Football team that play in the NFL. On the wall, close to the players' dressing room, was a quote that said: You are getting better or you are getting worse, you never stay the same.

The 49ers acknowledged and perfectly captured this enduring need to adapt constantly to the frequent and subtle changes in life. To stay above the performance/progression curve, to remain valuable, current and effective, we must relentlessly pursue individual growth (in the midst of change) through the investment of personal development. For without this 'daily' investment to achieving and maintaining excellence, our ability to outperform others ceases – frankly, we become ineffective, less valuable and begin to stagnate as others develop and grow.

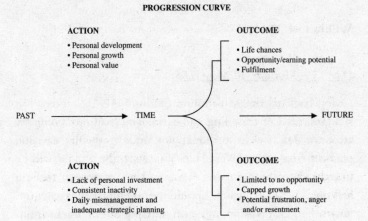

PROGRESSION CURVE

ACTION
- Personal development
- Personal growth
- Personal value

OUTCOME
- Life chances
- Opportunity/earning potential
- Fulfilment

PAST ———————→ TIME FUTURE

ACTION
- Lack of personal investment
- Consistent inactivity
- Daily mismanagement and inadequate strategic planning

OUTCOME
- Limited to no opportunity
- Capped growth
- Potential frustration, anger and/or resentment

Key Points:

- Sustained success is only possible if we accept and adapt to change. In this sense, although change invites (short-term) discomfort, it also provides a gateway to discovery.
- Staying abreast of the 'performance/progression curve' is vital for success. Resting on one's laurels and not undergoing progressive and sustained personal development exploration as an individual, only leads to a fading of skills and performance value.
- Change happens. Accept it, adapt to it, overcome it and thrive.

5

RECRUIT NERO

The construct of masculinity

WEEK 1 of 32

<u>*Day 15 – Monday 30 May 2005*</u>

Going back to the Millennium Stadium AGAIN today. I'm sick and tired of travelling and eating shit 'bag rats' (*military pack lunches*), I want some real, hot food! It's the first division play-off final today: West Ham v Cardiff, the winner will be promoted to the Premier League and it's rumoured to be a sell-out – 75,000, which should be a fantastic experience. Anything that takes my mind off starting our 32 weeks training tomorrow is welcome, because I'm absolutely dreading it!

It wasn't a bad day today, but I'm really tired and full of cold, which I can't shake off. 18 new lads join us this evening to start training – let's see if they can hack it?

<u>*Day 16 – Tuesday 31 May*</u>

Well, the first real day of training today – 32 weeks and counting. However, I must admit I'm not looking forward to it one bit, it appears an impossible task that defies human capability.

Been talking to a bloke in the gym, he's 30 years old and

has done 48 weeks training – 16 weeks in Hunter Troop, the Royal Marines rehabilitation troop – and was literally two weeks away from his Commando Tests and potentially completing the course, but his Commanding Officer has discharged him for failing Final Ex – the final exercise on the Commando training course, which accumulates all the knowledge and skills learnt over the past 30 weeks into a final exercise which includes the Killer Yomp – a 25–30 mile load carry over Dartmoor carrying kit weighing up to 100lbs.

I can't believe he's getting discharged so close to completing training – all that hard work and effort for nothing! He said it's because of his age (him being 30 and not younger).

Some of the new lads that joined us last night look so unfit – one or two of them are knobheads from my PRMC.

Just waiting for another Gym Assessment at 16:55 – we have to max out on the bleep test, pull-ups, press-ups, and sit-ups, plus other bits added in: it's awful. One of the new lads, recruit Nero, has been medically discharged on Day 1, and recruit Moore wants to leave tomorrow.

Day 17 – Wednesday 1 June

During inspection this morning I got caught play-fighting and was made to adopt the Superman stance – a plank position where you only have opposing legs and hands on the floor recreating the flying pose of Superman – which is very much a stress position for 10 mins – HANG OUT!

The new lads have their Maths and English test throughout the day, which we did in week one (*holding week*), so we've been told to iron and clean the accommodation until they get back. Think I'm starting to settle in now, some of us watched a DVD last night on 884 Troop that passed out two weeks ago. It was so brilliant and really inspiring. It made me want this even more and I wish I could watch it every week!

When we first arrived here, one of the Captains said: 'Some men never attain it, while some men bust gut and limb to wear it, and it only costs £7.' He was talking about the Green Beret and despite its monetary value, lads are willing to die to get it . . . quite unbelievable!

Day 18 – Thursday 2 June

Yesterday there was a clear gear-change in how we were treated; even the slightest fall in individual or team discipline and the training team were all over us – a really intimidating environment – feels very similar to being bullied. Only place you dare look is to the floor!

I went to the drying room to collect my bed sheets and on the way back to foundation a Corporal said, 'Show me your change.' He wanted to see if I'd used the dobie shop – washing machines and driers – which is forbidden while in the earlier stages of training. Everything must be handwashed and dried in a drying room. (*This elicits time pressure and is a good way of inducing sleep deprivation in recruits during the first phase of training.*) Anyway, I pulled out my change and he knocked it out my hands and walked off . . . ha ha, whatever!

Just received my English and Maths test results. I've done well, I got level 5 in Maths and level 2 in English, which means I can achieve the rank of Corporal. We had PT today – I think I'm getting into it now – although the emotions (*anxiety*) I have before doing it are horrible.

Now 21:00 and listening to 'Everybody Hurts' by R.E.M, it's fitting for down here – class!

Day 19 – Friday 3 June

It's 05:15 and I've had 3 hours' sleep. So hard to peel myself out of bed, but I need to get breakfast and get my bed and locker ready for a practice inspection in preparation for the real thing tomorrow morning.

We went to church third period, then got marched back to foundation and had 30 seconds to change into PT kit. Known as quick changes, they are designed to put you under maximum pressure and they work. After every change you get a quick inspection and failing one isn't worth living for!

Church was a small building on camp and was a place of recruit refuge. Inside the confines of the church walls, the laws of Lympstone didn't exist. You could almost 100 per cent relax and were often allowed to sleep for the entire period. Seeing church on the daily roster lifted morale amongst us all.

PT involved a 1.5 mile run at our PTI's pace to a checkpoint, then best effort back (*1.5 miles*) to camp. After the run, the Training Team lined us all up on the 'top field' and said: 'To that tree, it pays to be a winner.' This meant we had to sprint to a tree around 100m away and back. The first 4 back got to rest, while the others had to go again! I'm not the fastest, so I always have to go again along with the majority, until I manage to win.

The 3-mile run was the toughest thing mentally and physically yet. You have to keep going even though your body is screaming at you to pack in. I did the run back in 8.40 mins – happy – then we had a swimming circuit straight after, which included press-ups on the poolside, poolside dips, and front-crawl water sprints.

Got drill at 14:30 and then the troop photo – quality.

Day 20 – Saturday 4 June

We had 2 hours PT first thing this morning and it was a complete hammering. My body is aching all over and I'm so sluggish. We had to do two camp circuits – 800m each best effort – 2 × 30m rope climbs, double marking time (*high knee running on the spot*) – sprints and IMFC – a sort of synchronised full-body movement exercise to improve motor skills. By far the hardest session yet, the step up in intensity from the first 2 weeks is unbelievable – lads literally fall asleep standing, which is something I never thought possible.

During the morning inspection, Corporal M found 2 dead flies on one of the lads' windowsills and he made him eat them, saying he should NEVER leave anyone behind! I'm always so scared the closer he or the others get to inspecting me, it's just awful. You have to stand there that long; your feet start throbbing and legs start shaking.

Been ashore (*off camp*) for 6 hours leave this afternoon. Back now, cracked my admin, and have been invited to watch 'Rambo 3' in the lecture room – first time watching TV in 3 weeks.

Day 21 – Sunday 5 June

Managed to have a 'lie in' until 06:30 this morning – I was still falling asleep in the 'webbing lecture' (*personal load carrying equipment, which allows you to carry magazines, ammunition, food, water, and personal first aid kits*). Anyone that has been through this will understand how you feel day to day, constantly falling asleep everywhere.

It's 10:55 and we've had a double period of PT: first period was an introduction to 'Techno Gym', the second, co-ordination and routine practice ready for Parents' Day. It's going to be brutal. Apparently, the Parents' Day is tactical – they invite your parents down and then you go on your first leave home. This sequence is said to get rid of a lot of lads who are starting to have second thoughts.

Have just put my webbing together and it looks class. I've got my bayonet on there too, which looks the bollocks. Preparing all our field kit this evening ready for exercise 'First Step' Tuesday.

P.S. I didn't get my locker trashed this morning, only a handful of us didn't. Happy and relieved about that, because when it is, it means we have to stay up all night getting it ready for the following morning.

LESSON 3

The fallacy of judging a book by its cover: lessons learnt on 'stereotyping' from my early experiences at the start of recruit training.

Our brains create 'heuristics' – mental shortcuts that allow us to solve problems and form judgements with speed and efficiency. In the context of stereotyping others, these cognitive strategies allow us to categorise people into groups based on appearance; a process, however, that oversimplifies the individual qualities and variation each person possesses. In this sense, the benefit of speed when making snap judgements is at times to the detriment of accuracy.

It could be argued that our tendency to form mental shortcuts is socially constructed to some extent and based on pre-existing knowledge that we have acquired in previous social encounters, coupled with the social and cultural environments we inherit. Collectively, this serves to create a bias – to feel or show an inclination or prejudice for or against someone or something – that informs our expectations and beliefs about people based on appearances, and influences our attitudes towards them.

Although Recruit Nero was medically discharged, he encapsulated my stereotype of a tough, strong (both mentally and physically), masculine male – like many of the others who left shortly after him during the first few weeks of training. In the context of Royal Marines training, I thought, *he looks the part, he'll succeed*. I wanted to get to know this person, to associate with him, and to achieve my goal through cohesive like-mindedness. After all, he and the others like him were big, muscular in stature, and covered in tattoos – all attributes linked to aggressive, manly behaviour.

Most, if not all, of the men that I categorised with my 'faulty' stereotype were *extroverted* in demeanour – over-imposing their masculinity to intimidate others, perhaps in an attempt to mask their insecurity and lack of self-confidence. Those recruits left training before Week 8, whilst the lads who remained, who looked geeky, physically non-imposing and appeared *introverted* in demeanour, stayed in training and later passed out as original troop members.

My experience in the Royal Marines redefined my entire belief system of masculinity, allowing me to witness the unforeseen power that many people can embody when not judged at face value – for example, the introverts. This experience taught me never to judge a book by its cover, and caused me to harness an unreserved respect for all.

Stereotyping can act as a clever way to bunch people quickly together, but in doing so, it oversimplifies the complex make-up of an individual – disregarding their hidden and unique qualities.

It is a lazy cognitive shortcut that evaluates group members based on the identity of their whole social category, and often ignores the individual person. More dangerously, it can tarnish one's perceptual reality, and affect the ability to make informed decisions and assure strategic success when it counts.

Current and future relationships, and social group membership, can either facilitate or inhibit performance, opportunity and success. The people you choose to surround yourself with, to learn, to grow and get better and more effective with, will predict a successful or non-successful outcome. For instance, peer-pressure, negative evaluations of risk and adversity, poor attitude, professionalism, and so on.

It is so easy to fall victim to these influences when you are out of your comfort zone and searching for self-assurance and external validation. If I had latched onto 'some' of the extroverts at the start of training, their general approach to adversity could have negatively influenced my outlook on what was ahead of us all.

Key Points:

- For humans to process the volume of information we receive daily, our brains have developed shortcuts to categorise groups of people quickly, which is often to the detriment of the unique traits and qualities of individual variation.
- Our tendency to judge others based on appearance is hard-wired. Appearances, therefore, can be deceiving.
- If your goal requires the help of others, which it almost certainly will at some stage, then choose your associates wisely, thus assuring long-term success.

6

FATIGUE AND BURNOUT

Sleep deprivation, 'restorative environments',
and the benefit of time

WEEK 2

Day 22 – Monday 6 June 2005

I've been packing and preparing my bergen and webbing (*fighting order*) – ready for exercise tomorrow. Every item of clothing must be bagged up individually so it is waterproofed, and my bergen must be packed in a certain way to maximise space effectively. It's taken all day!

In the evening, we went to a careers specialisation fair to look at the type of specialised jobs we could go into after completing training. One of them is the Special Boat Service (*SBS*). I was talking to a young lad who had recently completed selection and had been 'badged' – that's what he called it. It sounded absolutely unreal and I would give anything to be where he is now. Another bloke who was with him was older and had done 17 years in the SBS and their stories were amazing, stuff you never hear about – Quality!

They had all the latest guns on a table in front of them: M4, Pump action shotgun, Sniper rifle, M4 with underslung grenade launcher, handguns, and a new gun that allows you to fire round corners with some sort of laser sight. The sense of excitement

I get when talking to these lads and looking at the weapons is unbelievable, and I know this is exactly where I want to be.

The SBS are the lesser known brother of the SAS (Special Air Service). Both are 'Tier 1' UK Special Forces units and undertake the same selection process. Historically, the Paratroopers have gone to the SAS after successfully passing Selection and the Royal Marines to the SBS – although in recent years, the routes of passage have become less sectarian. Other Army and Navy personnel can also go on Selection, and some do and are successful. The term 'badged' is used when someone has passed Selection and is now a Special Forces operator, and replaces their original cap badge with that of the SAS or SBS, for example.

Day 23 – Tuesday 7 June

First field exercise. Lights on at 05:00 and I've had around 2 hours' sleep. Final checks on my bergen and webbing then we are on the bus to Woodbury Common for exercise 'First Step'. My bergen is really heavy and uncomfortable – the straps are cutting into my shoulders and the base is rubbing the skin off my lower back, and the muscles in my lower legs are burning – it's horrible, and we've only walked 100 yards to get on the bus.

We were taught how to wash ourselves in the field today – one of corporals pulled his foreskin back and it was full of cheese (like when you have thrush) and then he bent over and scooped a load of what looked like shit from his arsehole and ate it – it was disgusting and some of the lads were retching!

I was later told it was Dairylea and peanut butter, but it was still gross to watch. Also, we were shown how to cook food, make shelter in the daytime, and then covertly in the pitch-dark without using any light.

I had to get on sentry at 23:00, it was freezing and having to get out of a warm sleeping bag to going and laying on the ground was so emotional. At 03:00 we were all woken up, we had to pack up and walk out to an RV point – shocking – and to top it all off, I've had 3 hours' sleep in 48 hrs.

Day 24 – Wednesday 8 June

No sleep from last night, I was freezing and hungry the entire time. There were worms and spiders everywhere, crawling all over me during the night. I had a little torch and I daren't turn it on for fear of what I would see.

It's 04:45: washing cam (*camouflage*) cream off and doing any form of personal hygiene cleaning while getting ready for a kit inspection and having to cook food is pressure like you wouldn't believe. It's really mentally tough being in the field, and if I don't do what I've been told to do, for example, look after my feet and keep them dry to avoid 'trench foot', I will go down. When we arrived at Lympstone, we had a foot inspection and Nath has got trench foot and that happened from just ONE night in the field. It's going to be so, so hard this!

We had a talk this evening from Colonel T, who did 17 years in the SBS. He was the most intelligent bloke I've ever sat and listened to – so much charisma but also very cold in how he approaches things: very inspiring – I love his mindset.

Day 25 – Thursday 9 June

It's 05:30: We have unarmed combat first period this morning – get ready!

Well, we did it. We are starting very basic, however, some of the moves will be interesting. After that we had section team challenge in the gymnasium. It was like a physical team problem-solving session, spread across multiple stances. One of them involved the assault rifles we will get at some point, the SA80s – class! So tired, I can't catch up on my sleep. All our lockers were shit this morning, so we are having another inspection at 22:00 and we've got to be in drill rig.

Now 02:30 and I'm just getting in bed. The lockers got absolutely trashed and we've been up until now sorting them out. Literally hallucinating and I have to be up in 2½ hours. That will be 6 hours' sleep in three nights!

Eliciting and maintaining sleep deprivation is a process that forms the fabric of the first fifteen weeks of training. Failed inspections are often inevitable and systematically carried out to inflict carnage on a recruit's evening routine. Having lockers turned upside down and then having to prepare for re-inspections throughout the evening and into the early hours – changing in and out of various military uniforms – keeps recruits up for hours and is the most effective tool for breaking recruits down over a sustained period of time. In effect, weeding out those who begin to question their motives for continuation.

<u>Day 26 – Friday 10 June</u>

Really struggling today and I started, for the first time, to lose sight of why I'm here! The Training Team are being bastards and constantly hammering us physically for everything.

We've passed this morning's locker inspection and we can now move out of foundation and into our new blocks – can't wait, some of us have spent 4 weeks in foundation instead of the usual two, and it's been hell.

We've got PT and swimming this morning then the annual Royal Marines sports day and I genuinely feel like I'm dying.

I don't know how I'm going to get through this at all. This is by far my hardest day yet – my eyes are starting to play tricks on me.

Colonel T ran the sports day. Apparently, he has the highest kill count in the British military, and he is soon to be knighted.

Day 27 – Saturday 11 June

We had swimming circuits all morning. One of the exercises was swimming quietly under the water with assault rifles on our backs – absolutely class!

Locker inspection at 14:00 – we've been told that if it's OK, we can go ashore straight after until 20:00.

Passed inspection – going ashore now to get steaming. Since we passed out of Foundation Block, we've had a lot more freedom to do what we want, and it feels good.

Day 28 – Sunday 12 June

Me and seven of the lads got kicked out the camp pub last night for pissing in pint pots and drinking them. Some of the lads were being sick in bins and the bar staff called the duty sergeant – Sgt R, the one bloke on camp you never want to turn up! We are in the shit big time now and have been told to expect 'mud runs' all week and a 'beasting' that will make 'our eyes bleed'. Looking back, it was funny though.

Also, yesterday, we nearly got into two fights in Exeter with local lads – they absolutely hate us round here.

I pulled my pants down and said, 'What can you say about me now?'

A girl replied, 'That is the littlest dick I've ever seen!'

I replied, 'I know!' and it completely shut her down.

Just heading to church now and then I think we have the rest of the day off. My right shin is killing me every time I apply pressure through jogging and running, and it's really worrying me because the last thing I want is a stress fracture, which is very common down here and gets rid of lots of good lads.

LESSON 4

Managing sleep deprivation and understanding the restorative 'scientific' qualities of savannah-type environments, and utilising their ability to replenish our attentional resources.

Fatigue and sleep deprivation resulting from heavy workloads and commitments elicit stress, frustration, and temporarily cloud one's judgement.

Royal Marines training arguably elicited the most intensive mental and physical fatigue I have ever experienced; followed by operating in hostile environments and more recently, undergoing the study of psychology. When decisions about our futures are made in this cognitive fog, they can have catastrophic consequences, especially when trying to attain arduous undertakings like that of Royal Marines Commando training.

Therefore, it is important to note some key scientific research studies, which have been conducted to investigate the 'restorative qualities' that natural environments can have on stress reduction; the rejuvenation of attentional resources, and how they can alleviate if not safeguard against cognitive burn-out.

The Biophilia hypothesis[2] suggests that humans possess an innate tendency to seek connections with the natural world

---

2   Edward O. Wilson, *Biophilia*, Harvard University Press, 1984.

and other forms of nature over human-built structures and urbanised, artificial environments.

To support this claim, the Attention Restoration Theory (ART)[3] argues that attentional fatigue due to the depletion of mental resources occurs, in part, due to a lack of natural features or vegetation in a person's environment, but can be restored and maintained by four qualities: 'fascination' – sensory qualities that have an inherent appeal; 'extent' – a sense of environmental vastness; 'being away' – from the demands of regular life; and 'compatibility' – relating to what one wants to do and what they can do in a given landscape.

Our evolution may play a key role here: scientists believe that green open spaces are representative of the 'Savannah-type Environments' from which we first evolved, and by stepping outside of densely populated towns and cities, and seeking green parks or the countryside, we can rejuvenate our attentional resources and cognitive processing – leading to better mental health, well-being and sustained performance.

Surprisingly, a Norwegian study[4] found that even the number of indoor plants nearby a worker's desk also had a very small but statistically reliable association with reduced sick leave and increased productivity.

Moreover, a study conducted by Roger S. Ulrich,[5] which was underpinned by his Stress Reduction Theory (SRT), subjected two groups of hospital patients to either a natural hospital

---

3   S. Kaplan, 'The restorative benefits of nature: Toward an integrative framework', *Journal of Environmental Psychology*, 1995.

4   T. Bringslimark, et al., 'Psychological benefits of Indoor Plants in Workspaces: Putting Experimental Results into Context' in *HortScience*, pp. 518–87, Vol. 42: Issue 3, 2007.

5   R.S. Ulrich, 'Aesthetic and Affective Response to Natural Environment', in Chambers University of Technology, 1983.

room view or one of a brick wall. He found that the group with the natural view needed to stay in hospital for a shorter time after their operation, took fewer painkillers, and received fewer negative evaluations by hospital staff.

According to Zhang and Zypnur,[6] many of today's mental health problems can be attributed to the artificial environments people inhabit. Therefore, understanding our innate evolutionary needs and inherent connection to natural spaces is vital for mental health restoration, well-being, processing, and sustained cognitive ability.

Key Points:

- Declines in mental and physical well-being, due to cognitive fatigue, temporarily change our perception of what we value as important. This can sabotage our desire to remain consistent when undergoing medium to long-term goal acquisitions.
- With the benefit of experience in training, a good sleep or adequate rest can often uncloud your judgement and assessment of things and is a key ingredient in getting a rational state of mind back on track. Unbelievably, many recruits often make decisions about their future, i.e., to leave and return home, in states of fatigue.
- Cognitive burn-out is often more deep-rooted and requires regular exposure to natural environments, as

---

6   Z. Zhang, & M.J. Zypnur, 'Physiological functioning and employee health in organizations' in: Colarelli, S.M., & Arvey, R.D. (eds.), *The Biological Foundations of Organizational Behaviour*, University of Chicago Press, 2015, pp. 139–67.

well as adequate rest, in order to replenish and restore our attentional resources.
- Even something as simple as putting plants on a desk can have a significant impact on productivity and therefore success.

7

STAYING MOTIVATED

*The fear of failure, knowing about motivation,
and managing emotions*

WEEK 3

Day 29 – Monday 13 June 2005

Really tired today, we've had three periods of drill and I've been falling asleep in-between each period. Shocking, I hate drill – you have to have your drill boot laces pulled together so tight that your feet go numb and it's horrible – real hangout! My right shin is playing up constantly, increasingly getting worried about it, but it's out my hands – I hope it sorts itself out.

We moved into the newest camp blocks today and it's class. I'm in a room with five lads, but have my own private bed space – heaven. A far cry from foundation and the open room with 51 lads.

Day 30 – Tuesday 14 June

I slept in this morning – didn't get up until 06:17. I slept with ear plugs in, because Evans snores so loud. I had to get out of bed at 03:00 and tip him out of bed!

Been to see the Company Sergeant Major (CSM) today to

find out our punishment for the camp pub incident. We must sweep the weapon teaching stances and ranges from 18:00–22:00 tomorrow night. We got off lightly, he had considered taking our leave off us.

I felt so lethargic during PT today. We practised the 'make-fast' for the first time on a 30ft rope. It's a way of securing yourself to a rope by your legs and feet mid-air, which allows your arms and hands to rest during fast roping operations from helicopters – if for whatever reason the landing site becomes unsafe to rope onto – really cool!

Day 31 – Wednesday 15 June

One of the lads – Recruit Cake – dislocated his shoulder while doing a rope climb last week and he got 'medically discharged' yesterday. Poor bastard, I feel really sorry for the lad, even though I wasn't keen on him.

The Training Team took us for our first mud run today, on the legendary Mud Flats. It was absolutely horrible – sinking down to our knees in fucking mud. We had to try to play football and rugby and had to crawl to checkpoint. At 18:00 I had to do camp duties for drinking piss in the camp bar last Saturday. It's 22:00 now and I'm absolutely WORN OUT.

P.S., I was talking to Cpl Dite today about his time serving as a sniper in Ireland and Iraq . . . Unreal!

Day 32 – Thursday 16 June

Weapons training this morning in the stances – we were taught the characteristics of the SA80, and how to do safety checks; load and unload, make safe, and what impact a bullet has on the human body – CLASS! (*Weapons stances are small, specially designed teaching huts on the south of camp, where recruits are taught the fundamentals of weapon handling and manipulation.*)

Two periods of military and soldiering lectures this afternoon. Literally couldn't keep my eyes open and was told to come to front of class and submerge my head in a bucket of 50% water and 50% ice cubes. After, it was PT. We were rehearsing our gym routine ready for Parents' Day while getting absolutely hammered in the meantime. If we manage to pull it off tomorrow in front of our parents, it will look amazing.

At 22:00 we had rounds (*accommodation inspections*), which we failed and had to throw everything we owned out the window. Cpl C said it was a wake-up call! It's 00:00 now and having washed all my clothes, I now need to wait for an ironing board to start ironing my kit for Parents' Day in . . . 5 hrs!

Day 33 – Friday 17 June

Looking forward to seeing my mum and grandma today and then going home – it's been 6 weeks now that I've been away. I've had very little sleep, around 2 hours, because I have to get all my kit sorted after failing rounds. Two periods of PT first thing – and we have to look flawless, as up to 100 parents will be watching from the gymnasium viewing platform.

PT was absolutely brutal – the hardest session in the past 6 weeks. We gave everything and were completely exhausted after – with some lads throwing up. PTI B said our movement around the gymnasium was too slow. He said, 'There are two speeds around the gym – lightning fast and perfectly still!'

So, after the parents left the gym to go and get lunch, we stayed behind and got thrashed. Wall-to-wall sprints, stress positions, crabs, and dragging our bodies using only our arms, which burnt all the skin off my knees.

Just on my way home now, what a feeling! I have Saturday off, which will involve large amounts of booze, then I have to return by train on Sunday afternoon.

I would later learn that Parents' Day was strategically placed at Week 3 and the failed locker inspection the night before, plus the thrashing after the parents left, was all done to cast motivation doubt in recruits' minds once they got on leave . . . Indeed, a few lads never returned to training after that weekend and for those that did, some left by the end of Week 4.

Day 34 – Sunday 19 June

It's 15:20 and I'm travelling down to Lympstone again. Really don't want to go back, but something inside me is pulling and I know I must, but I'm completely gutted. I feel so conflicted today. I've seen all my mates and had a great weekend, it's been brilliant. If I break it down, though, it's only the same old shit in Hemsworth.

One of my trains got cancelled – an absolute nightmare, had to change twice and I'm now due to arrive at camp at 22:00 rather than 18:00. I wanted to be in bed, all admin done for ten, not just starting at daft o'clock.

WHAT AM I DOING WITH MY LIFE!

LESSON 5

Staying on course by 'understanding' and manipulating Extrinsic and Intrinsic motivating factors, and how to manage emotions when going from the in-group to the out-group.

A scientific understanding of motivation

Intrinsic motivation is subjective and comes from within. It is the internal drive to do things purely because they are interesting or enjoyable. For example, we may be motivated to exercise to benefit our physical health, or to promote and maintain our self-esteem.

Extrinsic motivation is more objective and involves the actions we perform to gain rewards, or to avoid things that are personally unpleasant. It could be more calculated in nature; for example, going to work to earn money, or doing something to receive a favour in return.

A *crossover* occurs when a behaviour performed for money or a favour becomes enjoyable or rewarding. In relation to Royal Marines training, a recruit works hard to achieve the Green Beret, and admiration from others (*extrinsic reward*). In turn, and over time, the discipline and training becomes part of who they are, generating *intrinsic rewards*, such as increased self-esteem, self-reliance, and self-discipline.

Real world application

If we are aware of what our motivations are, then we can use them to our advantage; to stay on track towards attaining our goal. From my own experience, I harnessed the fear of failure to motivate me both intrinsically and extrinsically throughout training.

There was one thing that enabled me to continue on

61

towards my end goal. Chipping away at the back of my mind was what people said when I first revealed my intention to join the Royal Marines: 'See you in a month's time. You can't do the Marines, no chance!'

This was a typical reaction and it strengthened my resolve to succeed: I had to dig deep and prove them all wrong.

The dynamics of in-group and out-group biases[7]
In-group: *People who are categorised as belonging to the same social, ethnic or age group.*

My conduct prior to joining the Royal Marines was reckless and misguided. However, among my peer group at that time this type of behaviour was 'the norm': it was expected, accept-able and even valued. It represented the behaviour of my in-group. Opportunity and life chances did not really form the fabric of my social structure and connections at that time. I had to leave.

Out-group: *People who are categorised as not belonging to the same social, ethnic or age group.*

When I started to leave my in-group, my local village community, and to take the bold step of trying to join the Royal Marines, I began to attract negative labelling from those who were deeply embedded in the in-group that I was leaving. This was an uncomfortable period emotionally and one that created tremendous anxiety and risk if I had not completed training.

---

7 H. Tajfel & J. Turner, 'An integrative theory of intergroup conflict', in M.A. Hogg & D. Abrams (eds.), *Key Readings in Social Psychology. Intergroup Relations: Essential Readings*, Psychology Press, 2001, pp. 94–109.

The message

In times like this, it is absolutely crucial to stay positive. It is fundamental to engage in the regular mental exercise of positively reinforcing your rationale for why you want to achieve something. It might be preparing for an arduous endurance event, a weight-loss goal, a course (degree) to open doors of opportunity, or a significant and life-changing shift in career.

I used negativity and indirect attacks on my personality and character to fuel my motivation to continue. The fear of failure, of returning home and validating general opinion, provided such a solid anchor of intrinsic and extrinsic motivation, that the notion of returning home without succeeding at my goal, was never an option. Failure, in this sense, was such a powerful ally.

Key Points:

- If harnessed correctly, negative endorsements can be immensely powerful motivational drivers for success.
- Everyone has an opinion – positive or negative. Not many people have been exposed to what it takes to achieve significant life-transforming experiences. It is important to remember that, when you are seeking advice or comfort. Therefore, select your support network wisely.
- Instead, seek like-minded interaction with those who have already taken the journey you wish to travel and, crucially, have been successful in that endeavour.

8

LOSING SIGHT OF THE END GOAL

Remaining resilient in the face of adversity

WEEK 4

Day 35 – Monday 20 June 2005

Can't explain how depressed I feel this morning! I feel so pissed off and gutted to be back down here. We have 2 lectures on soldiering this morning then double – 2 periods – of PT.

One of the lads, Recruit Moore, is AWOL; he hasn't returned back from leave and the Training Team have said he's in the shit BIG TIME! They said if he comes back, he'll get 28 days in Colchester (*military prison*). We all knew he didn't like it down here, but he could have just come down and wrapped (*given up or quit*) today.

Afternoon was spent doing weapons lessons. It's 20:00 now – going to the NAAFI (*camp shop*) then going to wind up some of the lads and get the banter going, which usually involves me throwing buckets of water over the toilet cubicle doors when lads are either masturbating or having a shit. I'll hopefully be in bed for 21:30.

Day 36 – Tuesday 21 June

My 21st birthday today and somehow managed to sleep in until 07:00!

We were introduced to a new circuit this morning call IMFS, it's like IMFC but is a weights/resistance circuit that prepares the body for the Bottom Field assault course, which looks and is rumoured to be absolutely brutal.

The circuit was good, I really enjoyed it – very much like the kind of circuits I did at Leeds Rhinos – but hammers you like everything does down here. After the session, we had to do a makefast and two full rope climbs – 3 of the lads spewed up into their tucked-in gym T-shirts . . . so glad it's not been me yet, but I'm sure my turn will come.

When it comes to scran time, the Training Team keep putting time limits on how fast we need to get down to the galley, eat and come back. On most days we have to run to the galley, frantically wait in the epic queue, get food, find a place to sit and shovel it down, and then run back – awful.

After lunch, we had two periods of weapon training – going through; firing positions, safety checks, ways of regulating our breathing and how to aim. It was very interesting! Then we had another collective talk from Cpl Dite; he told us about his career in the Royal Marines, from training to being in a Commando Unit. He talked candidly about his time in Sierra Leone, Iraq, Ireland, and his time with Recce Troop as a sniper. So fascinating, really gave me a reality check and reinforced why I'm doing this!

P.S., My birthday was wank. I put my cards round my bed and the Training Team came around and ripped them all up, saying, 'There's no fucking birthdays down here.' Anyway, whatever!

Day 37 – Wednesday 22 June

The two lectures this morning were on global security – IRA and Al-Qaeda – very interesting. PT involved a three-mile run. My right shin is playing up again. After lunch we had two weapons training periods and I just managed to close my left eye for the first time. Absolutely buzzing!

At 16:30 we deploy on exercise 'early night' with our SA80s. Not sure what to expect, but will probably involve zero sleep, little food and being cold and wet throughout – CAN'T WAIT – Not.

The exercise went OK, although we were late on loads of details (*timings*) and had to 'repay' the Training Team with fourteen minutes of PAIN . . . stress positions!

Day 38 – Thursday 23 June

I had to get out my sleeping bag and go on sentry at 00:00 until 01:00 with my SA80. During sentry, Cpl Brown crept up on me and pretended to slit my throat. It's unbelievable how close he got to me without me knowing!

Got back to camp around 16:00 – we've had no sleep, very little to eat – rations are fucking awful, and now we have to strip and clean our weapons, de-service (*wash, iron, and clean*) our kit ready for inspection in the morning. This will take me and the rest of us all night to sort out and get it to the correct standard. Not looking forward to it at all. Yet another night of no sleep.

Where can I start with military rations, aka 'Rat Packs', especially the ones of old. You would get handed a small cardboard box containing twenty-four hours' worth of food rations that had to be broken down and packed in your bergen.

The contents were, for example: French onion soup, savoury biscuits, fruit biscuits, chicken pâté (absolutely honking), bacon and beans (breakfast), something like corned beef hash (lunch: absolutely honking) and maybe curried lamb (dinner), and finally chocolate pudding (dessert: the only food item capable of resurrecting morale!). Along with smaller items like: Hot chocolate, milk chocolate, electrolyte powder, boiled sweets, and chewing gum.

In all, the contents were about 50 per cent edible and 5–10 per cent enjoyable. The meals had to be cooked by digging a portable Hexi cooker into the ground and heating up the contents in a metal cup of semi-boiling water before enjoying the rare culinary delight. Tabasco sauce was the only thing that could make the cooked meals remotely edible without gipping. However, we weren't allowed to take this 'silver bullet' into the field before Week 15.

Day 39 – Friday 24 June

Had one hour's sleep and had to get up and lay out my kit muster and open my locker ready for inspection. I feel so shit, run down, and dizzy! As I am writing this, I'm driving my pen into the page, I'm that frustrated and tired.

Periods three and four were spent doing weapons lessons, looking at bullets and what they do upon impact on the human body – unreal. PT was shit and PTI B said we didn't work hard enough so period nine, he absolutely thrashed us on Bottom Field – fireman's carries and 200m crawling – dragging our bodies, etc.

Two lads are leaving, can't handle it. Training has really increased dramatically in intensity – every day is a pure struggle now. It's the fact that you have absolutely no control over your life! The only time when I'm completely free is late at night when I'm in bed and about to go to sleep.

Day 40 – Saturday 25 June

IMFC, the new weights-related circuit this morning, which includes rope pull-ups, squats, hyper-extensions, fireman's carries, and bridging up on a large fixed object called the penny. This helps to develop the upper body and core strength to get over the 6ft wall on Bottom Field wearing kit. It's all done at 100 mph and it's really challenging, but I enjoy it, so I don't mind this session when it comes around.

Planning to go into Exeter today, I need a few things from an army surplus store in town for our exercise next week. The guy who runs the store is an ex-Royal Marine apparently and and knows how to charge us.

Day 41 – Sunday 26 June

Nice lay-in this morning until 09:30 and we've got all day off. Just cleaning magazines and ironing, then chilling out. Might go into Exeter and lay on the grass outside the church and sunbathe.

Ended up staying round camp, I watched 'Kill Bill 2' – shit! Going to Torquay next Sunday to meet some lasses we met in Exeter yesterday.

LESSON 6

Strategies that you can employ in order to remain focused and resilient when you start to lose sight of your ultimate aim.

The reality is, regardless of how much you want something and how committed you are to achieving an aim, at some point and quite possibly on numerous occasions, you will lose sight of why you are doing something.

Acknowledging that losing sight of the end goal will happen, learning to cope with it and accepting that this is all part of the journey, forms a key, foundational ingredient in the construct of mental resilience, which keeps at bay 'cognitive dissonance' – physiological stress caused by competing and contradictory ideas, beliefs, values and subsequent behaviours that arise towards an event that bring discomfort.

Mental strategies that can mitigate disillusionment and uncertainty

Loading value onto your end goal is essential to safeguard the acquisition of that goal or the pursuit of a goal coming to fruition. For example, write down or visualise what achieving the end goal will do for you; reinforce how it will alter the trajectory of your life; what opportunities will come after achieving it and, notably, why you are choosing to leave the environment you currently inhabit.

Often, when heavily entrenched in a plight to attain something that brings discomfort, human beings tend to look back with 'rose-tinted glasses' to what was before. This assessment of a previous existence often exaggerates the positives and downplays the negative aspects, making them appear less problematic than they are.

For example, it could be a lack of job opportunities; the emergence of alienation from your social peer group; a faulty past relationship, or the complexities surrounding your living arrangements. When times get tough, it is easy to overlook these complex 'past' negatives and proceed irrationally to take them back on.

69

Be aware of this, it is an illusion. Take the time to invest in positive reinforcement and visualisation – key practices that enable you to load 'value' (glue) onto an end goal.

I told myself repeatedly how training and earning my Green Beret would radically alter the trajectory of my life. I believed wholeheartedly that it would open doors of opportunity that were both expected and unexpected prior to joining. For instance, in my personal case, going on to hostile private security operations after leaving, and you could say, the creation and publication of this book.

I fully understood and crucially acknowledged the magnitude of the task at hand, but time and again I took steps to reinforce mentally how entering into the hardest military training in the world, and seeing it through, would be a very short-term sacrifice – a 'sacrifice-to-life ratio' that I quietly told myself was not a difficult trade-off.

For example, after enduring nine to ten months of utter hardship, a loss of autonomy, risk and uncertainty, upon completion I could live the remainder of my life with pride, internal satisfaction and external respect, and drastically improve my life chances. It absolutely did that!

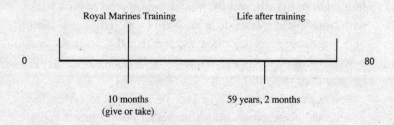

Royal Marines Training   Life after training

0   80

10 months   59 years, 2 months
(give or take)

*Based on a recruit at 20
and a lifespan of 80

70

In short, visualisation of the end goal, and the positives it will bring when achieved, coupled with regular acknowledgements of the sacrifice – the hardship or discomfort it will take to attain it – are fundamental processes that 'prepare' the mind for what lies ahead, thus safeguarding success. Basically, reflect on and learn the value and power of the sacrifice-to-life ratio.

Key Points:

- Losing sight of the end goal is natural and part of the journey. With experience, you will discover this is often only temporary and disillusionment comes in waves – some larger than others, but the storm will eventually subside – often with adequate rest.
- Loading value onto your end goal is key to seeing it come to fruition. Write down the positives and repeatedly visualise life after your goal has been achieved. This will steady the ship when temporary disillusionment creeps in.
- Remember, if it was easy, everyone would do it! Take comfort in that and acknowledge the small (relative to life) sacrifice it will take to achieve a significant, life-changing goal.

9

ERADICATING COMPLACENCY

*The lessons and applications of the Wet
and Dry routine*

WEEK 5

Day 42 – Monday 27 June 2005

The morning started with a four-mile run. I then had my weapons handling test, which was pretty challenging. In the scenario, I walked into the weapons stance and came across an SA80 lying on the ground. Unaware of the weapon's state, I had first to make it safe by unloading then performing the safety checks. After, I had to completely strip the weapon and name each part. On completion, put the weapon back together, get a magazine and load, then go through the motions of firing while encountering various stoppages that I had to rectify quickly and continue. To finish the test, I had to load a magazine with 30 rounds in 60 seconds. I PASSED. I can now live fire on the range next week at 40 Commando – can't wait!

Three of the lads are leaving: Dutchy, Moore, and Ward. It's funny, Dutchy was asked in Week 1 what he wanted to specialise in once/if he completed training and he said arrogantly: SBS. Ha ha ha, fuck off mate!

Had a full kit muster at 20:00, getting in bed now at 00:30.

I've got loads of washing to do, but I'll just re-iron my clothes from today and see if I get away with it.

Day 43 – Tuesday 28 June

We had three periods of drill first thing – I hate it – so boring. During drill, Sir Jimmy Savile came to talk to us. He walked onto the drill square wearing a Green Beret and in a full blue and pink shell suit – covered in gold and diamonds. He's quite funny, but has an arrogant side to him – maybe a shit bloke, if I'm honest? He apparently comes down to Lympstone once a year.

I still get really nervous before PT, because you know each session is going to push you to your absolute limits and today was no different: 3 × 30ft rope climbs, twenty mins high intensity circuit, two camp circuits, and 40 mins of swimming – brutal.

It's getting to a stage now where I'm struggling to describe how hard this is. My idea of what's hard is not even on someone on the outside's radar – it's impossible to explain, you have to experience what it's like down here. Complete lack of sleep, none at all some nights, and constantly under time pressure.

Just prepping my kit ready for exercise 'Quick Cover' tomorrow. Three-day exercise including: camp concealment, firing positions, section fire, evasion, stalking, wet and dry, observation, and judging distance.

While writing this some years later, I find it necessary to explain what the term 'wet and dry' means and the misery this routine creates while on exercise in the field. In order to maintain the heat and sustained integrity of one's sleeping bag, a recruit must learn the harsh discipline of changing, often in pitch-darkness, from wet clothes into dry clothes (that are kept in their bergens) before getting in their sleeping bags to sleep.

Operationally, this enables teams and troops of soldiers to stay out longer on operations and in a better, more hygienic state. A lack of discipline in the wet and dry process can lead to soldiers contracting hypothermia, becoming a liability not only to themselves, but the troop or mission. It is therefore essential that the habitual techniques of locating dry kit in the dark are learnt and that the process of wet and dry is executed on exercises and live operations without fail, even though it goes against every natural human instinct.

There is a big downside to this, however. We started training in the summer and throughout all of our summer exercises, the late evenings/early hours were spent getting submerged in the most atrocious cesspits the Training Team could find on Woodbury Common or other exercise locations. Every single night, or morning, between 22:00–03:00 the Training Team would scream to us, 'Get out of your sleeping bags!', which were often located in the thick, dense Woodbury undergrowth. 'Three fucking lines on the track!' they would shout, and we knew what was coming.

Now, getting out of wet clothes and putting on dry clothes isn't really the drama. It's when you have to get up for your allocated one-hour sentry duty during the night and/or get up for reveille at 05:00 in the field, and then have to get out of a warm sleeping bag and take your warm, dry clothes off and put your cold, wet clothes back on. A process that breaks even the strongest of minds eventually.

Come winter, and it becomes a whole new beast altogether: recruits can be seen smashing frozen trousers off trees to get them on – it is one of the most brutal things anyone can experience during training – especially when you can be sat in them for hours until they eventually dry off during the winter months. With this in mind, it becomes easy to imagine how recruits pray all day for no rain, because rain means carrying out the wet and dry routine.

Day 44 – Wednesday 29 June

Exercise Day 1: It's been really tough today, but the most interesting day yet. We have to do Wet and Dry later, which is going to be the biggest test this far mentally. It's said it finishes loads of the lads off.

We've been through camouflage and concealment, 'why things are seen', it was so interesting. We also saw parts of the legendary Endurance Course and Peter's Pool, which is part of the course and one of the notorious Commando Tests at the end of training. It is actually the one that the young lad is running through on the Royal Marines Advert: 'What's your limit? Here? Here? Here? Compose yourself! Compose yourself! Off you go, good lad, get away! . . . 99.9% Need Not Apply.'

Just had our rations – disgusting – and been given 2 blank rounds to load into a magazine plus taught various firing positions.

Day 45 – Thursday 30 June

Exercise Day 2: Woke up in the field, it's 05:00 and I now have to put shocking wet clothes and boots on. Mentally the biggest test of my life. We got marched down to Peter's Pool on the Endurance Course last night at 23:00. It was absolutely pitch-black, cold, and I was half-asleep walking into the water.

The sheer disbelief of what was happening soon came when the water rushed over my boots – the coldest water ever! Once the water was up to our waists, the Training Team made us completely submerge ourselves three times, then we had to get

75

out of the water and turn in at a designated RV point, quickly change into dry clothes and get into our sleeping bags. It was 00:15 by this time and I was due back up at 02:00 for sentry duty.

Getting shook at 01:30 to get ready for sentry is the worst experience any man can experience. Knowing that the process of wet and dry immediately awaits in pitch-darkness, and having to put cold, soaking wet clothes on, makes you wish briefly that the ground would open up and swallow you and is by far my most stressful test yet.

Day 46 – Friday 01 July

Exercise Day 3: It rained all day yesterday, which meant my clothes didn't dry out and I had to sit in cold, wet clothes all bastard day. Same again this morning. I'm cold, wet, and absolutely starving hungry. I don't want rations, I want a McDonald's or Kentucky Fried Chicken.

We've learnt basic stalking today, as well as ways of moving for different situations from front rolls, crawling, and ghost walking. Just gone through various section attacks, practising doing 'hard target' – running not in a straight line to avoid being shot – and recce tasks, where we got to fire our blank rounds. This is why I joined the Marines (class).

Just arrived back at camp! Stripping weapons, magazines, and cleaning then de-servicing my kit. Absolutely broken now, mentally and physically.

Day 47 – Saturday 02 July

Waking up in a warm comfy bed is such an unbelievable feeling. In the field, I would see the odd sight and hear the distinct sound of a car. I felt so angry and envious of these people that were going home to nice warm food and a warm bed, while we were getting submerged in cold water and eating rations.

Looking back over the past 4 days, I've encountered many challenges: wet and dry, five hours' sleep total, and very little food, so I feel proud I've come out the other end. I joined the Royal Marines to see who I was as a person; I think and hope I'm starting to get to know.

Well, fuck it! I'm going on the piss at 14:00 with the lads. Ha ha ha . . . 'Half man, half beer barrel.'

Day 48 – Sunday 03 July

I'm feeling so rough this morning, although I was treated to a nice 10:30 sleep in. Going into Exeter again today for a portable DVD player, then chilling and watching movies.

LESSON 7

The Subtle Edge is forged in the shadows and refined by the mundane: what we can all take away from the harsh practices of Wet and Dry routine to enhance our performance and optimise our lifestyles.

Conducting Wet and Dry routine properly in the middle of a harsh winter requires a recruit or trained soldier to harness and apply most, if not all, the other lessons within this book. Having the internal self-discipline and mental resilience to execute each morale-sapping, gruelling phase of the Wet and Dry process goes against human instinct. Its application, however, is a funda-mental necessity that allows frontline soldiers to stay combat effective and thus operational in the field or theatre for sustained periods of time.

At the beginning of training, a recruit is checked systematically after each exercise. A simple check of a sleeping bag conducted by the Training Team reveals if wet clothing or boots have been worn in it during the exercise. However tempting the urge is to get into a sleeping bag in the middle of winter, when you are wet through and exhausted, it must be resisted – that is where resilience and self-discipline come in.

As seniority grows throughout training, sleeping-bag checks become periodic as habit, trust and expectation intertwine, and once a recruit 'successfully' leaves Commando Training Centre Royal Marines, they are never checked again, because they are absolutely, without question, expected to do it and not cut corners. Come the end of training, the standard is set, and the understanding of expectation embedded.

The transferability of Wet and Dry routine

Wet and Dry is most often conducted in the thick of night, in pitch-darkness. Nobody watches you do it nor do they heap praise on you for doing it correctly. What we do behind closed doors, when the spotlight is not on us, matters the most. It is the investment, commitment, and self-sacrifice (or lack of it) that we do without hesitation, when nobody is watching, that makes us either incredibly average or furiously unstoppable.

If you can harness the self-discipline to do the less desirable tasks in life well, with purpose and attention to detail, then the enjoyable, effortless things in life get done to a higher standard. Quite frankly, you develop a Subtle Edge to how you conduct life, which is (a) immeasurable in its nature and (b) unattainable by those who do not practise it.

For example, the New Zealand All Blacks Rugby Union

team would practise for hours in their dressing room the simple and mundane process of putting on their socks correctly; they had to make sure the heel part of the sock sat perfectly on their heel. This not only prevented blisters, but it safeguarded the team as a 'whole' by acknowledging the fundamental role of the individual.

For the All Blacks, it was all about 'preparing for success', and that meant deconstructing what people see in public, on TV and in the stadiums. It goes right back to a focus on mastering the basics. That is the lesson to take away from the Wet and Dry routine.

The philosophy of Wet and Dry routine applied in a non-military sense

It is about not making excuses when it comes to living and maintaining a disciplined and professional lifestyle. It is about getting up early on a cold winter's morning to go for a run or attend a fitness class before work, staying consistent and up to date with work commitments, like reports or university assignments, for instance. It is about transferring the principles and commitment needed to carry out a successful Wet and Dry evolution and applying them to your philosophy of life in the form of non-negotiable behavioural actions, in order to gain an edge in ability and performance.

Key Points:

- It is what you do in the shadows that makes you unstoppable when the spotlight is on.
- Master the mundane and the easy, enjoyable aspects of life become effortless.

- Not cutting corners and appreciating the seemingly insignificant impact small actions make, gives you a Subtle Edge.
- Forming new, positive, and potentially life-changing habits takes up to 90 days. Whereas extinguishing bad habits takes between 14–30 days. What are you waiting for?

10

ACHIEVING MASTERY

Corporal Dite and the 2p coin

WEEK 6

Day 49 – Monday 04 July 2005

PT this morning was really hard. We are getting ready for gym pass out, which is in Week 9. If we pass this, we can move on to Bottom Field.

In the afternoon, we had two weapons lectures, an alcohol and first aid lecture, and to finish the day, a full kit muster: everything had to be gleaming – no water in water bottles, no dust on weapon internals, etc.

Cpl M inspected me and my room mates. Everyone is scared to death of him; if he doesn't like you, your kit and everything you own will either be thrown out the window or down the stairs. He seems to like me and Wrighty, so we got a 900 Troop team stamp on our foreheads. However, Evans and Softly weren't as lucky and he soaked all their kit with water, ha ha ha.

Day 50 – Tuesday 05 July

Map reading, and navigation lessons all day today. I'm OK with it and find some of it interesting. For instance, at night, you can't read a map with night-vision goggles on, because you can't see the red lines and borders on a map, so you have to use a torch in certain tactical ways. They hammer it home, though, that any overuse of a torch in the field and the enemy will see you, so having an awareness of this and minimising the light output is crucial.

Our Troop Captain was among the first Royal Marines that went into Iraq and he was telling us classified information about the Americans and their satellite systems – unbelievably interesting!

Day 51 – Wednesday 06 July

The runs are increasing, today's was five miles at 07:50 and we were running 7-minute miles – my legs were hanging out!

Period eight was IMFS, my body is proper fucked from the run, but I did well. We've started practising rope re-gains on a 15ft high beam in preparation for the legendary rope re-gains on Bottom Field wearing full fighting assault order (29lbs plus weapon).

Exercise 'Marshall Star' next week is playing on my mind. If I'm honest, I'm absolutely dreading it. Everyone down here talks about it and how gruelling it is. I'm trying to change my mindset on it and draw out the positives, but I can't.

Day 52 – Thursday 07 July

Been to 40 Commando today to see what life is like outside this 'concentration camp'. It's unbelievable how relaxed and laid back this place is; the fully trained Marines were playing football, rugby, and golf. The camp is brilliant as well.

Also, we did our first live fire shoot with forty rounds on

a 25m range. My shooting was good, but all the factors that go into shooting correctly are so difficult to master. The power of the bullet is unreal.

Cpl Dite – the recce sniper – hit a 2p coin without zeroing his weapon from 100m away . . . AMAZING!

Day 53 – Friday 08 July

Weapons inspections first thing then two lectures and swimming. In one of the lectures, we watched the US Marines training. What a complete joke, they have girl recruits and their training for both genders is 12 weeks, as opposed to ours which is 32 weeks long. They are compared to our Army and we are like their Navy Seals!

We have four weeks of hell coming up, starting with Marshall Star from Monday to Thursday and then gym pass-out in Week 9 – that's a full week of tests. If you fail gym pass-out, you get back-trooped. If you pass, it's on to Bottom Field to start battle scenario physical training.

Can't stop thinking about what's ahead. I'm scared and worried.

Day 54 – Saturday 09 July

Four periods of drill complete – fucking terrible that shit is!

Anyway, it's 11:30 and I'm going on the piss with some of the lads.

Day 55 – Sunday 10 July

Rough as shit this morning – wow, Exeter was OK, the weather was boiling, and I burnt my shoulders badly, which is bad news as I have Marshall Star on Monday and have to carry a 70lbs bergen.

Woke up at 00:00 this morning covered in sick, I must have spewed up in my sleep – weird one, unless one of the lads spewed on me? I had to sleep on a roll mat in my sleeping bag all night.

17:00. Everything is now packed for Marshall Star and I'm dreading it. If the grapevine down here is to be believed, it's the worst exercise of them all and its sole aim is to get rid of lads that don't really want to be here now!

LESSON 8

The art of mastery and the commitment required to produce unbelievable feats of human capability, relies on the investment of 10,000 hours of practice.

When Kev Dite hit that 2p coin with an un-zeroed weapon (an SA80 assault rifle's barrel that had not been aligned with the rifle's SUSAT telescopic sight), I viewed that as sheer excellence. From growing up and being surrounded by professional rugby league players, I had an awareness and fascination with people that were exceptional – who were elite amongst the elite. I had witnessed first-hand how difficult the road was to achieve excellence – the meticulous attention to detail required in order to make complex skills look effortless.

That day, Kev made shooting – a highly technical and complex skill – look effortless and it left us all gasping for breath, including the rest of our Training Team.

But my fascination did not end there. Playing rugby as a child and into my late teens at a high-level exposed me to some truly remarkable players. I have always wondered what makes somebody so good, so effortlessly talented at sport. For example, a Roger Federer, a Jessica Ennis-Hill, or a Cristiano Ronaldo? These are world class athletes who make extremely difficult, technical, and often unimaginable skills look easy. Floyd Mayweather (love him or hate him), the unbeaten 15-time world boxing champion, is another who springs immediately to mind.

Is such exceptional skill and talent driven innately through a complex mixture of genes and traits that we inherit? Or does it come from the social and cultural environments that we are born into – external factors that surround and shape us, influencing our personalities and behaviours throughout childhood into adulthood?

That is the elusive million-dollar question and a debate that will likely continue to rage for some time. However, studies and intensive investigations[8] exploring how people achieve mastery at highly skilled disciplines have revealed that 10,000 hours of practice is required to achieve that level of competency.

Granted, it would be careless to discount the role that genetic propensity and intellectual capacity plays on one's journey towards success – their unique drive, motivation and determination to succeed. For example, Kev may have been blessed with the inherent properties of exceptional eyesight and motor skills. That said, there is absolutely no substitute for hard work, dedication, and 'deliberate' practice – 10,000 hours to be exact.

---

8   K.A. Ericsson & K. Harwell, 'Deliberate practice and proposed limits on the effects of practice on the acquisition of expert performance: Why the original definition matters and recommendations for future research', *Frontiers in Psychology*, 10, 2396, 2019.

Indeed, when Kev Dite hit the 2p that day from 100 metres away, he had been in the Royal Marines for six years. Researchers estimate that depending on the person, 6–10 years is what it takes to achieve 10,000 hours of deliberate practice and thus achieve mastery in a chosen field.[9]

Key Points:

- No one person's success can be attributed to themselves. Success requires the help of others and is a complex mix of timing, social and cultural environments, opportunity and innate capability.
- Achieving mastery and excellence takes on average 10,000 hours of 'deliberate' practice. Roughly 6–10 years (individual dependent).

9   M. Gladwell, *Outliers: The Story of Success*, Little, Brown and Company, New York, 2008.

11

REDEFINING EXPECTATION

Acceptance

WEEK 7

Day 56 – Monday 11 July 2005

Exercise Day 1: I have never felt like this prior to an exercise. We depart camp for Woodbury Common at lunchtime and I don't want to go at all. Absolutely dreading it, NO sleep for three nights and piss wet through. I feel really fed up today, but I need to snap out of it QUICK!

Day 57 – Tuesday 12 July

Exercise Day 2: Wet and dry last night was the worst thing in the world. The Training Team led the troop into a harbour position (*tactical sleeping area*) at 23:00 in dense woodland undergrowth. We literally got our ponchos up, roll mats down, and sleeping bags out – in pitch-darkness – then the Training Team came back in at 00:00. (*They sleep in a proper tent, with cooking facilities and camp beds.*) They gave us a massive shake: 'Stand to! Get on the fucking track! Three ranks on the track! 3 – 2 – 1 – On the fucking track!'

We knew exactly where we were going. They marched us hard to the 'Sheep Dip' on the Endurance Course, making us crawl through puddles of minging water and thick sludge on the way. After the Sheep Dip and covered in mud and piss-wet through, we went for a lecture at 03:00 on 'light and sound' and how both travel at night. We were using Night Vision Goggles (NVGs) and CSWs – that's an infra-red imaging scope. Both were brilliant and for a moment I forgot I was covered in shit and shivering my bollocks off.

I've had 1½ hours' sleep since Monday and have every bug and insect crawling all over me, plus ticks in my armpits and groin!

Day 58 – Wednesday 13 July

Exercise Day 3: It's 05:30 and I've just changed into my freezing wet clothes. I've been bitten to death, it's horrible out here. Passed my kit inspection (just), which means no 'flank' – the Training Team's 20 minutes of 'special attention' for failed kit inspections.

I was watching wild deer last night through the NVGs – the view you get is like it is on the 'Splinter Cell' Xbox game – quality! Loads of lectures this morning and then Field PT. We had to crawl through gorse bushes that are covered in spikes – it's like crawling through razor blades – my legs are now cut to ribbons and I'm bastard constipated too because of the rations.

The Training Team are really trying to break us. They won't let us have even a second to ourselves and it's wearing us all down. I've had only 1 hour sleep again – 2½ hours since Monday and had to do wet and dry routine constantly.

Day 59 – Thursday 14 July

Exercise Day 4: GOING BACK TO CAMP!

Had four hours' sleep now since Sunday and my eyes are playing games with me. I'm mucky as shit and the stink coming from my body is unreal. Mentally broken now. Words can't explain how painful and hard this is, I'm totally exhausted, and we are all pushed to the limits now. Just had PT – lads were falling asleep stood up – I've honestly never seen anything like it. We learnt how to make booby traps and trip flares this morning – loved it!

HOLY FUCK . . . they just handed out more ration packs . . . I think we are staying in the field? Just been told we are doing a night navigation exercise tonight at 22:30. I'm wet, cold, and starving – had 4 hours' sleep and this ex will go on until 03:00 apparently.

Day 60 – Friday 15 July

At 04:15 our harbour position got infiltrated by enemy (_Training Team_), we had to jump out of our bags, put on our wet clothes, pack all our kit in two mins flat and get to an RV point which was 1km away. Once there, we yomped 4–5 miles back to camp! I've now had five hours' sleep since Monday morning – my feet are fucked, I've got massive blisters, and trench foot starting.

We messed up sentry last night, so Captain W has put my section on sentry duty from this afternoon at 16:00 until Monday morning – two hours off / half an hour on sentry. I feel like wrapping and going home, but I know this is what they want, so I'm determined to get through this.

This is the most emotional test and the biggest hurdle I've been up against this far in my life. It's me that's going to win, not them!

Day 61 – Saturday 16 July

I had to attend sickbay this morning because I can't get my boots on – my feet are in bits. They gave me a trainer's chit (*note*) for one day to let my feet recover, which means I miss drill today . . . YES!

Got my 'Battle Swimming Test' (BST) this afternoon. We must jump off the diving board wearing combats, webbing, and weapon and swim 100m then take off the webbing and weapon and tread water for 3 mins.

I found the BST fairly easy and passed, which is another tick in box, however, two of the lads failed it. Just doing my sentry now – non-stop until Monday. I'm gutted because the lads are going to Torquay on the piss. Watched my PTI and three others do unarmed combat today with baseball bats and weapons – it was class!

Day 62 – Sunday 17 July

Been up five times in the night for this sentry detail. I'm so tired and we've got three big weeks coming up.

Just ironing my kit and then going to watch 'Man on Fire'.

LESSON 9

Learning to accept sudden and often negative outcomes is fundamental to reduce emotional distress, therefore preserving high performance levels, and in a military context, sometimes life.

In Commando training, the Training Team simulate false endings, usually towards the end of arduous exercises. For example, in the case above, mentally preparing us to return to camp only then to issue us with extra rations, which meant another twenty-four hours in the field. That is a classic false ending, which destroys morale. The same happened again on subsequent exercises; we would be waiting for helicopter extractions, only to be told they had been cancelled and therefore to 'prepare to yomp'.

Now, this may seem cruel. Indeed, such incidents affect if not break even the strongest of minds until 'acceptance' creeps in. However, these situations are by no means confined to the military and have extensive real-world applications, and are thus vital lessons in life.

In the context of the military, getting to and from missions via use of military land, sea, and air-based transport is not always assured. It may become too dangerous to infil or exfil from hostile enemy territories via transport, as situations are always rapidly evolving.

In Royal Marines, we are taught to expect the unexpected, and that things never go to plan – to stay both 'reactive' and 'adaptive'. Such instances often leave military personnel to walk into hostile engagement after travelling considerable distance by foot – carrying extreme amounts of heavy kit – then to fight and 'hopefully' win. Likewise, having to return to camp or FOBs (Forward Operating Bases) after fierce, sustained and physically exhausting enemy contact, often with some personnel injured.

'Acceptance' in these moments of realisation is crucial, a cognitive skill that must be practised and maintained constantly. Like all things in life that create disappointment, frustration and disbelief, acceptance is the remedy.

Consider the more common example of losing a mobile phone, a wallet, or a purse. Initial realisation sparks uncomfortable human emotions that trigger the five stages of grief – a theory first devised by Elizabeth Kubler-Ross,[10] in which humans experience denial, anger, bargaining, depression, and finally acceptance – that if left unmanaged, can be vivid and debilitating.

However, after 1–2 weeks, those emotions have normally subsided if not disappeared completely, and that is acceptance. It is an emotional cycle that can be shortened and with practice, even eradicated. For instance, knowing at some point that you *will* accept it (based on previous experience), will enable you to get over it and resist the urge to attach too much expectation onto certain outcomes; thus getting over things quicker if an alternative reality is presented.

Not to undergo and crucially acknowledge this process of acceptance can have massively negative implications on the short to medium-term, when on military operations. Dwelling on what could have been, or what you expected to happen, takes your mind away from the reality that you are now living in. This invites dips in performance and attention, which can lead to mistakes – and mistakes on the field of battle can have catastrophic consequences.

In short, when I experienced these moments of realisation, when the helicopter did not arrive, or when we were issued with more rations, I learned to say to myself: 'Just accept it!' This simple internal process over time made a huge difference to my interpretation of disappointment. A process or reaction I have applied to every aspect of my life since then. It makes taking risks in business easier to handle mentally, and safeguards myself against negative emotions.

---

10 E. Kubler-Ross, *On Death and Dying*, Macmillan, New York, 1969.

Key Points:

- Anticipate the unexpected – things rarely go according to plan.
- 'Acceptance' alleviates negative and uncomfortable emotions such as disappointment, despair, frustration, and disbelief.
- It is likely that you will start to accept the disappointment of a negative realisation in 1–2 weeks; after losing your mobile phone, for example. With this insight, why not take steps to shorten that timeframe?
- Remember, it has happened, it is now in the past – 'just accept it' and refocus.

12

SELF-CONTROL

Resisting the urge

WEEK 8

Day 63 – Monday 18 July 2005

Sentry finished this morning. I'm exhausted and can't be bothered with anything or anyone. Still can't get my boots on, so I've been told to get to sickbay and get them checked out – I have big holes in my heels. They gave me a light duties chit for the day, but I missed a four-mile run and IMFC – not happy. I really want to take part, this light duty is not me at all. There's a stigma attached to sickbay and I'm not one of them blokes!

We have Company Commander's inspection tomorrow and we've just had a run-through of what to expect at 22:00. Some of the lads have been hiding mucky kit, so we've all been told to 'fucking standby'.

It's now 02:00 in the morning, so work out the rest . . .

Day 64 – Tuesday 19 July

Got in bed at 02:00 and had to be back up at 04:00 to start cleaning ready for inspection – I wish I was at home now more than ever.

We failed inspection, in fact, Major B didn't even come around because some of the lads are taking the piss and staying in bed when they should be up cleaning. Wankers! So we all must report to the drill shed tonight and in the morning for kit musters. Honestly can't even begin to describe how shit I feel.

Swimming circuits this morning were OK, but I'm broken at the moment. After, we had 'realities of war' lectures and the videos on Op Telic (*Iraq*) and news clips of 40 Commando we watched were graphic, blokes getting shot and everything! All I want to do is get in bed and sleep.

Day 65 – Wednesday 20 July

We had drill this morning, I got put on the flank for my hair – even though it's shaved – and for being rats (*ugly*). I've got to report back to the drill shed at 19:00 in drill rig for another inspection.

After, we had a four-mile Fartlek run. Don't know what's up with me, but I'm absolutely hanging out all the time and not performing well during phys (*PT*). It may be due to the fact that I've just eaten, or because I've had 20 hours' sleep since last Monday.

Map reading period 9, then we have the rest of the night off – PRAISE THE LORD.

Day 66 – Thursday 21 July

Two weeks to leave!

We've been to Stallcombe Wood today for survival training with the Royal Marines Mountain Leaders (MLs). It was awesome, they taught us how to make animal traps, shelter, fire, and filter mucky water. One of the MLs claims to have done a lot of work with Ray Mears.

Then at 14:55 we had first aid, which was discussing 'battle-field shock'. We all couldn't keep our eyes open and our heads were nodding like dogs – hence the reason that trained Marines nickname the recruits down here 'Nods'.

Day 67 – Friday 22 July

Instead of the planned schedule, which was supposed to be IMFS, the PTIs made us do five rope climbs – two normal and then two with heaves (*rope pull-ups, where you stop midway up a 30ft rope and do 1–5 fully extended pull-ups, close grip*) – and the final rope climb was a normal 30ft one; then one makefast and two 400m camp circuits. Apparently that's super-human, the other troops down here do only 3–4 max climbs in one session!

It's 08:55 and we are boarding transport to Woodbury Common for a static map-reading stance. The focus is on 'back bearings', 'map to grid' and 'line bearings'.

I did OK, but it got boring after a while. We have the rest of the day off. Around 15–20 lads have left now either through injury, or because they've decided it's not for them. Treating myself to an early night – 20:30.

Day 68 – Saturday 23 July

'Royal Marines Dancing' (*drill*) this morning. Cpl N is a right bastard, he puts you on extra parade for fuck all, but today he was OK. Period three was a swimming circuit, which was pretty tough – I don't think it ever gets easy, you just get fitter and stronger and push more. After, PTI B was talking to us about gym pass-out next week. It's a full week of gym assess-ments, from runs to IMFC, to rope climbs, etc., all of which has to be executed with perfect technique.

He's picking his 'Gym Superiors' on Friday – 6–8 lads who demonstrate exceptional physical ability are awarded with a red T-shirt to wear throughout gym pass-out. I so want to get a red T-shirt, but I'm also very anxious about next week.

He dropped a right bombshell and told us that he's been drafted to FPGRM in November, which means we don't have him to take us through the Commando Tests at the end if I make that far . . . Gutted!

Day 69 – Sunday 24 July

Bit of lie in this morning – 08:45. Me and some of the lads are going to watch 'War of the Worlds'.

What a shit film! Can't stop thinking about the week ahead, it's by far the biggest test of my life and I need to dig really deep. The week begins with a three-mile run in the morning in combat boots – 1½ miles out in 11 mins 30 secs and 1½ miles back to camp best effort. It's going to be horrible, this test wearing trainers is bad enough, never mind wearing boots!

I'm at a really low point here and constantly have an awful, anxious feeling.

LESSON 10

Rewiring the hardwired: what we can learn from the conduct expectations of recruits on the gymnasium floor when it comes to elite performance outcomes.

97

Where it starts: deconstructing human behaviour

The cognitive impulse to wipe sweat off your face, or to scratch an area under siege by the tickling sensation created by cascading droplets of water, is an almost irresistible, subconscious natural reaction. So why then are recruits on the gymnasium floor consistently corrected by the PTIs and told *not* to touch their faces or fidget, when sweat is pouring out of them?

Answer: self-control

You may think this meticulous attention to detail is insignificant or needless, and I did too, until I learned later in my Commando unit of its necessity during training. The process is one of an underlying reprogramming that works to reset and then reinforce a recruit's ability to regulate self-control (to manage impulses, emotions and behaviours); a key element of 'executive function' – a process that enables individuals to plan, monitor and achieve long-term goals.

Where it matters

During OPs (Observation Posts), ambushes or other instances of concealment and poise, lying there, quiet and motionless is often the difference between life or death – success on a mission or its failure; and unlike any other job at that level, failure on an operation often has catastrophic consequences. In such cases, Royal Marines must lay in wait, focused, and undeterred by detrimental environmental elements, distraction, or our evolutionary response to insects or arachnids such as spiders.

They must go above and beyond what the enemy is capable of and, crucially, where they are prepared to venture mentally, in order to gain 'the edge' and survive.

Therefore, in these scenarios, harnessing the ability to exert self-control allows Royal Marines to direct their attention to assure a desired outcome, despite the presence of competing stimuli.

Take the 2018 Royal Marines advertisement that depicted a Commando lying motionless in wait of passing enemy insurgents. Whilst in position, a large spider can be seen crawling over his face, and he does not even flinch – he remains emotionless. For to react in some way, by shouting, losing composure or moving to brush it away, would likely compromise his position. This encapsulates the notion of self-control and reflects his relentless (trained) commitment to achieving his objective. Indeed, such outcomes are born and cultivated in the Royal Marines gymnasium and during other subtle and carefully contrived training serials at CTCRM – forged through an intricate and consistent focus on behavioural adjustment; constantly nudging the subject(s) to rectify their body language and body positioning until technical perfection is realised through self-control and discipline.

Transferability to the everyday, and the production of cutting-edge performance outcomes
Producing and then maintaining self-control and discipline in moments of fatigue, discomfort or emotional despair is critical in assisting the collective team, troop or organisational group in the cohesive and unifying effort to achieve complex goals. What's more, self-control and thus harnessing emotional regulation can also be applied to personal development ventures (achieving a degree) and corporate world settings, like optimising sales teams to secure long-term strategic business deals.

Quite frankly, resisting the urge to succumb to subconscious reactions (habits) that facilitate the easier route, and afford short-term comfort, produces outcomes (when devised and structured correctly) that allow an individual and team to operate with elite level performance capabilities.

It goes without saying that self-control is tightly woven into the fabric of what makes an elite soldier. Learning to self-regulate protects Royal Marines from heeding to innate reactions to what can be detrimental stimuli, thus safeguarding sustained success.

Key Points:

- Elite performance outcomes are only attainable by meticulously and consistently deconstructing and rewiring human behavioural responses.
- Resisting temptation requires the application of our attentional resources, which is underpinned by self-control.
- Applying self-control to avert misfortune is fundamental when 'easy options' and potentially unforeseen negative outcomes present themselves. Like social influence (peer pressure) and/or external environmental factors.
- Withstanding short-term discomfort, distraction and torment by learning to apply self-control is key to staying resilient during the acquisition of objectives and goal aspirations.

13

REGULATING DISAPPOINTMENT

Extracting the positives, refocusing and going again

WEEK 9

Day 70 – Monday 25 July 2005

Gym Pass Out Week! It's like living a nightmare down here, I'm finding it difficult coming to terms with what's in store this week. I feel snappy and pissed off and like my life is shit.

We failed drill pass out. We were shit, so we can't move on to drill with weapons until we come back from leave.

Period 4 and 5 was a Battle Fitness Test (BFT): 70 sit-ups, 5 pull-ups, 1.5-mile troop run in boots and then 1.5-miles back best effort. I ran the 1.5-mile back in 09.25 mins – happy with that, I hammered it, but it was really hard. ONE TEST DOWN!

Self-Reflection (in 2005)

I now feel completely cut-off from the outside world. I haven't watched television or read a newspaper properly for eleven weeks. I have no idea what is happening with the London bombings, or what is going on with Big Brother and other shit like that – we only really get information through word of mouth.

In fact, I have no interest in those things anymore – all the things you take for granted. Before I came here, I did them every day, and I do feel that I'm changing . . . maybe? What this experience has taught me this far, is that if you really want something bad enough, you can adapt to any form of new surroundings. Very scary, I suppose!

Bear in mind that mobile phones back then did not offer the kind of global access, connection, and mental escape that we enjoy today. They were still extremely basic in their technology and searching Google for news and entertainment was problematic, if not impossible on some devices.

Day 71 – Tuesday 26 July

Company Commander's inspection again this morning, everything was absolutely gleaming so hopefully we passed, but haven't been told yet. If we get our 'Blue Passes', we can stop out or go home every weekend, which is an UNBELIEVABLE FEELING.

I'm writing this during first aid lecture, because I'm bored! Although the lectures after are on survival, so should be better.

It's Gym Test 1 – first encountered on the PRMC – in the morning: Max out on bleep test, press-ups, sit-ups, and pull-ups. I really want to earn a red gym superior T-shirt for Friday, so I'm going to leave it all in the gym and keep my fingers crossed. Only my body will stop me!

Day 72 – Wednesday 27 July

Feel anxious this morning for Gym Test 1, we are getting ready to head over to the gymnasium now. The tests are all done to a beep, so beep – chest to floor – beep – press-up, extended arms, and so on. The targets everyone at Week 9 should meet are:

VO2 Max: Level 13 +	Sit-ups: 70 +
Press-ups: 50 +	Pull-ups: 10 +

I went above all the basic requirements, sucking air through every hole on my body. B said, 'Only a maximum of ten will be picked for the gym superior T-shirts, and it goes on the past nine weeks' performances and general attitude. Whoever gets them usually tends to go far in training and are good men for any troop.'

I WAS PICKED! I got a red T-shirt along with another six lads: Wrighty, Col, Mike, Brad, Halfpenny, and Goldsbury. We wear them for Friday's gym pass-out now and it goes in our service record forever. Proudest moment of my life so far!

Day 73 – Thursday 28 July

One Week to Leave. It's been a boring day today; we had a weapon bore sighting lecture, followed by swimming and flexibility in preparation for tomorrow.

After that it was down to the stances for three periods of Light Support Weapon (LSW) familiarisation. We also got fitted with our NBC kit and equipment (gas/chemical suits, boots and masks).

It's 20:20 and I'm ironing my PT kit ready for gym pass-out tomorrow. There's added pressure on me wearing the red T-shirt, which is making me really anxious and nervous. All my movements during the tests have to be executed with perfect technique and timing. I hope to God that I perform well and pass, then I won't give a shit about exercise 'Hunters Moon' next week, which is supposed to be as bad if not worse than Marshall Star!

Day 74 – Friday 29 July

Gym Pass-out! I've never been as nervous and scared in my life as I was this morning. When B came to the blocks to collect us, he said: 'Prepare now, this is where you must harness the "Commando Spirit", because you are about to go through the hardest session to date and quitting will be easy – only mental strength will get you through. Be cheerful in adversity and you will all make it through.' Loads of lads were being sick and B was saying, 'Let the fucking weakness out – that's just weakness leaving the body, let it escape.'

I did my 'liveners' (*warm-up exercises*) and three 30ft rope climbs, then a camp circuit. When I arrived back at the gym, I knew I was already wrecked. I quickly got under a rope to do the fourth rope climb. A PTI shouted, 'To the top, climb!' and I headed up midway and started my first of three full extension heaves (*rope pull-ups*). I did the two, then on the third, once I'd fully extended, I couldn't bend my arms to make the 3rd pull-up – ascend to the top of the rope and touch the metal clasp. My bastard arms would literally not work.

One of the PTIs was watching like a hawk and PTI B was looking up too in disbelief shouting: 'Timmins, don't come down!' I knew at this point I had freddied (*failed*) it and lost the superior title. Although I passed with ease, I lost my vision midway through and felt like I was going to collapse, which cost me the red shirt. I left it all in there and couldn't have done any more, so I feel a bit of comfort there. Well . . . not really, I'M GUTTED.

The lads have been ripping me all evening, because I was walking round in the red T-shirt last night taking the piss and telling them how physically superior I was to them. Having failed to keep the T-shirt at the end, I must suck this up now and take it on the chin . . . oh well, I won't hear the back of this for a while.

It's 21:30 now, I'm aching all over, and full of cold. SOOO

looking forward to three weeks' leave. You win some, you lose some – shit happens!

Day 75 – Saturday 30 July

Been live firing today with the LSWs. We were firing on rapid fire and automatic. I'm doing well with the shooting and getting good groupings.

Cpl Dite was telling us about the 50 cal Barrett sniper rifle. He was saying that if one of the rounds (*bullets*) passes your head within a 30 cm radius, the vacuum created from the bullet will rip one side of your head off. So, you don't even have be shot to get killed . . . unbelievable. I love this shit.

Just packed my bergen and webbing while psyching myself up for Hunters Moon tomorrow. No sleep or food again for at least four nights. Beautiful, can't wait!

Day 76 – Sunday 31 July

Hunters Moon Day 1: Deploying back to Woodbury today – the devil's playground! This exercise covers stalking, day and night navigation, map reading, camouflage and conceal-ment and observation. All looks great on paper, but the reality and rumour is that this is absolutely horrific and designed, like Marshall Star, to weed out the weak ones among us.

I'm really down today and don't want to talk to anyone, just want to be on my own. I don't want to go, thoughts of finding excuses have crossed my mind, but I couldn't live with myself if I did that.

Waiting outside for transport to Four Firs, a region on Woodbury. Cpl M walked up to us rubbing his hands together. He scares us all to death that bloke and looks to break anyone and give them the most uncomfortable and miserable time as humanly possible. They mess with your head down here with every waking minute, keep you in a constant state of anxiety and pressure.

The transport was a complete lie, they speed marched us four miles up to Woodbury Common wearing full kit and that's before the nightmare started. The thought of going home on leave is overwhelming and all that's keeping me going right now. I'm counting down the hours and sleeps.

Known as the 'gruesome/terrible twosome', exercise Marshall Star and Hunters Moon are notorious during training. They are two opportunities to get recruits away from Lympstone and absolutely hammer them to within an inch of their lives (in 2005–6). No sleep, time pressure, wet and dry, systematic physical thrashing and relentless mind games all provide the ruthless ingredients to break down recruits and weed out those having second thoughts about remaining in Commando training. Nothing saps the morale of an individual or effectively breaks down their will to continue more than these two exercises during training.

LESSON 11

Dealing with disappointment during large challenges and how misfortune along the way is often not a predictor of success . . . it is merely an illusion.

Look, I was devastated at not getting PT Superior. For me prior to the gym test, it was a foregone conclusion, which made the outcome a bitter pill to swallow. However, through a period of reflection, I was able to deconstruct what went wrong and learn from it. I had gone too hard. I tried to make a positive impression on the PTIs present, and it backfired.

My interpretation of what would impress them was short-sighted. The primary error was that I failed to assess the task requirements adequately – I wasn't strategic in my approach and consequently did not execute the action plan (conserve/control the gas tank) needed to achieve the end result. In my inexperienced attempt to impress, I went all out and burnt out. I attacked that 90-minute assessment as if my life depended on it.

Consequently, I did not pace myself, or preserve my gas tank to last the duration of the session. I went at it like a 100m sprint, when what was required was the philosophical approach that one takes to win a marathon – controlling pace to regulate output. In hindsight, my approach lacked maturity and life experience.

Now the positives

Firstly, my performance up until Week 9 had clearly been recognised and acknowledged. As a result, I was awarded a Red Jersey prior to Gym Pass-out. Secondly, and more compellingly, all those (barring Mark Goldsbury) who retained the Red Jersey at the end of the assessment (winning a certificate and acknowledgement in their personal records) subsequently left training in the weeks that followed, or got back-trooped for poor performance, for failing to grasp key skills during the tactical phases of training.

Therefore, retaining the title of PT Superior was not a key marker of success, nor did it predict one's ability to go on and achieve a Green Beret. In fact, out of the seven of us that were selected, only two of us completed training: myself and Mark Goldsbury.

Disappointment is an enduring part of the journey of life, however sour it may taste. Like failure (Chapter 32), disappointment has hidden assets that we can harness, and with a hard lesson learned, we can overcome it and continue forward by extracting the positives. When my initial disappointment was put into perspective, it was merely a minor blip in the road whilst on the journey to becoming a Royal Marines Commando.

More significantly, upon reaching the end of training, I wouldn't have been able to tell you a single name of those who got selected with me, nor did I give it a second thought – at that stage, it was insignificant! In the instance above, I took the best approach, which was to put it straight behind me, to move quickly on to the next challenge and assessment. Also, by undergoing the process of acknowledgement, I was able to establish what went wrong and learn from it. This safeguarded my self-confidence, allowing me to progress on and complete training.

Dwelling on what could have been is the epitome of wasted energy. The Royal Marines philosophy on misfortune is to acknowledge where you went wrong, learn from it, and move on to the next opportunity – which in my case, was exercise Baptise Run.

Key Points:

- Hidden assets reside in every disappointment that we can harness and use to our advantage, in order to perform better.
- Reflection facilitates this and allows us to analyse and extract the positive elements that exist in disappointment and/or shortcomings.
- Don't waste energy dwelling on what might have been: reset, readjust, adapt and overcome.

14

LIVING WITHOUT COMFORT AND CONVENIENCE

Hunters Moon

WEEK 10

Day 77 – Monday 01 August 2005

Exercise Day 2: I woke up at 05:30. We didn't get bumped (*potentially compromised or attacked by the enemy, which in training is always the Training Team*) last night, which is crazy. Just cooking my breakfast – corned beef hash (gipping), scrubbing the cam (*camouflage*) cream off my face and will then shave. After, I need to lay out my kit muster, make sure my water bottles are full to the brim, my weapon is stripped down and absolutely gleaming – completely free of dust down the barrel ready for inspection. I hate these inspections!

Putting wet clothes on and washing in the middle of a field full of gorse bushes is the most miserable and morale-sapping experience anyone can have. It's swings and roundabouts on exercise – one minute you're dealing with things well, then next, no matter how mentally strong you are, you think of ways of getting off and being in a nice warm bed on camp.

I want to be at home for 95% of the time during exercise. I'll never be able to explain the strain and consuming depression that comes over me in the field. 4–5 Royal Marines

Commandos (*Training Team*) have complete control over your life and scrutinise every move you make, and any fall in discipline from perfection results in punishments of absolutely disgusting physical retribution. Done about seven miles today carrying full kit, with little food and sleep.

Day 78 – Tuesday 02 August

Day 3: Woke up and immediately thought of how many days we have left . . . back to camp tomorrow! I was completely covered in spiders' webs this morning and had stuff crawling all over me. The weather is dull, cold, and foggy. I feel really fed up today and starting to lose sight of why I'm putting myself through this mental torment and torture.

Passed kit inspection at 07:00. We have stalking and observation stances this morning which should be OK, probably with a little bit of extra phys thrown in for good measure.

Stalking was class, sneaking about while under observation by the enemy trying to stay undetected. The Royal Marines call it being Ninja. During the observation stance, I had to lie in a puddle for 4 hours watching for enemy movement. We have a night navigation tonight at 23:00. That's got no sleep written all over it, which will mean no sleep in three days.

Day 79 – Wednesday 03 August

Day 4: Me and another lad got lost during the nav ex. I knew we were going to get fucked when we managed to gather our bearings. While lost, I was thinking of ways of getting out of the Marines – one way was to tell them the truth, a secret I hold dear, that I have asthma – that would get me out. Stupid thoughts looking back, as I couldn't live with myself if I quit this course and that keeps me locked in.

We arrived back to the camp base at 02:40 and I was punished by the Troop Commander; lying down side by side with a fellow recruit he emptied a full Jerry Can of oggin on us, most of it over my face. We then got marched to what can only be described as a cesspit of stagnant water and mud – absolutely horrific. We had to walk in showing NO emotion and completely submerge ourselves, then walk out and fall in three ranks ready to go back to camp base.

On return, we were told to occupy our patrol harbour and draw up a sentry routine. I'm on first at 03:00, which means I will go straight on – this is such a massive bonus, because it means I won't have to put on dry clothes to get in my bag, then have to get up and do wet and dry in the night for a later sentry slot.

Laid on sentry now for one hour freezing my bollocks off. I'm off at 4:00 and we all have to be up at 05:30 to start our morning routine, then we have a nine-mile yomp carrying full kit. I keep thinking of home and good memories and for 3–4 minutes it offers me some distraction from this bullshit.

So, we did a 4-mile speed march with the equivalent of six stone on my back, then at a checkpoint we marched 5 miles back to Lympstone. I was hanging out like the rest. My lower back is rubbed raw from the bergen and my feet are full of blisters.

Day 80 – Thursday 04 August

GOING HOME!

Leaving, on a jet plane, I don't know when I'll be fucking back again. HA HA HA.

My exploits and conduct on leave:
OK, I have been strictly honest throughout the book and I
feel a need to uphold that integrity, because not to do so would
paint an unfair reflection of the environment in which I once
lived, and the reckless and self-destructive behaviour I often
engaged in during my leave periods from training. There was
once an elephant in the room . . .

Eighteen months prior to registering my interest to join the
Royal Marines at Leeds careers office, I was heavily involved
in the part-time (weekend) but consistent taking of recreational
drugs. I was from an old mining village and all my social group
– you could argue, most of that generation – partied for days
on a cocktail of alcohol and illegal substances. From being
18–19½ years old, once rugby was over, my weekends were
spent consuming as much drink and narcotics as humanly
possible – often in dwellings where the owner or tenant didn't
even know who I was. It was virtually inescapable.

I joined the Royal Marines in an attempt to break out of
this lifestyle, this deep trench of despair and incessant lack of
opportunity. The Royal Marines was by no means a free or
guaranteed ticket out, in fact it was my ultimate risk. The odds
stacked against me were incredibly overwhelming.

That said, I knew and acknowledged that the sacrifice of
putting myself through Royal Marines Commando training
to reach my end goal, if I succeeded, would completely transform my life – propelling me into different and more desirable
networks, increasing my life chances and, in turn, my earning
potential. Even at a very young age, I was extremely motivated
by money and all the trappings that significant earning potential could bring.

However! After Hunters Moon and then periodically
throughout training when I returned home on leave from the

Marines, I fell straight back into old habits. I could be found on a council estate with practically anyone, taking drugs for days. It was as if the strict discipline, mental stress and focus that Royal Marines training demanded, needed releasing – and my release was booze and drugs. I wanted 'me time', but all that youthful energy was displaced into negative behaviour and outcomes, and like everything I did at that age, I did it to the extreme.

The Royal Marines drinking culture at that time also indirectly encouraged my outlook and propensity to behave with excess; in many respects it felt acceptable and I was simply being a boy – what the Corps calls being 'Royaly', minus the drugs!

For me, Friday night would spark a chain of events where I lost days and my grasp of time. My ultimate destination was often Sunday morning, walking home to my Dad's in a fragile mental state, having not slept, eaten or touched a drop of water in days. A disorientated scramble would then place me on a late afternoon train back to CTC, and upon returning to Lympstone, this had a hugely detrimental effect on my performance at the start of each week back from leave.

Whereas most of the lads were probably at home resting and maintaining fitness, I was getting smashed and abusing my body, not letting it eat and recover. Looking back now, it totally jeopardised my success on the course.

Day 81 – Sunday 28 August

Massive sad and miserable face – or wow, the last thing I want to do is write this entry, but I feel compelled to do so. I'm travelling down to CTC and I've never felt as down in my life. I've had all the freedom in the world and that will be taken away in three hours when I arrive by train outside Lympstone.

The last three weeks' leave have been brilliant – just being home was such a great feeling.

Well, I've been on camp one hour and the lads are arriving in trickles. Wrighty and Mike are talking of opting out of training, which has really surprised me, as they're really strong lads – everyone is devastated to be back, not only me, which gives me comfort.

I watched the Ricky Hatton v Kostya Tszyu world title fight while on leave and I keep drawing on that to give me the inspiration to settle back into life here . . . COME ON!

LESSON 12

During times of restricted privilege and undesirable living conditions, establishing new routines and making the most out of new living areas begins the process of environmental integration.

Living and operating in the field during training is a mental test like no other. The second you leave the relative comfort and confines of camp, the small amount of freedom and solace you do have (a mattress and duvet, cooked food, convenience store, warm accommodation or shelter, shower, and so on), ends abruptly.

In the field, the Training Team controlled our every second: time pressure on cooking and eating, time pressure to get to and from locations, and then to complete various educational stances (such as soldiering, fieldcraft, or personal administration); then they dictated when, where, and for how long we could sleep. We lost our freedom and independence, in every sense of the word, during the first half of training.

It is quite remarkable what you miss when taken-for-granted privileges are pulled from under your feet. Vivid fantasies had us all pining for a warm bed, a warm shower, and cooked food (not rations); Dutchy's, the onsite fast food (fast death) outlet, dominated all our thoughts, as well as daydreaming about hot bacon sandwiches each morning, and for some, enjoying a cigarette.

Leaving a safe and comfortable 'home' that provides basic life support for an environment that is stark, exposed to the elements and lacks stimulation, can suck the spirit and optimism out of recruits like a 'moral vacuum', especially during the harsh winter months; these moments leave even the strongest of minds searching desperately for consolation. However, accepting this brutal transition, and thus preparing for it mentally, is imperative if soldiers and troops are to remain effective.

Therefore, establishing the new routine is essential when faced with a remote and often harsh and restricted living environment. For example, working efficiently to set up camp, servicing and maintaining operational kit (clothing, fighting order and weapons) and prepping food. It's about 'taking control' of what you can control; the familiarity of sorting out your own kit and equipment establishes the foundation of routines and affords comfort when living in extremely uncomfortable environments – especially during a very cold and treacherous winter on the likes of Woodbury Common or Dartmoor.

Indeed, at the base of Abraham Maslow's 'Hierarchical Theory of Human Needs',[11] he argues that at the physiological

---

11 A.H. Maslow, *Motivation and Personality* (2nd ed.), Harper and Row, New York, 1970.

level, which encompasses the very basic, but self-preserving needs of human beings, we require sleep, water, and shelter before we can work our way up the hierarchy to undertake and satisfy more complex needs. In this notion, we cannot go on to achieve other goals without achieving the basics (the foundation and formula of success!).

The skills learnt in the field during training will equip a recruit to become a soldier who possesses the ability to adapt and thrive in any environment in the world; from the Arctic conditions in Norway to the inhospitable mountains of Afghanistan. Constructing new living means, establishing new and effective routines, servicing personal kit and equipment, and maintaining good personal administration, all make environmental and cultural change seamless and bring comfort in new surroundings, which optimises performance.

Key Points:

- In new environments or situations of restricted living means, it is essential to 'take charge of what you can control' and 'establish new routines' (ways of living).
- Simple actions, like unpacking kit, familiarising yourself with the immediate area – finding local amenities (if available) and establishing places to exercise, all bring comfort in new environments, lifting morale and maintaining effectiveness.
- Don't succumb to new surroundings, own them.

15

COPING WITH AND THRIVING UNDER PRESSURE

Winning the Shooting Medal

WEEK 11

<u>Day 82 – Monday 29 August 2005</u>

First morning up at 05:30 in three weeks and it hurts. I have no motivation and I don't feel as mentally sharp as I did before I left on leave – just need to get back in the rhythm.

Should have had PT first period, but it got cancelled, which is bizarre but very welcome. Double map reading, then onto the ranges to zero our weapons; my grouping was brilliant – all rounds in the centre, which has made me really happy.

Just packed my bergen, we are heading to straight point ranges for two weeks, it's going to be absolutely class. Night firing with tracer, moving target shooting, automatic firing, bullet penetration demo, knife and bayonet fighting, and firing long distance, where I'll have to aim off for wind, etc. The two weeks finish with a big test of shooting, which is pass or fail!

Day 83 – Tuesday 30 August

First day at straight point ranges. We've been live firing at 100m targets from all different positions – quite tricky. I didn't do too well – panicking and overthinking the shots too much.

The Training Team have brought AK47's, an UZI, a 9mm pistol, and an LSW. I hope I get chance to fire them all. That will be awesome! It's really relaxed – something is wrong – it's too good to be true!

Our accommodation for the next two weeks is a gimping old ducker underground, 60ft × 30ft, full of stagnant water, spiders, and all sorts of creepy crawlies. Very hard to relax. (*This building was condemned shortly after our stay!*)

Everyone must finish the food the Training Team bring out – it's a massive pot of warm 'range stew' and we have bets on who can eat cold potatoes and honking 'pussers' (*standard military issue*) Cornish pasties – a culinary delight that must be experienced (not). The food is that bad, lads are burying their food so the Training Team can't find it!

Day 84 – Wednesday 31 August

Up at 05:30, covered in spiders – absolutely minging. PT first thing at 07:00 was a 4½ mile run, which was a proper dangle because we were up and down hills for 40 mins.

Then we went onto the ranges; firing at 100, 200 and 300m with the iron sight, which is so hard at 200 and 300m, but I did really well. I got 121 shots on target out of 136 – very happy with that. After, we moved on to electronic pop-up targets at the same distances. We had to carry out quick exchanges, from standing to kneeling – I was the only one in the troop to pass first time!

Really enjoyed today, hope I can maintain the same performance tomorrow. Hungry as ever to get that Green Beret today and pass out of training. I'm in great spirits, but worrying slightly about exercise Baptise Run, which is an assessment exercise – pass or fail at Week 15.

Day 85 – Thursday 01 September

The ranges overlook a holiday caravan park to the east, which is right on the beach front. So, we got hammered this morning on the beach; leopard crawling and sprints, then sit-ups and press-ups in the sea with the waves crashing over our heads. After the beach session, we had to speed march uphill back to the ranges carrying 10lbs of kit.

Been going through firing techniques today with Cpl M. I did proper shit and he gave me a really hard time, which made me panic even more. He started opening my magazine pouches whilst I was firing and then asked, 'Why the fuck are they open, Timmins?' I had to say I didn't know, which makes me so angry. As punishment, I had to do 'the sandbag run'. This is an absolutely horrific punishment, and we were all scared to death of receiving it.

You were given an empty sandbag at the ranges, then had to run 1.5 miles up and then downhill to the beach below. Once at the beach, you had to fill it to the top with sand and submerge it in the sea, then run 1.5 miles back UP to camp with a heavy, wet sandbag wrapped around your neck and shoulders in under 30 minutes – which chaffed the hell out of the skin around the base of your neck and shoulders. If you got back and didn't have enough sand in it, or you were a second over, you had to go again . . . Horrendous!

Hope I do better tomorrow for the actual test. If you get

over 85% on the shoot, you get awarded 'Marksman' when you pass out of training. It's a mega-achievement and you get to wear a badge on your blues uniform of two crossed rifles for the rest of your career.

Day 86 – Friday 02 September

Really nervous today, I want to get marksman badly! The APWT is a series of shoots at 100, 200, and 300m followed by a 400m shoot in various positions under time limits. For the 100, 200, and 300m shoots, there's a possible of twenty points on offer. I got 19, 19, 19, which was the highest score in the troop. One of the corporals said, 'Timmins, providing you hit all five targets at 400m, you will get Marksman.'

Each lad got fifteen rounds for five targets at 400m – that's 3 per target! It took me seven shots to hit the first target because of the wind adjustment. I thought it was over! This meant I had only two rounds per target for the remaining 4 targets – a massive feat and pressure in strong wind. I only went on to hit the next four targets with four rounds and had four to spare, achieving MARKSMAN!

I now get to wear the badge on my blues and will be presented with the shooting medal for best all-round shot in training, providing I'm an original troop member at the end. Really happy and proud of myself. Only five lads achieved marksman and I got the most shots on target with a score of 62/65 and won £36 that had been put in a winner's pot.

Day 87 – Saturday 03 September

Bullet penetration demonstration was first thing this morning. There was an old car, a house door, a tree trunk, and a wall made of sandbags (hence the reason for the sandbag punishment) and brick wall. All the Training Team were lined up seventy yards away from the targets with a variety of weapons: sniper rifle, 9mm handgun, LSW, GMPG – a devastating weapon, an AK47, an SLR, and me with my SA80 – I was the only recruit allowed to shoot as I got No.1 marksman.

All my shots went straight through all the objects – small entry hole and large exit hole. Corporal P then started firing the GPMG and it destroyed the wall of sandbags and smashed the car to bits, I got to fire the 9mm and sniper rifle. It was a brilliant experience.

Just boarded the bus ready to go back to Lympstone for the weekend. Happy, happy, happy!

Day 88 – Sunday 04 September

Hungover! I woke up this morning in bed with Rich and had a thong on . . . Strange?

We hit Torquay last night (good night) and apparently a girl in a hen party asked me to put on the thong so they could take a picture, which I did – obviously – but never returned it, ha ha.

On the ranges again in the morning, which is moving targets and night shooting. Then on to Dartmoor for more complex firing scenarios. It is fast approaching exercise Baptise Run, which is a mid-training test exercise. Feeling apprehensive and nervous about that.

LESSON 13

Shutting out the external (negative) distractions and focusing on what you can control . . . the internal.

I had absolutely no idea I had a gift for shooting (in the most modest of ways) until this week in training. I have since tried to analyse what goes into shooting and makes some better than others. For me personally, I can only think that it was perhaps my good hand–eye co-ordination, developed through years of playing rugby, that gave me a subtle edge.

I found the following marksmanship principles easy to master in unison:

1. The shooting position and hold must be firm enough to support the rifle.
2. The rifle must point naturally at the target without any undue physical effort.
3. Sight alignment and sight picture must be correct.
4. The shot must be released and followed through without undue disturbance to the position.

That said, when it came to the 400 metre shoot, I fell apart under pressure. I was leading on points by this stage of the assessment, and success here meant I would win the 'Charnock Trophy' and the 'Shooting Medal' come the end of training, providing I remained in the troop as an 'Original Troop Member'. (*Tragically, and in acknowledgement, the Charnock Trophy is named after Recruit Charnock of 711–712 Troop, who died during the 30-miler, and was due to receive the Shooting Medal on his Kings Squad Pass-out.*)

All eyes were on me as I stepped up to attempt the shoot;

the lads were cheering, goading, and a few were offering general words of encouragement. I buried the first six shots in the sand behind the target – not only was wind playing a factor, but I had succumbed to peer pressure from the Troop. Both were external factors that I could not influence, but I could control how they affected me by applying the pillars of mindfulness and focusing my attention.

During times of pressure in rugby, I would take a brief moment and visualise what I needed to do, breaking each part down. For example, when kicking a rugby ball from a cone or kicking Tee, I visualised it leaving my boot and going over the post at obscure angles. I applied this same principle to hitting the target at 400 metres. I even pinched a small gathering of grass and threw it up into the air to gauge the wind speed and direction.

Visualising the round leaving the barrel (in my mind) and following its trajectory through to the target, whilst aiming off for wind and systematically executing all the marksmanship principles correctly, enabled me to both shut out the external distractions and hit five consecutive targets at 400 metres. As a result, the accolades were all mine and the prize fund came in especially useful for beers in Exeter.

Sometimes you must shut out the noise, focus attentional resources, take a few deep breaths and crucially, visualise the action. In doing so, it settles nervous energy – ultimately keeping you in state of composure. This provides the mental clarity needed to optimise concentration and thus reinforce self-confidence and belief.

Key Points:

- In times of 'perceived' pressure, take a moment; breathe and visualise the various stages you must execute to achieve the desired outcome.
- You may not be able to control external distractions, but with focus – underpinned by the practice of mindfulness, you can mitigate against them by applying attentional resources and utilising visualisation techniques.
- 'Starve your distractions, feed your focus.'

16

COMPOSURE

Fighting in Plymouth

WEEK 12

Day 89 – Monday 05 September 2005

Back on bus to straight point ranges again today. Really cannot be bothered at all – feel down today, depressed.

Done an automatic shoot with the LSWs this morning, which was shit. Sick of the ranges now after a week and a half solid of it. One of the lads was heard slagging Cpl M off and it got back to him, so because no one would own up to it, the Troop Sergeant marched us up and down the beach from 00:00 to 01:30 and made us do press-ups and sit-ups in the sea – so emotional!

We now have to sleep outside under our ponchos – the wind is that bad I feel like we are going to get blown off the cliff edge, so up to now at 03:00 I haven't slept a wink at all. I'm cold, wet and absolutely fed up.

Day 90 – Tuesday 06 September

Woke up to more punishment this morning. Wet and dry. I've had no sleep at all, and we've got a three-mile speed march in one hour with full kit. This marks the start of prep and conditioning for the Commando Tests – in particular, the 9-mile speed march.

After, we were back on the ranges, firing with gas masks on – which made things really difficult. Can't see anything through them and it's so hard to get a decent shot off trying to look down the SUSAT (*weapon sight*).

Really surprised we are going back to camp tonight, then going to Dartmoor in the morning. Can't wait to jump in a nice warm bed. Cpl M has made my eyes bleed today, constantly thrashing the shit out of us. One of those days when you wonder what you're doing here.

Day 91 – Wednesday 07 September

Up early, boarded the bus and arrived at Dartmoor at 08:00. Literally can't see my hand in front of face, it's that foggy and it's cold as hell.

Shooting laterally moving targets today, which was pretty tough, but the best range we've been on thus far. Out of a possible 64 marks, I scored 63, which was the highest score again in the Troop.

It's 23:00 and we've just completed a night shoot using CWS (*night-vision scope*), flares and tracer rounds to see how fast bullets travel. It is something to witness – absolutely unbeliev-able how fast bullets travel and the best buzz and experience down here yet.

Day 92 – Thursday 08 September

All up at 06:00 for another shoot but the weather is howling, so we've been stripping and cleaning weapons all morning.

We had a bet with Cpl M last night that England would beat Northern Ireland (he is Irish). The loser would get in the lake in the middle of Dartmoor. Well, England lost, and we had to get in the lake first thing this morning. Absolutely Baltic. Just been told if we work hard tomorrow and don't screw up, we can have the weekend off . . . Buzzing!

Cpl Dite – the sniper – leaves next Friday to join the fire service. He tried to get in the police on CO19, but they wouldn't have him because he has confirmed kills on his record – what bollocks! Apparently, he could have gone to Poole (*SBS*) as a recce sniper, but still decided to go outside. On the bus back to Lympstone. So happy.

Day 93 – Friday 09 September

Three periods of drill this morning. For the first two periods we watched Kings Squad's passing out parade (the lads who have completed training). It was class and gave me goosebumps, I really hope that's me next year.

Just returned all the field stores we took to Dartmoor, then after a quick inspection we can go ashore for the weekend.

Going to Plymouth this weekend, staying at Pearce's house with Goldsbury, Mike, Whatley, Mourn, and Laws, which should be class.

Day 94 – Saturday 10 September

I knocked someone clean out last night. Some bloke was acting like a right clown and wouldn't leave us alone, so I hit him and knocked his teeth out. Had a tooth stuck in my left knuckle, so had to go to A&E for it to be taken out and sterilised plus four stitches. I'm flapping big time now as they said I could lose my finger if it gets infected. What's more, I could end up being back-trooped!

My hand's really swollen now – I'm worrying it's broken.

Day 95 – Sunday 11 September

Went out again last night, but didn't really enjoy myself because my hand is worrying me so much. Going back to camp at 13:00.

Told the Troop Sergeant what happened, thinking I would be in the proper shit. He was really happy and impressed with me and I had to explain everything to the Training Team. They all said, 'Fucking good effort.' Ha ha, buzzing with that!

They said I'm now the Troop hero.

LESSON 14

Complacency and spontaneous, uncharacteristic behaviour fuelled by alcohol, and how the 'Group-mind Theory' of individual behavioural influence can sabotage everything.

My lack of composure that weekend in Plymouth was in part fuelled by alcohol and the influence of the 'Group Mind';[12] a theory about group behaviour, which purports that an individual loses their 'individuality' and 'rationality' and instead acts in ways that conform to the 'pack', the collective group.

This relates back to the notion of the 'in-group',[13] the

12 B.A. McClure, 'Metaphoric illumination in groups', *Small Group Behavior*, 18(2), 1987, pp. 179–87.
13 H. Tajfel & J. Turner, 'An integrative theory of intergroup conflict',

people we want to be like and the group that offers security and makes us feel comfortable; and the 'out-group', people who are different from us in some way, or whom we want to move away from. The group's behaviour that night, and my influence upon it, not only nearly halted my progression on the course, but almost destroyed my dream of becoming a Royal Marines Commando.

Upon arriving at A&E, the nurse practitioner took one look at my hand and said, 'I must prepare you – you may lose your finger.' I said, 'What!' The other guy's front tooth was still embedded in my left-hand base knuckle.

Unsurprisingly, this news sobered me up instantly. It was no longer my knee, eczema or asthma that was the enduring threat to my goal; no, it was an act of spontaneous, unnecessary idiocy. The wound was cleaned profusely and injected with a number of different antibiotics, then I was told literally to wait it out . . . to see if my finger and hand became discoloured with infection.

In the meantime, training continued. I still had to complete the 30ft rope climbs on Bottom Field. Every time I did the climb, the wound opened up right down to the bone. The risk of developing a life-changing, dangerous infection was enormous. Not only this, in line with the natural progression of training, we then went in the field and I had to conduct Wet and Dry routine, like the rest of the lads. This again put me at massive risk of serious bacterial infection.

Those tense few weeks after that incident brought me the worst worry, uncertainty, and anxiety I felt throughout my

in M.A. Hogg & D. Abrams (eds.), *Key Readings in Social Psychology. Intergroup Relations: Essential Readings*, Psychology Press, 2001, pp. 94–109.

whole time at Lympstone. The worst thing was that it was all so avoidable – nothing more than self-inflicted sabotage.

In short, my spontaneity, a split-second momentary loss of composure, which the Royal Marines breeds into recruits throughout training, nearly cost me everything. Had I lost my finger, you would not be reading this book today, as the Royal Marines would have medically discharged me. I would have been sent home to the people I had left behind, to those who had become my 'out-group', and thus had to face the very people who doubted that I could make the grade to be a Royal Marine.

Key Points:

- If going out and drinking alcohol, like in my case (when I was younger), puts you, your goals and ambitions at risk, then cut out the problem: Don't drink, or drink responsibly, or even better, don't go out at all.

- A lack of composure is the direct result of a lack of 'emotional self-control' (discipline). After this night, I learnt to conduct myself better, to apply self-discipline and try to lead by good example.

- Dependent on the social or cultural group you inhabit and its expectations, succumbing to Group-mind Theory can have incredibly detrimental effects on individual behaviour, causing you to perform acts you would not do if you were alone or part of another group.

- Small, negative, and seemingly insignificant actions can have potentially life-changing consequences. Therefore, stay focused and committed to the acquisition of the end goal, even if that is a painful sacrifice at the time: it's just not worth it.

17

MANAGING FEAR

Dunker Drills

WEEK 13

Day 96 – Monday 12 September 2005

I've had to attend sickbay this morning to see the camp surgeon; he said my hand will be OK for 'Dunker Drills' – helicopter emergency underwater escape training. I'm well happy now.

We've been gassed today down on Bottom Field in the gas chambers. The NBC instructors made us enter and start walking around while they burnt CS gas pellets and threw them in. The whole room started filling with smoky gas, which immediately started burning my neck around the seal of the mask and suit. On their command, we had to take off our masks and say our names and PO numbers.

Hell fire, I took my mask off, took a natural breath in (BIG MISTAKE) in order to speak, and I could not breathe, it was like being drowned and trying to talk underwater. My eyes were gushing with water and my throat and mouth was full of foam – I couldn't talk at all. The instructors were shouting: 'Say your name! What's your fucking name! Talk to me, where are you from? Give me your PO number . . . !'

Once they saw my mouth had started foaming, they let me

out, where I was sick all over. One of the most shocking experiences I never want to go through again.

Day 97 – Tuesday 13 September

Been doing Bowmen Signals (*radio communication*) today – learning how to use the radios and headsets. It's all Gucci kit, but boring to learn.

Can't stop thinking about Baptise Run in 1 ½ weeks' time. I could never have imagined I would make it this far, and now it's fast approaching, I'm in a bit of disbelief and shitting it. I would be absolutely devastated if I failed the exercise and had to leave the Troop, but I have a quiet confidence I'll do well.

I'm getting closer each day to reaching my goals, dreams, and ambitions!

Day 98 – Wednesday 14 September

Been in the classroom all morning, then after 'scran' (*food*) we had grenade lessons – arming and disarming, impacts, types of grenade and their uses during operations. Really interesting.

Had a surprise locker inspection this morning. I got caught out and have got extra parade later – and to top it all off, a map reading 2 resit test at 18:00.

Been a decent day, but a lot of screwing around.

Day 99 – Thursday 15 September

Dunker Drills! Heading to Yeovilton this morning for the notorious Dunker Drill training. Some of the lads are shitting it, but I'm excited, not fazed by anything water-based.

You must sit in a helicopter hull that's suspended above a deep tank of water. Three crash simulations are then conducted in daylight, daylight without control – the hull spins upside down under the water – and the final one in complete darkness without control. Each of us was strapped in like we would be in a Heli and then the hull was lowered or dropped into the water depending on the simulation: 1, 2 or 3.

Once the hull stopped – underwater you had to unstrap your seat belt, push out the window to your immediate left or right, and jettison (*exit*) through the window and up to the surface. Divers were in the water in case anyone panicked or got stuck. It was scarier and more frightening than I antici- pated, but the adrenaline was pumping. In all it was quality and one of the best things I've done this far.

Day 100 – Friday 16 September

Went for stitches out of my hand this morning, ready for Bottom Field PT. Five mins after having them out, it opened up again and the doctor said it could be the early signs of infection . . . possibly due to doing the ducker drills.

I can't do Bottom Field now and having spoken to the Troop Sergeant, he said if it does get infected, I could be sent into Hunter Troop (*Royal Marines rehabilitation troop*). I'm really worrying now and praying for the best.

This afternoon we went up to the grenade range at Woodbury Common to throw live grenades. What a mint experience. Cpl Dite was telling us about '14 INT' – the UK's covert and top-secret military intelligence service – absolutely love hearing stuff like this, fascinating!

Day 101 – Saturday 17 September

I've had to report to sickbay again this morning. My hand is looking better and will be OK, fingers crossed. I'm missing drill (not bothered) and Bottom Field again, which I'm not happy about – I feel proper shit when I have to miss phys.

Got exercise 'Running Man' next week – not looking forward to that at all, it's supposed to be a right hang out! Then test exercise Baptise Run the week after. If I pass that, it's all good – I'll be classed as a trained soldier, then I progress into phase two of training: The Tactical Phase.

Since summer leave, the Troop has pulled things together and the Training Team appear happy, which is a great feeling.

Day 102 – Sunday 18 September

It's 08:45 and we are going to church this morning. I'm feeling threaders, we went to Jolly's (*camp pub*) last night and got steaming.

It's Running Man this week coming, rumour on the 'Nod Vine' (*grapevine*) is that it's the worst and one of the hardest exercises in training. One of the lads has opted out of training, because he's been back-trooped to us (*900 Troop*) and doesn't want to do the exercise again. Holy shit!

Apparently, the exercise is constant yomping with full kit: 98lbs. I don't know how I'll do this and where I'll pull the strength from, my body is fucked. By now though, I'm learning that it's all mental down here.

LESSON 15

Fear is a state of mind created by an illusionist, a trickster of emotion, that deceives our perception of an event – manipulating our reactions by constructing a version of reality that will likely 'never' happen.

Sometimes, the unnerving emotion(s) of fear – created by a 'perceived' impending or future threat of danger or harm, must be confronted. In my experience, nothing is ever as bad as the mind projects it to be. Looking ahead into the unknown tends to breed anxiety and signals an invitation to fear.

The misrepresentation of a 'future' event
Controlling fear takes practice and skill (through experience, by resisting the temptation to succumb to emotion), but understand that fear is an illusion created by the mind around an event that is yet to happen. It is testament to the fact, that not all people fear and create anxiety about the same event. Therefore, the perception of fear is merely a prediction based on individual interpretation of an event, which the mind tries desperately to evaluate. In doing so, it maximises the potential outcome to prepare the body for the unknown.

For example, have you ever pre-empted an event yet to happen, perhaps a flight when you have a fear of flying? Well, reflect on that for a while, or something else that you fear . . .

The reality of a 'past' event
Now fast-forward to the actual 'past' real-time exposure (a real flight experience). I bet when you were seated and waiting to take-off, or in the air, the process did not match the increased emotions you had experienced beforehand.

Bringing yourself – your mind – into the present moment is vital to gaining an accurate representation of reality in these moments. Take a step back, breathe, visualise the process in your mind; what you need to do and the various procedures in the entire evolution, and try not to let your mind or emotions wander.

Events in real time

When faced with exposure to the event, remember what you have been told in relation to the outcome. Nine times out of ten, I can guarantee that the instructions you were told by the 'professionals' were delivered in an extremely basic way; broken down into bite-size understandable stages for all intellectual abilities to understand. Follow the process, focus, and execute the instructions. Even when faced with an unexpected event, life experiences up until that point will have equipped you with the valuable solutions and strategies to overcome such challenges.

The example

Admittedly, being dumped into the water, submerging, and being rotated upside down in pitch-darkness whilst strapped into a helicopter hull, is not particularly ideal; but I was told when it stopped to follow my right or left arm (which is fixed to the window) > Push the window out > Alight and swim to the surface. Reiterating the simple process internally countered unwanted emotions of fear and made getting out a manageable and, crucially, a composed and successful experience.

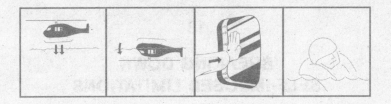

Key Points:

- Fear is an unnerving emotional response to a 'perceived' threat of danger that will never unfold as envisioned. Left unmanaged, it can ravage the mind, exhaust emotions, cloud judgement and destroy progress or aspiration.

- The event outcome rarely, if ever, matches the expectation one places on it. In this sense, worrying is a waste of emotional energy.

- Not everyone fears the same things, so its interpretation resides solely within the individual, therefore, it can be controlled and/or alleviated.

- Break distressing events down in stages and visualise them. If applicable, recall the instructions you were told and systematically put them into action in your mind.

- Remember, fear is an illusion the mind creates to prepare the body for the very worst outcome – an outcome that is 'statistically' extremely unlikely to happen.

18

BREAKING DOWN
SELF-IMPOSED LIMITATIONS

Running Man

WEEK 14

<u>*Day 103 – Monday 19 September 2005*</u>

I should have PT this morning, but my hand is still fucked; it's healed, as in there's no signs of blood, however, there's a gaping opening about an inch down my knuckle, which the lads keep calling a fanny. I'm really pissed off, because feel like I could be falling behind – I hate watching the lads do PT when I can't get involved, however honking it may be!

This afternoon, we were all fitted for our Lovetts (*green passing out uniform*). They look class and make me feel really special. It's a weird feeling looking in the mirror and seeing yourself in this uniform and the Blues uniform. I finally feel like I'm making real progress and just cannot believe it. February 10th can't come quick enough.

Evening now and I'm packing my bergen whilst trying to psych myself up for exercise Running Man tomorrow, which I'm failing to do – I'm nervous and totally dreading it.

Day 104 – Tuesday 20 September

Exercise Running Man: On our way to the drop-off point, I was really nervous and didn't speak much to the lads – I always feel so low and threaders on the way to exercises, like my world is about to end. It's the unknown, the lack of control, and the fact someone else is completely in charge of your life once you leave the relative safety of Lympstone.

We got dropped off at the RV and as soon as I put my bergen on, it nearly broke me in two. The weight of it numbs the shoulders straight away and stops the blood going to the arms, so they start getting pins and needles in them and you lose feeling in your hands – it's brutal. We yomped 7k, about five miles, up and down small mountainous terrain; it was so painful on my shoulders and lower back.

Once we arrived at the harbour position, we were all exhausted – to think in 10 weeks or so, on Final Ex, we must yomp about 25 miles with full kit. That's not possible, is it? It has been mentally and physically hard today and we've just been told to expect 10k tomorrow and a 7k night navigation. I feel like shit!

Day 105 – Wednesday 21 September

It's 05:00 and I'm putting my wet clothes on – it's so emotional this process. They got us wet at 00:00 and by that time we'd only been in our bags around 50 minutes. I've had around 3 hours' sleep (if that) and we are due to do 10k this morning with full kit. Even though my hand is a risk, a massive risk as far as I'm concerned, they still made me fully submerge it underwater, whilst crawling through a deep, muddy stream. I keep covering it in iodine spray to keep the infection at bay hopefully.

Anyway, just completed morning routine in the field – which involves getting rid of any sign of cam cream, shaving, brushing my teeth, wiping myself down with scent-free wet wipes (so dogs can't smell them and locate you in live operations), cooking breakfast and eating food – maybe even taking a massive field shit then burying it, and finally stripping and cleaning my weapon and laying out all my kit in a set way ready for inspection . . . all before 06:30!

I passed inspection – so that's a massive bonus – it's always the same lads who don't and end up on the flank, ha ha. Getting geared up ready for the 10k nav ex, I'm stiff as hell.

Just arrived back, it's been a killer mentally, the pain from the bergen was unbearable and the skin on my lower back has been rubbed off. It took us around 5½ hours to complete. Just can't explain how I felt while doing it.

It's late evening now and we've just done a stalk, which was absolutely class. We had to creep up on an enemy position and get close enough to read what was on a board without being detected – all the while changing our camouflage when needed whilst we transitioned to different areas. Really cool stuff. Going on a 7k night nav now.

Day 106 – Thursday 22 September

Got 30 minutes sleep last night – usual story on exercise. The lack of sleep and eating rations is making me feel sick. This morning, we got a shake off the Training Team and had 20 mins to get out our bags, change into our wet clothes and pack our kit up ready for a tactical stand to (_a defensive formation ready to fight off an enemy attack_) – a near impossible task, all designed to add maximum time pressure and stress – it works brilliantly!

No kit inspection this morning, that's the first time ever, I think it's because we are close to phase two of training. The night nav ex last night took 4½ hours to complete and I didn't even want to do it. Since Tuesday morning we've had 3½ hours' sleep! I'm gutted, as today we should have got a helicopter to the survival part of the exercise – this would have been my first time flying in one – but there was a problem, so we are yomping to the RV point, which is going to be a killer.

Once I passed out of training, I learnt that the helicopter never comes, it is all designed to apply 'unexpected' adversity and to see if recruits break as a result.

So, we started yomping at 08:00 – it's raining and my bergen is piss wet through and the pain on my lower back is brutal, rubbing constantly on the blistered and raw areas from the days before. We yomped 3k away from the harbour position and I was preparing for a rest at some point, but we cracked on straight through to the next checkpoint. 'False endings' appear to be the theme of this exercise . . . absolutely soul-destroying!

I feel like quitting more than ever, my feet and shoulders are numb and I'm sure I'm on the verge of exhaustion. I keep imagining eating a Double Decker (*chocolate bar*) or a warm bacon sandwich, and in some cases I can even taste it. These thoughts offer temporary release, which helps to distract myself from the pain – maybe it's why I do it.

The Training Team are playing proper mind games with us now; the lack of control and independence you have over your own existence is absolutely massive, they direct your every move. Their games are working; I want to be anywhere other than here.

One of the lads has just passed me a boiled sweet, and I'm opening it frantically like I've never been fed. Osborne has given me one of my best presents ever and immediately lifted my morale. Loads of lads are struggling now and fatigue is evident. In some cases, blood is literally pouring out of a lad's boots. Two blokes have wrapped on it and asked to leave training!

Finally, after 12–15k, I saw the 4-tonners in the distance. I was walking towards them, but they didn't seem to be getting any closer – I'm exhausted now. Made it to the 4-tonners and passed out into a deep sleep en route to the survival phase of the exercise. The sense of both achievement and relief is indescribable.

We arrived at Gidleigh Wood, where we were greeted by the MLs – the Mountain Leaders in the Royal Marines are elite amongst elite man. They love it – the cold, the rain and generally living in harsh, horrid conditions – and give recruits some of the worst thrashings ever. Not ideal with 3½ hours' sleep in 3 days.

They're going to show us how to kill chickens and rabbits, how to skin and then cook them. Some of it was difficult to watch, especially in my fragile state.

I was given a chicken and had to hold its legs and wave it back and forth upside down allowing its wings to open fully, which appeared to relax it. I then had to lower it carefully so its head touched the ground, and then pull its head and neck along the ground before putting a stick across the back of its neck; then stand on either end of the stick, trapping its head and neck, and quickly and aggressively pull it up by its legs, detaching its head from its body.

Once I'd done this, the fucking thing – with no head – set off running and flapping its wings all around the woods! You could see starving lads chasing headless chickens through the dense undergrowth – unbelievable scenes.

After this madness, I was handed my rabbit and told to grab hold of its back legs again and stroke its back whilst it was upside down. Once it was fully relaxed, I had to give it a swift and direct chop to the back of its neck with my strongest hand to break its neck. I wasn't fully committed – I didn't want to kill it and managed to knock its two front teeth out – this sent me into a chopping, bastard frenzy and in the end I killed it.

Then I had to break its legs and make a small incision with a knife in its groin area, and then put my lips over the cut and blow it up like a balloon, inflating the poor thing. Once inflated, I had to push the broken legs out of its leg skin – so its legs were in its body, under its skin – then skin it from its bum up to its head and screw its head off with all the skin and fur coiled up round its neck. I did the same with the chicken, only I plucked it first and then gutted them both.

I've just made shelter with my oppo (*friend/mate*), which is wank and made a fire, because this is survival ex now – we have only the clothes we are wearing, no sleeping bags, food (apart from the dead chicken and rabbit), or anything. I honestly can't say how cold I am – it's absolutely freezing, to the point where some of the lads have started to develop the first signs of frostbite!

Day 107 – Friday 23 September

Walked out of my makeshift shelter this morning at 06:00. Me and one of the lads who shared the shelter with me spooned each other all night – shivering violently and passing out at times through sheer exhaustion, then waking up shaking – it was absolutely horrendous. We didn't even eat the chicken or rabbit, because me more than him was scared to death of getting food poisoning and being back-trooped, so I just ate raw onions that the Training Team gave us to put in our stew.

However brutal that past twenty-four hours was, it was a great experience. Survival is such hard work. I'm mucky, stinking, tired, and cold. We've just been collected by the 4-tonners and are on our way back to camp – exhausted. Can't wait for Dutchy's later! Since Tuesday, I've had 5–6 hours' sleep. I'm so ratty now and have retreated within myself, not talking to anyone, I just want my own space – everyone can fuck off!

It's 19:00 now and I've got the weekend off. I'm shattered but determined to go out for a drink, you don't get many chances down here, even though I look and feel like a heroin addict.

Day 108 – Saturday 24 September

Nursing a hangover, so just chilling today. Thinking about going to some health club in Exeter with Ste and Wrighty. Then probs a few pints . . .

Day 109 – Sunday 25 September.

Baptise Run next week: when I started out I never in my wildest dreams thought I would make it to Week 15. Now I'm scared to death. It's a big test – pass or fail. A pass means moving on to phase two of training, where it starts getting good and you do all the Gucci stuff. A fail, and I stay in phase one . . . back-trooped!

LESSON 16

The zone of proximal learning, and the discovery of the outermost boundaries of the self, lie just outside the Comfort Zone.

Going through the pain barrier is part of the fabric of training at Commando Training Centre Royal Marines (CTCRM). It is fundamental in the process of reshaping a recruit's belief-system: of what the human mind and body is capable of withstanding and, therefore, overcoming.

I have often described the experience of life, and the journey of self-discovery at CTC like this: Royal Marines Commando training constantly redefines your understanding and assessment of what is humanly possible; a difficult, gruelling, often mentally and physically demanding undertaking that shatters self-imposed limitations, thus cultivating self-confidence and reinforcing mental strength and resilience.

Throughout the years I have been asked the same question, 'How hard is training?' by young hopefuls fuelled by intrigue and desperate to join up, as I did, when I was 18–19 years old. However, this question cannot be answered accurately and here's why.

Nothing in life can prepare you for the adversity that Royal Marines training creates. It is a process of redefining your 'perceived' limits and boundaries, of penetrating the unexplored frontiers of your mind, and redefining new possibilities and capabilities beyond what you could have ever imagined.

Dare to venture

You must harness the courage to venture into the unknown (uncomfortable places mentally), because the ignition for 'growth' and 'proximal learning' resides there. The experiences that you believe will compromise you – perhaps negatively exposing your true character – instead provide you with the opportunity to develop, to become better, more well-rounded than you ever believed was possible. Therefore, you must take steps to redefine your capabilities.

Reflection

We inhabit a world of cultural and social structures, all of which have been created by us, human beings. The fact that we have created all that we have come to know in our lives (occupations, challenges, education, exploration, and so on) means that what has gone before – a road taken by another person – is possible, it can be done again and surpassed; but only if the right Mindset, Study, Preparation, Determination and Understanding are applied.

Key Points:

- Self-assurance, self-confidence, and endless possibility lie beyond the pain barrier.
- Everyone has their own interpretation of what mental and physical adversity means to them. This can be redefined.
- The vast majority of people will never push themselves beyond their 'comfort zone'. Therefore, going beyond the pain barrier will enable you to benefit from the riches that lie beyond it. In turn, you will gain a crucial performance advantage enabling you to attack life and confront obstacles that would otherwise overwhelm most people.
- Nothing is impossible, what has gone before can be repeated and surpassed with study, preparation, application, dedication, understanding and a desire to succeed.

19

ATTENTION TO DETAIL

The Subtle Edge

WEEK 15

<u>Day 110 – Monday 26 September 2005</u>

Baptise Run: Trying to peel yourself out of bed is a test in itself. This morning was PT on Bottom Field. As a Troop, you make your way down through camp to the top of the assault course and stand in three ranks outside the NAAFI, waiting to see which PTIs you get to take you for the session. On the dot, they burst open a rear door to the gymnasium and a handful of them start coming outside – it's so intimidating! The sight of JR would fill any man with terror – he's one scary bloke and everyone's heart sinks if he comes out – because that means you're in for a horrid 1–2 hours of PT. He's the stereotypical vision you have of a Royal Marine Commando.

After PT we boarded transport to Woodbury Common for a Baptise Run revision day. The tests seem fairly straightforward, which has made me more confident. Still proper shitting it though.

Well, we screwed up straight away on the stalking element and we've been fucked around all afternoon back on camp for it. We all had to get everything we owned and throw it out the window, plus do a room/bed change to mess us about even more. It's now 03:26 in the morning and I need to iron all my clothes ready for inspection at 07:00. Winner!

Day 111 – Tuesday 27 September

A 4-mile speed march with full kit (21lbs) and weapon this morning with 2 hours' sleep. I was dreading it, but it was absolutely fine – easy!

Then we deployed on Baptise Run. We immediately went into the stalk we failed the day before, then map reading tests, observation stances, target indication, and fire and control orders. After scran, it was camouflage and concealment and a full kit inspection – all of which was scored out of ten.

Finally, at 21:00, we started our night navigation ex, I was shitting this – Woodbury is pitch-black at night and trying to reach different checkpoints under time pressure whilst following 'only' a compass bearing is the key to maximum anxiety. Get lost on Woodbury, and you've failed. The nav was 4–5 miles individual effort and I managed to complete it in 2 hours 20 minutes. Finally, at 02:00, we did wet and dry routine – WANK – and then managed to get some rest.

Day 112 – Wednesday 28 September

Just gone 05:15 and I'm about to climb reluctantly into my wet clothes. It's a groggy, cold, wet and misty morning on Woodbury. I've got to get through morning routine then it's an 8-mile load carry (41lbs) back to camp. I've had 3 hours' sleep since Monday!

Back at camp, we had a CBRN test, which is part of Baptise Run. Passed that and I think I've passed everything so far. We now have sixteen hours to fully de-service our kit ready for tomorrow's final day of tests on Baptise Run.

It's 03:00 and we've just finished sorting out all our kit. I'm up in 90 minutes ready to clean, wash and lay out my individual kit along with the rest of the lads in the drill shed ready for inspection.

Day 113 – Thursday 29 September

Well, everything went well with the inspection, we are due to get our results later. I'm confident I passed, but fear failure. A fail would turn my life upside down.

Just done Bottom Field, a brutal session as always. Doing 30ft rope climbs wearing full kit – 21lbs plus weapon – in full combat clothing and boots is a mammoth effort. We then re-did drill pass out that we previously failed, and passed it this time round, which is awesome – I still hate it though.

I PASSED BAPTISE RUN! I'm so happy; I came seventh on the points tally overall out of all the lads. Got to stay up now most of the night squaring my drill rig away and polishing my drill boots ready for tomorrow, but that's the least of my concerns – so happy!

Two of the lads failed Baptise Run and will be back-trooped now.

Day 114 – Friday 30 September

We are passing out of phase one this morning, the camp flags have been raised and the Training Team have arrived in their Lovetts . . . WOW! I feel very special today, I finally get a sense that I'm making real progress here. I'm now classed as a trained basic soldier. Seems like only yesterday that I was sat on that sofa with my best mate Chris Snowden, pissed up, talking shit and watching the Royal Marines on Sky News in Iraq. Now I'm halfway to becoming one – unbelievable.

A progression on to phase two: the tactical part of training means all the bullshit and messing around stops, or at least it isn't as bad. Now the emphasis is on learning the complex military tactics and Commando skills. In phase two we are allowed to buy our own Gucci kit for exercises ready for life in our units and no longer have to wear the wank issued shite you get when you first arrive.

I'm so happy with my life and what I'm doing, just hope things keep going well for me. Lads keep getting stress fractures and are being withdrawn from training for various injuries – I've started drinking a pint of whole milk daily to keep my lower leg bones strong.

Day 115 – Saturday 01 October

Leave: heading home!

Day 116 – Sunday 02 October

Travelling back down to camp, I'm really motivated now for phase two.

I didn't enjoy going home this time, felt a bit detached and wanted to be at Lympstone cracking on with training – that's scary. Funny, everyone back home still doing the same shit week in week out, thank fuck I left to do this!

LESSON 17

Planting the seeds for future success, and 'possessing' the awareness, that thorough care and daily investment facilitates their growth: Attention to Detail!

When you consistently enact the philosophy of 'Attention to Detail' in your daily life, it begins to breed and nurture the seeds of excellence. Having an awareness of the need to apply attention to detail in all of life's commitments, tasks, responsibilities, and ventures of personal development, truly gives you a Subtle Edge. It is what sets the Royal Marines apart and safeguards our success and reputation.

It may seem simple; indeed, it is. However, its simplicity is the hidden assassin, as people often cut corners and overlook the things that are required to accumulate and produce successful outcomes, because they don't believe they matter, nor do they understand the power of the 'Compound Effect'.[14] This results in them not staying the course.

To highlight the relationship between behaviour and its influence on the compound effect, I will draw hypothetically on the contrasting attitudes of two people and how their approaches to responsibility produce vastly different outcomes.

Type 1: The Controller
The Controller remains reactive to change and is ruthlessly efficient with time discipline. The Controller understands the value of self-discipline – the often harsh and mundane undertaking of getting up earlier than the majority to set their day up for success; for example, to exercise, shower, and conduct

---

14 D. Hardy, *The Compound Effect*, CDS Books, New York, 2012.

personal administration. In the context of recruit training, also to clean the accommodation ready for daily inspection.

The Controller does not put off their tasks and responsibilities throughout the day, nor do they let them lapse into the following day; actions that begin to apply unnecessary 'self-induced' pressure. They maximise time and opportunities to stay abreast of their daily responsibilities, performing all the small but fundamental actions with control.

Indeed, the efficient management of essential daily routines such as personal admin – washing, drying and ironing clothes and bedding, cleaning the accommodation – and also 'accepting change' and making the necessary adaptations as soon as possible, are what subtly separate *ordinary* from *extraordinary* performance outcomes in the medium to long term.

Type 2: The Dismisser

The Dismisser, on the other hand, lacks the self-discipline to control their environment and thus fails to acknowledge the power and consequence an absence of daily control and time management brings when trying to achieve long-term strategic success.

In isolation, one day of inaction and lack of control may not affect performance in the future, but cutting corners and delaying the inevitable personal responsibilities forms habits, and habits can become deep-rooted. Fundamentally, it is about consistency; resulting in either positive or negative behavioural outputs.

Those who opt for short-term comfort, who consistently put things off and don't control time and opportunity effectively, are inviting pressure to build – and when pressure compounds, their capacity to learn new skills and maintain upward performance trajectory becomes compromised.

Over a period of say 3–6 months, the disparity in the performance and technical ability between the Controller and the Dismisser can be absolutely startling. All because of their contrasting subtle approaches to daily and often mundane, but essential, responsibility management.

Why we appear to be predisposed to cutting corners
Over many millennia, human beings have developed ways to find and manipulate shortcuts. From an evolutionary perspective, when we were 'hunter-gatherers', this strategy reserved energy and assured our survival when food was scarce. These prehistoric cognitive structures are still present today and to a large extent help us to navigate the social world efficiently, but they also create complacency.

When it comes to acquiring the subtle edge that separates you from the rest, there is no substitute for attention to detail; doing the small, seemingly insignificant things that people don't think will make a difference. Trust me, they are the building blocks of unbelievable success and fulfilment.

Reflect on this
The creation of the Great Wall of China, one of the seven 'man-made' wonders of the world, started with a single brick, which over time became one of the most awe-inspiring feats of human engineering ever created. All from a single brick . . .

Key Points:

- The small things that most people overlook produce excellence and are the fundamental building blocks of unimaginable success.

- Every daily action taken – small or large – has an effect, whether that is subtle or substantial. Therefore, doing the small, 'positive actions' repeated over time will give you an Elite Performance Edge.
- Our ancestral past as 'hunter-gatherers' created cognitive processing shortcuts to allow us to preserve energy in-between successful hunts. These shortcuts are still present today.
- Attention to detail = Quality = Excellence = Elite Outcomes.

20

REACHING THE HALFWAY POINT

Staying focused

WEEK 16

Day 117 – Monday 03 October 2005

The start of the tactical phase of training!

A boring morning of signals and radio voice procedure to start the day. Then a double period of Bottom Field, which was an absolute hangout: 3 × 30ft rope climbs with 7lbs of kit and weapon, 1 × 200m fireman's carry – carrying someone of similar height and weight with their kit (horrific) – 1 × lap of the assault course (sub 5 mins), and a full regain over the tank . . . dangling.

Just received orders from the Troop Commander. We are now allowed quilts on our beds, instead of sheets and itchy, scratchy brown blankets. I can't tell you how happy we all are about this news. Buzzing!

Day 118 – Tuesday 04 October

Commando 21 structure (*tactical*) lecture looking at how the Commando Brigade (*Royal Marines*) is set up – pretty boring. We played football period five . . . FOOTBALL? What the fuck is going on? Then we did 1½ rope climbs with 10lbs of kit. That was really hard, followed by a full regain over the tank. I cracked it though and stayed dry, so I'm happy with that.

Capt W (*Troop Commander*) was telling us about how the Russians dropped land mines in Afghan from planes. He was saying that once some poor bastard stands on one, they shoot out the ground and detonate at waist to chest level – honking that, but interesting!

Day 119 – Wednesday 05 October

This morning was spent learning the NATO sequence of orders, tactical signals, and surveillance techniques. The surveillance was mega, we were discussing infra-red bands, radars, spy planes, NVGs, CWS, and PNG (*image intensifiers*) and visible band MKII – that's what standard our eyes will be at the end of training. They'll train us to pick up things visually that the average person won't detect – CLASS.

PNG is what Sam Fisher uses on the video game Splinter Cell. It's an NVG and Thermal Heat intensifier in one headset that's interchangeable. I'm loving this new phase of training, it's mostly fascinating stuff. Later, if/when I do pass out and go to my unit, I'll be using all this stuff on operations. Absolutely awesome!

Day 120 – Thursday 06 October

Woke up this morning in a terrible mood. Not helped by the fact that we have a signal voice procedure test, then a recce patrol lecture. After, double Bottom Field . . . I've been dreading this day all week.

Sky News filmed us during Bottom Field, which is due to

air on Saturday at some point, so we all knew we were in for a right thrashing. They were filming because the Royal Marines has the highest percentage failure rate across the armed forces and Sky wanted to know why. We got hammered big time, lads were spewing all over and I picked up a calf injury. After lunch, it was more signal voice procedure with the headsets, which I enjoyed.

Day 121 – Friday 07 October

We have had an intro into amphibious warfare this morning, which was really cool. I can't wait to do this later in training. Afterwards it was back down on the Bottom Field – what a place that is, so bleak and depressing and fills any man with pure dread. I'm aching and feel so run down at the moment. I really cannot be arsed to do PT today.

PT was a technique session, which was very welcome and chilled, but still a bit of a hangout. Wank signals last period. I can't wait to see the back of this week; it's been proper shit.

Just been told I'm on poor admin routine all weekend for not putting my name in my Gore-Tex Socks. What a load of bullshit, it's complete bollocks. Fuck it, I'm still going out, even though I need to be up and ready for inspection at 05:00 – no one is ruining my weekend!

Day 122 – Saturday 08 October

I'm rough as hell and on poor admin duty all weekend. Just trying to lay all my kit out for inspection and I can't even think straight or see properly.

I can't believe I'm on this detail for not having my name in my socks. I have to be ready for inspection at: 05:45, 09:00,

14:00, 19:00 and 20:45 – Saturday through to Sunday . . . wankers!

Day 123 – Sunday 09 October

Really fed up today, every Sunday I get depressed, it's a horrible feeling. I just seem to sit and psych myself out of training.

The next 15 weeks are going to be so challenging and sometimes, like now, I wonder why I'm putting myself through it. Everyone back home said, 'See you in one month,' and that's what keeps me going here, I would rather die than give them that enjoyment and satisfaction.

It's 18:25 now and I'm getting ready for my inspection at 19:00. So hacked off with this bullshit now. I need motivation and inspiration more than ever. SHIT!

LESSON 18

Staying focused; resisting the tendency to become complacent, and refraining from expressing the undesirable embodiment of self-adulation.

In my experience and through observation, three things can happen when you reach the halfway point (or the end goal for that matter) to achieving a long-term, significant goal: Self-adulation, Disillusionment, or Complacency. All three can be dangerous, but I will focus on complacency and self-adulation, although I acknowledge that disillusionment can strike at any point.

By this stage of the course, you will take military training and life in the Marines for granted, to varying extents. The training and environment will start to become your norm, your way of life; and your existence before Lympstone – the recruit's previous way of living – will be slowly disintegrating and becoming a distant memory.

The lesson

It is important not to get complacent. I have frequently observed people in fantastic positions in life, who then self-sabotage their success. Most, if not all of these people have become accustomed to the power and prestige that success brings them and their surroundings. They take their lifestyle for granted; it becomes such a part of their reality that they fail to recognise that success – the trappings of it, the status symbols and adulation it affords – is only temporary. Catastrophic change through self-sabotage is always just around the corner. Therefore, maintaining and producing the desired results requires an understanding that continued success necessitates a daily investment.

High-profile examples

Complacency is the silver bullet, along with an element of self-adulation (feeling better than, and untouchable from the rest); it strikes when your guard is down, when you haven't reflected on life and taken account of the fortunate position you find yourself in. For example, look at the high-profile instances involving golfer Tiger Woods, former US president Bill Clinton, and cyclist Lance Armstrong. These are only a few of the phenomenally successful people that have had it all and then severely self-sabotaged their success and reputations.

Training to become a Royal Marine won't bring you massive wealth and notoriety, but you will quickly find yourself in a position that many wish and have failed to attain, as you make progress through each stage of Royal Marines Commando training.

Becoming disillusioned

At Lympstone, it can be easy to look back to the not-so-distant past through rose-tinted glasses. You may remember all the good points, maybe even the positives of your former life, but remember this: there is a reason why you left it, why you began this and other journeys of self-discovery. You did not like where you were and what was on offer.

My previous existence before the Royal Marines depressed me. Personally, it is a life that is still trapped in time to this day. Therefore, keep reflecting on and reinforcing the reasons that put you on the path to where you are now; your path towards achieving something incredibly significant and life-changing. Remind yourself why you left, why you started, and what the positives will be after achieving such a huge undertaking.

Self-control and patience are like muscles that must be flexed. The more we exercise restraint and self-sacrifice, and take periods of reflection and visualisation, the better and easier it becomes to safeguard and achieve our goals. Reflection and reinforcement of the reasoning, behaviours and actions that put you where you are, are important processes to apply in order to maintain and achieve success.

Key Points:

- Reflect on where you are, how far you have come, and don't become complacent because that invites negative consequences. Training is not over until you have your Green Beret on your head.

- Looking back to the past can sometimes be viewed through rose-tinted glasses. Remember, there is a reason why you left, why you started a significant journey towards life-changing achievements.
- Exercise emotional self-control and be patient. Reflect on and reinforce the reasons that put you where you are – this is fundamental to maintaining and acquiring future successful outcomes.

21

YOU CAN'T CONTROL THE WEATHER

Enduring discomfort is part of the journey

WEEK 17

Day 124 – Monday 10 October 2005

We've been doing harbour entrance and fishhook ambush drills *(rehearsals)* all morning in preparation for ex 'First Base' tomorrow – they never get easier to bear mentally.

After scran, we were down on the Bottom Field for double PT: three rope climbs; one with full kit (21lbs) + weapon – one with only weapon and one loose order. After it was a lap of the assault course (sub 5 mins) followed by a full regain over the water tank. What a hangout!

It's evening now and I'm packing the good old bergen for tomorrow and weighing my webbing *(fighting order)* ready for a 5-mile speed march first thing tomorrow morning. This one has to be in full kit: 21lbs plus weapon – I'm DREAD-ING IT.

Day 125 – Tuesday 11 October

Eleven of the lads creamed in and had to get in the safety wagon during the speed march. I would literally rather die than ever get in that wagon – even though it was brutal. Again,

I found myself saying, 'What the fuck am I doing here?' We then boarded transport to take us to the Perridge Estate in Devon. Cpl Drainey said, 'In parts, this place is like the jungle.' Absolutely buzzing – NOT. I do like Cpl Drainey though, he knows his shit and is hard-faced, but I reckon a good bloke if I was fully trained.

The bus journey to all exercises is spent fast asleep. You know that cold, awful feeling when you've been sleeping in a warm car and you suddenly arrive at your destination and have to get out into the cold – like a full-on assault on your senses? Well, we arrived at the exercise RV and were told to 'Get out!' and 'Grab your kit!' and line up in three ranks in a forest-type car park. It was, however, absolutely coming down in buckets and they left us there for 2–3 hours – the most soul-destroying short experience I've ever had – well, it certainly felt that way as I stood there thinking HOW SHIT IS MY LIFE.

It's early evening now and we've been practising tactical harbour occupation drills, patrolling, actions on enemy contact, and cave clearances – like you would do in Afghan – apparently that's where we're going straight after training . . . I hope so! Apart from the heavy rain, which has been unrelenting, it's been a great day in the field and very interesting.

Day 126 – Wednesday 12 October

Wet and Dry last night was horrendous. We were positioned in dense foliage in a wood block, just off a gravel track. Once it got dark, you couldn't see a thing. Trying to get it right – leaving no traces or clothing behind, when tactically you can't use any white torchlight – is near on impossible, but we must learn to master this.

We stood to at 06:45 – taking momentary tactical firing positions ready to return fire if needed. Then cracked our field and hygiene admin – rammed some breakfast rations down and stripped our weapons for inspection. Shortly after, we were taught how to set up and conduct OPs and Recce Patrols.

At 21:00 Delta Fire Team (*my team*) moved off to recce an old paintballing facility, which had been renamed (*for the purpose of training*) as an enemy position. We had to gather as much info on the place – including drawing pictures – without anyone being alerted by our presence then or after. It was class and I loved it – really starting to feel like a Royal Marine now.

Day 127 – Thursday 13 October

It's rained solid now for three days! Just come off sentry, I've been on since 03:40 – it's now 08:20. It's been ninja (*skilful, hard, complex*) this exercise so far, we've started using headsets and hand signals to communicate in the harbour area. No one can know we are here, it's brilliant sneaking about.

We've started sleeping through the day and operating at night. My fire team (*Delta*) are going on an OP (*Observation Post*) tonight using NVGs to observe a likely enemy patrol. Our mission is to assess the following: their weapon capabilities – whether that be long or short range, their morale, daily routines, and uniforms. We are going to be there concealed for fourteen hours – no sleep!

I feel like a Marine more than ever now, I'm loving this – this is why I joined for sure. Loving this new tactical phase of training.

Day 128 – Friday 14 October

We are yomping to an extraction point 5 miles away this morning with full kit: 80–90lbs – not looking forward to it at all, as I'm fatigued mentally and physically and generally drained. All I can think about is going to Dutchy's – the camp fast-food stall – even though he knows how to charge us recruits, and that food will kill any man after a period of time, it just has to happen.

The ex has been good, a far cry from the others but still a lick (_hangout_). On the bus now, the yomp back was OK, but my feet are covered with blisters and my arms kept going numb from the shoulder straps digging in. Brutal, fucking brutal.

Just arrived back at camp, cleaned all weapons and de-serviced (_washed, cleaned, dried and ironed_) all my field kit. Going for a drink with Gold's, then getting a good night's sleep in.

Day 129 – Saturday 15 October

Our Troop Commander, Captain W, gathered us all up on the stairs this morning and said, 'The weather we have just experienced on that exercise was absolutely shocking.' He went on to say that he has seen finer men wrap their tits in.

'It was Nod (_recruit_) breaking weather and you didn't wrap. I came with thirty-five men and left with thirty-five men and that's a credit and massive chuck up to all you lads.' He continued, 'The originals that started day one with me, come the end of training they – you – could go on and pass SF (_Special Forces_) selection, no problem.'

What a compliment that is – wow! That gives me a brilliant

feeling and a lot of confidence that I can do this. This course is mine for the taking, providing I don't get injured now.

Day 130 – Sunday 16 October

On reflection, I'm so proud and happy at the stage of training I've been able to achieve here. It's Week 18 now of Royal Marines Commando training!

You hear all the scare stories about lads getting injured and then medically discharged, and also lads opting out and returning home because they no longer want to continue, or through girlfriends. I absolutely love it when lads leave – it empowers me, makes me stronger and more determined to do this. When someone opts out, I automatically lose all respect for them and think they're weak.

However, a good mate of mine down here, Cutler, has got a stress fracture in his shin – apparently, he's had it since Week 9 and has been in Hunter Company to try and get it sorted. Just been told he's leaving training and going home, which is a great shame. He's a great lad with plenty of guts and determination, but his body let him down.

LESSON 19

Embracing discomfort is what makes the journey so worth-while, and reaching the end goal such a fulfilling experience.

Today, when I try to recall my previous life at CTC, only significant snapshots in time are retrievable. One such picture, however, stands alone, a vivid recollection of the moment when the Training Team left us to attention in that heavy rain for three hours, while they went in search of hot food and shelter, and failed (unsurprisingly) to communicate their ETA with us. It was a soul-destroying experience, which those present remember even to this day, and one of the moments in training that left me contemplating my rationale and life choices.

I had experienced other times like this in the field, on Running Man and subsequently on Dig Ex, when temperatures dropped below freezing. In civilian life, you can take measures to evade the rain and apply more clothing when exposed to freezing temperatures, or you simply don't go out. In training, however, and during subsequent operations in the Middle East, respite from the environment is not a possibility. You must simply 'accept' the conditions, mentally prepare, and understand that at times life will be an unbearably uncomfortable experience, which you will have no option but to endure.

I remember vividly on Salisbury Plain during Dig Ex, we all felt the need to dig with such purpose and intensity for our sheer survival – not to get the job done quicker, but simply to keep warm – it was that cold. Brief moments of rest, to stop and take on water, were met with instant cooling and exposure. It was the same on Final Ex, when Tom Curry and I were so cold that instead of sleep, we chose to exercise (discreetly) throughout the night in order to stay warm. In any case, sleeping was almost impossible; at times you would suddenly pass out into a deep sleep, only to wake up moments later, shivering violently. It was absolutely brutal.

Knowing and crucially 'embracing' the environment and reality you are going into, not only prepares the mind, but it allows Royal Marines to operate and be productive when others (enemies) shut down. It is a matter of acknowledging the distinction between internal reflection and the impending reality, and therefore accepting 'temporary' discomfort.

Key Points:

- There are situations in life and external factors that simply cannot be changed or avoided. You must accept temporary discomfort.
- Embrace these challenges and take comfort in knowing that many have been deterred, whilst you remain resilient and productive.

22

CONSISTENCY

The construct of an elite mindset

WEEK 18

Day 131 – Monday 17 October 2005

I've never felt as down or as shit about things as I have done this morning. Really can't be bothered – I have zero motivation and we have failed inspection, which has compounded my misery. Just got back from PT, I was dog shit – we all were, and got an extra thrashing for being wank. What a day . . . I'm depressed, frustrated, exhausted, broken, tired and lost.

It's the evening now, and we've had our duvets taken off us, so it's back to bed sheets, itchy and scratchy blankets, and making our beds for inspection every morning. In addition, we've had to change rooms with each other (*known as room changes*), which is designed to massively fuck the lads around and lower troop morale – yeah, it works.

If that's not enough, we've got to be in drill rig every morning now for two weeks – loads of ironing, polishing drill boots, etc. every bastard night. What a JOKE, I feel like rapping my tits in with this SHIT. I'm up at 05:00 to clean the block and it's now 02:00 and I'm getting in bed for three hours' sleep!

Day 132 – Tuesday 18 October

POW (_prisoner of war_) handling lectures this morning. It's howling it down with bastard wrap juice (_rain_) – pitch-black outside and we are going on ex 'Second Empire' in two hours' time until Friday. That's us piss wet through, freezing cold, and doing Wet and Dry routine all week.

Just arrived at Woodbury Common. It is some place this; always bleak, wet, cold and depressing. Same place we did Marshal Star – I've had nightmares and still do about that exercise!

We've been going through section attacks, actions on ambush, and patrolling all day. Then in the evening we rehearsed a troop level attack ready to raid and take out the 'Hunter Clan'. (_The injured but physically mobile lads in Hunter, who provide enemy for recruit troop exercises._)

Day 133 – Wednesday 19 October

It has rained all night. It's horrible being in the rain, freezing cold, when there's nothing you can do about it. Well, they say, 'What doesn't kill you makes you stronger,' but I can't really relate to this at the moment . . . in fact, it can FUCK OFF, that quote!

The Troop Commander has picked me to be his Radio Operator (_RO_), which usually means he thinks you're a shit bloke and wants to keep a close eye on your drills and field skills, i.e., speed of doing wet and dry, basic field admin, and hygiene maintenance. That's BRILLIANT. In real operations the RO is in effect the Troop Commander's bodyguard and his main source of communications.

This evening we had orders, and everyone now knows what

their jobs are and timings. It makes things very real and I feel the part. I'm going to show the Captain – he's clearly got a 100% wrong impression of me. Now bombing up my mags (*loading them*) with blank rounds and getting cammed up.

Just arrived back at the harbour, the attack was awesome, they sprung an ambush on us and we had to fight through it and ended up taking all but one out, so now we have a POW to interrogate. Love this shit!

Day 134 – Thursday 20 October

It hasn't stopped raining since Tuesday morning, the Troop's morale is uber low and I'm proper pissed off, can't wait to go back to camp.

Being the Troop Commanders RO, I have to share a poncho with him, which means doing wet and dry at the side of him, cooking, stripping and cleaning weapons – and conducting general basic hygiene (brushing my teeth, drying my feet and applying talcum powder, wiping my balls and knob down and cleaning under my arms, etc.) – all part of 'morning routine'.

The bastard was still in his bag for 'stand to' while I was smashing through wet and dry and cracking my morning routine. Gen, he said, 'Fucking hell, Timmins, you absolutely smashed that wet and dry routine, great effort!' In all fairness, we all normally drip (*moan*) while doing it – but on this occasion, I did it with zero emotion to prove a point. So happy he's seen what I'm about now.

Anyway, having interrogated the POW, he gave us INT that Hunter Clan are using a supply track to deliver ammunition, so we are going to lay an ambush tonight. We've been going through the rehearsals most of the day and had 2 hours of orders – covering everything about the mission. We are due to leave the harbour at 00:01 hours in the morning and it's started raining again!

This below was written shortly after arriving back, because I couldn't write during the ambush.

At 06:30 we spotted the enemy. Once the truck got into the 'kill zone', I fired all thirty blank rounds into it on fully auto, did an uber quick mag change, then went again with another 30 killing the enemy – collectively as a troop. At the end of the attack, one of enemy who was still alive was trying to restart the engine. Although you know it's not real, it's still a massive buzz!

We only had to wait 7 hours in the pissing rain, perfectly still in one position. I'll be honest, I was dying to get my head down and Wrighty, at the side of me, was even snoring – something you just cannot do, or at least get caught doing – but I was the Troop Commander's RO, so I had to hold my eyes open all night, because he was on my other side. I reckon Wrighty will get hell for that, because the Troop Captain kept saying, 'Recruit Wright, open your eyes!' but Wrighty had gone, snoring like a pig in a tactical ambush.

Day 135 – Friday 21 October

Been conducting wood clearances this morning. Fairly good, then we yomped 6 miles back to Lympstone with 90lbs bergens – emotional. Just cleaning weapons and comms kit, then having a mission debrief.

Well, apparently ten lads were caught asleep during the ambush. They're now on phone sentry from 19:00 tonight until 07:00 Monday morning. This means 2 hours off, ½ an hour on, when they must wait for the phone to ring and if it does, answer it within 1 ring or they get fucked . . . GOPPING.

It's a shocker, but it's not me this time, so I couldn't give a toss!

Day 136 – Saturday 22 October

Nice lay in, chilling all day and going into Exeter this aft.

Surprise, surprise, they wouldn't let us in anywhere – they hate Marines round here. Anyway, just looking at the lads on phone sentry is enough to cheer me up . . . ha ha ha!

Day 137 – Sunday 23 October

Really looking forward to this week – first time since being here. It's 'Adventure Training' (AT) week. Never in a million years did I think I would see AT week.

LESSON 20

The 'Access Override' key, to gain entry to the off-limits, most exclusive level at the top, has the name 'consistency' on the head.

When called and relied upon, Royal Marines need to perform without fail. Our reputation of excellence is underpinned by consistency, a key aspect that separates the 'ordinary' from the 'extraordinary' and produces elite performance. Consistency is not born overnight, however, it is the result afforded to those who undertake months and often years of accumulated and dedicated hard work.

Consistency is a habit; it is performing the same, 'desired' behaviours to produce a particular result, day in day out, until they become habitual; behavioural outcomes that are then performed subconsciously, the product of 'muscle memory' of both mind and body. Royal Marines and other elite forces not only work harder than everyone else, but they are more consistent than everyone else.

Elite level thinking and behaviour, which encompasses most, if not all, the lessons within this book, allows you to apply yourself in a way that facilitates the attainment of your chosen goals. It is harnessing the power of your mindset to study and research consistently with the intent to get better and become a subject matter expert. Likewise, it's engaging in consistent, constructive physical training to achieve unimaginable feats of human capability.

Take Michael Phelps, for example, one of the greatest Olympians of all time. When he was asked about his preparation for the 2016 Olympics, he said he had been in the gym or in the water every day for five years. For him, that amount of time and consistency was crucial, just to swim events that may have lasted a matter of seconds or minutes. Therefore, you must make consistency a part of your everyday life if you wish to develop an Elite Mindset and outcomes. But notably, you need to achieve consistency despite the pulls from both enduring and ever-changing external factors, such as maintaining good relationships, raising children and managing work commitments.

Key Points:

- You cannot perform at Elite Levels without sustained periods of 'consistent' behaviour. Put simply, it MUST become a way of life – underpinned by personal sacrifice and commitment.

CONSISTENCY

- Consistency is developed by performing the same 'desired' behaviours repeatedly until they become habits.
- Developing an Elite Mindset and behaviour allows the facilitation of large and complex goal attainment.
- Consistency is what separates you from the rest.

23

TAKING CONSTRUCTIVE CRITICISM

The inherent value of an external evaluation

WEEK 19

Day 138 – Monday 24 October 2005

GPMG (*General Purpose Machine Gun*) training all morning. This weapon is devastating, its design has not changed for years and it smashes through walls like they're made of polystyrene. The power is unreal: 7.62mm belt-fed ammunition!

After scran, we had the second fitting of our blues uniform and we've now been able to keep our Lovetts uniform in our lockers. I can't believe what's happening to me here, I'm really doing this! To top it all off, my blues have been sent off so they can stitch my Marksman badge on it. What a feeling – makes me feel so proud of myself.

Just had my TRC (*Training Record Card*) Report off Cpl Rikards. It was quality, saying: 'The previous exercise didn't faze him at all. Rct Timmins is very quickly becoming an accomplished field soldier.' Wow . . .

Day 139 – Tuesday 25 October

First day of Adventure Training today. We've waited a long time for this week to come and it feels quite surreal that I'm here at this stage of training – it's seen as a key milestone down here and allows a welcome and chilled break away from training for whoever makes it this far, and a rare opportunity to be treated, at least for one week, like a fully trained Royal Marines Commando.

Half the lads have gone to Chivenor. Whereas Section 3 and 4 (*my section*) are in Exmouth boathouse doing powerboating, banana boating, and sailing. This will be a good time away from training.

Just been to Tesco to get loads of beers in. We are watching a film later called 'Dead Man's Shoes', which is supposed to be good. Sailing today was boring!

Day 140 – Wednesday 26 October

Last night, Cpl Rikards told us about the 354 radios. Apparently, you can communicate from one side of the world to the other with them and signallers have reported hearing historic conversations from the Vietnam War, etc., because radio conversations bounce around the world and never really die. How mad is that?

Sailing again this morning – I hate it. However, after scran we are doing banana boating, which should be quality and a top laugh.

Going around Exmouth for first time tonight – this place is off limits and a location only reserved for trained Royal Marines. The next time we go out here will be after Kings Squad . . . just hope I make it. That's the thing down here, you can't get excited, because you never know if you will get injured or fail something. I mean, lads get injured on the 30-miler – breaking legs, ankles, and so on – and 3–4 lads have even died during it, so you must always stay grounded.

My lower left shin is killing me when I apply pressure, worried it may be the early signs of a stress fracture.

Day 141 – Thursday 27 October

Power boating today was brilliant, but made me feel very sick. It looks easy, but there's a lot to it.

I'm threaders again today – in a general state of 'fuck off everyone'. We've really felt part of the Marines family for the last three days. Cpl Rikards even called me 'Royal' last night – a term exchanged only between fully trained Royal Marines – it felt awesome. Crashing straight back down to earth tomorrow morning with double PT first thing. Honestly, I find it all so hard, not only doing it, but preparing for it mentally. Butterflies every time – it's pure hell.

I'm sick of training now. I can't wait to pass out of this place!

Day 142 – Friday 28 October

Three of the lads were late for our first detail this morning, which has sparked a right chain reaction. Everything has spiralled out of control now. We've been messed about all day like never before: Quick Changes – from one uniform to the next in 30 seconds – one Mud Run, Room Changes, and then to top it all off we had to throw absolutely everything we own, including the contents of our lockers, down the middle of our 4-storey accommodation block.

The pile of clothing and personal shit that we have created is 10 feet tall. We now have to sort it all out and find what bits are ours, which is honking because everyone has the same stuff barring names inside. Then wash it all, iron it all, and fold it all (global and laurel size) ready for inspection at 10:00 tomorrow. It's now 23:00, so we have 11 hours = 100% all-nighter coming up!

It gets better – straight after inspection, it's down on Bottom Field for double PT again with 18lbs and weapon.

This turned out to be the most horrific mess around we ever received at Lympstone by our Training Team. It took hours and hours to sift through all the kit; many lads were broken – shouting, punching walls, and arguing amongst themselves – myself included. It was a frantic rush to find your kit first and then make it across camp to the limited amount of washers to start the cleaning process. Not everyone could wash at once – not even half the troop – and we all knew that, which only heightened the tension between us. It was utter carnage!

Day 143 – Saturday 29 October

Zero sleep! We've been fucked around even more this morning. The rumour around camp is that this is common after AT. It's designed into the training schedule to lull you into a false comfort zone then be violently ragged back out of it, to get rid of the lads who are starting to show a small element of psychological self-doubt in themselves coming up to the Commando phase of training. So clever, if true!

If this is the case, I'm not going anywhere, and they can ram the AT up their arses, because coming back to this shit is absolutely horrible.

Day 144 – Sunday 30 October

I'm finding this part of training really tough mentally, the pressure is unbelievable. It's Bottom Field Pass Out in two weeks!

Self-Reflection (in 2005)

When people ask me, 'How hard is it down there?' I don't know how to answer, because everyone has their own perception of what 'hard' means to them. For example, a civilian's idea of a hard day mentally and physically might be a two-mile run, or a keep fit class.

Mine is three days without my eyes closed, little to no food, doing wet and dry every morning, and sleeping with wet socks under my armpits to dry them out during the night, so my feet don't go down with trench foot. Then throwing a 90–100lbs bergen on my back – the weight digging into my shoulders so bad the circulation is cut off, making my arms and hands go numb, and losing general control of my fingers. All this while carrying injuries, which we all are to some extent, and then pouring blood out of our boots at the end of an 8–10 mile yomp. That's how hard it is and it's only Week 19 of 32!

It goes against your human instinct; it's the biggest mental and physical strain imaginable, an experience you have to endure personally to get even close to understanding. Each day is so mentally taxing – like a constant cloud of fear and anxiety that never leaves you until you are able to get in bed. Once in bed, that is your time, your only bit of control, comfort and freedom.

It is torture, a rollercoaster of emotional ups and downs: I can do this, I can't do this . . . I love it here, what am I doing here . . . I miss home, fuck home. It's just insanity.

We all eat Pro Plus tablets like they are getting discontinued – any glimmer of the fade off and a load more go flying down range (*down the throat*) just to make it through the day. Then it's a matter of tackling the dreadful comedown each evening, because of the caffeine overdose; the jittery paranoia and extenuating anxiety caused from plummeting back down to earth. This often results in sleepless nights and the terrible realisation of crashing straight through to the following day with no sleep – knowing that the process of heavy stimulation must be repeated again to survive. Absolutely mental, the whole thing.

I'm just praying (to no god) that my body will hold out for another 12 weeks. I did a brutal six-month fitness conditioning build-up prior to joining, which near enough mimicked what we did at Leeds, during pre-season. I think it's all catching up with me now though.

There are 16 originals left out of 51 who started training 20 weeks ago – including that extra two weeks the first lot of us did, that's 22 weeks. I'll bust guts and limbs to be there at the end – passing out with the lads in February next year.

LESSON 21

Ditch the persona, unlock the door, and welcome in criticism. An external evaluation of your conduct and ability is the best thing you could ever wish for.

Throughout a soldier's career in the Royal Marines, taking on board constructive criticism forms an essential part of their development. It is a crucial part of self-improvement and maintains the collective standards of excellence.

In a culturally competitive working environment, characterised by an expectation that an individual will continually push the boundaries of possibility, an external evaluation forms a key component; for example, the routine TRC (Training Record Card) appraisal I received above on Day 138. Instances like this provided me with an insight into my performance;

identifying areas of improvement, aspects of soldiering I was doing well at, and the steps I needed to take to ensure my success on the course.

It is not always easy hearing about your flaws, especially from a person like Corporal Rikards, who was where I wanted to be and whom I desperately wanted to impress. But it is a vital part of learning, and it enables us to refocus our attention onto areas we may have overlooked, or not even realised were having an effect on our ability.

Without this type of valuable insight into the areas in which you can improve, where you fall below the standards of your organisation, or in this case, expectations of training, you will never get better at what you do. So it is essential to welcome these opportunities for feedback and personal investigation, and not to get defensive or take it personally when you hear some home truths. Take notice of the criticism and view it as a chance to develop professionally and more importantly, as a person. Use it as an aid to create stronger working relationships, optimise your performance and lift morale.

How others become successful is really interesting. In recent years, I have become fascinated with other people's success, or lack of it (this would fill endless books, I know). The question is: are they just lucky, or do they take steps to make themselves successful? What drives them? Is it the thought of getting what they want in life, or the thrill of the chase, or does the fear of failure push them to work harder?

I have observed and tried to understand some of the barriers to professional development and successful outcomes, and one thing I can say is that if people don't listen to constructive criticism, and fail to take it on board and use it to improve themselves, they are more likely to stagnate and never reach their full potential.

Although constructive criticism is fundamental to maintaining excellence in the Royal Marines, it is also, at times, an uncomfortable truth that we must all seek and learn to welcome.

Key Points:

- Taking on board constructive criticism is an essential part of learning and getting better, both professionally and personally. Without it, you could fail to address the areas in which you could benefit from improvement.
- However uncomfortable these encounters may be, if we are to reach our full potential, then it is a fundamental process that must be undertaken. Finally, don't let your ego get in the way of learning and personal development.

24

EXERCISE HUMILITY

Remain an adaptive student of life and opportunity

WEEK 20

Day 145 – Monday 31 October 2005

Cannot believe it's the start of Week 20 – I am about two-thirds of the way there and I must say I feel like shit – my body is fucked. We are due to go on ex 'Dorset's Leap' later on today, which means staying in Stanley Barracks until Wednesday morning, learning the Viking (*all-terrain armoured vehicle*) and how to utilise it during operations in various attacks and ambushes, whilst also learning of its capabilities. It can navigate over any kind of terrain and can even go amphibious . . . it's a hoofing bit of kit!

This morning, however, we've been going through boring Health and Safety. We have got an 8-mile yomp tomorrow night with 69lbs + weapon. I'm dreading it big time and it is pass or fail.

Day 146 – Tuesday 01 November

Worked with the Vikings all this morning. They are mega – 6 mounted smoke-grenade launchers and a mounted 50 cal machine gun – devastating weapon! It's 21:00 and I've just weighed my kit as we are due to depart on the yomp in 30 mins. It's two laps of a 4-mile dirt track circuit and is supposed to be honking.

Back at the accommodation at 23:50. It was really hard and the pace was intense. We did it in 2 hours and 10 mins – my feet are in absolute pieces now. After the 4-mile checkpoint, realising we had to go around again was mentally GOPPING. Yomping that distance at speed carrying weight is so demanding – it's a case of zoning out and staying in a positive place mentally, which is not easy to master and maintain when you're hanging out!

Two of the lads failed because their kit was underweight at the end. Some lads weigh in correctly, but then ditch weight prior to doing the test to make it easier. However, the Training Team sometimes re-weigh our kit after, and it looks like these lads have been busted so will have to retake and/or get back-trooped.

Day 147 – Wednesday 02 November

Woke up stiff as a board and we are heading into the field this morning supported by the Vikings. It's bastard throwing it down with rain – it literally hasn't been dry on exercise since phase one, and even then we were made to do wet and dry every night. Basically, during the past 20 weeks I have never got into or out of my sleeping bag without having to do the wet and dry routine.

The next few days will consist of section and troop attacks in the Vikings, so that should be good. The first part of the day covered the cam and concealment of the Vikings, which was boring. However, we were then introduced to a new vehicle cam net called the 'Barracuda', which stops any vehicle from emitting a heat signature. You can't see in but you can see out of net – it's like a stealth net, which is absolutely class.

Four of my section are going on a recce at 02:00, which means I'll be on sentry in wet kit freezing my bollocks off nearly all night, with no sleep – WINNER!

Day 148 – Thursday 03 November

Yesterday was non-tactical, which means you can operate in the field using white light during dark hours (game changer), you can also cook as and when you like and talk to each other in the harbour area, and generally means things are more relaxed. However, for the next two days it's fully tactical – so no talking, just PRRs and hand signals. We are going on section attack at 12:30 in the Vikings. In prep, I'm bombing up my mags with blank rounds and prepping my smoke grenades.

We were cutting around the common/training area looking to get into a contact (*firefight*). We got a left contact ambush. We dismounted the Vikings to the right using them as cover and formed an 8-man baseline, whilst taking cover. Three enemy wearing balaclavas were firing down at us from an elevated position. My section laid down fire with the GPMGs while 2 section fired and manoeuvred to kill the enemy – it was brilliant. I buzz off this shit.

I must admit, though, riding around in the back of a Viking – all squashed in with no windows, while getting thrown all over the place and bouncing off the solid seats – made me feel really sick. I was so happy when we got attacked so I could get out the fucking thing, and all us lads felt exactly the same . . . it was gipping!

Day 149 – Friday 04 November

Yesterday at 19:00 we were given orders to prepare for an attack on Hunter Clan. The mission was to find and stop 3 enemy engineers trying to fix 3 tanks, who were being protected by 4–6 enemy combatants. Orders lasted about 90 minutes and then we did a series of rehearsals before finally getting our heads down.

We all were shaken at 04:00, started prepping our kit and weapons, and boarded the Vikings – journey time to the FRV was 45 mins. Waking up at silly o'clock and thinking about getting into the Vikings for 45 minutes made me feel threaders, as I was fully aware of how sick it would make me feel – with each bump you completely left your seat and smashed your head on the steel roof!

We attacked at 06:15 with GMPG suppressive fire, while using smoke grenades to help us fire and manoeuvre 300m towards the target, which was a hangout over uneven ground. We went in hard and fast and the attack lasted 20–30 mins, killing five men and taking one POW. We then jumped back in the Vikings and fucked off. I love stuff like this, it's mint – just what the Marines are about: in and out – shock troops, as they call us.

Once we arrived at camp, we started de-servicing our kit and stripped and cleaned all our weapons. We then had to de-service the Vikings, which took 4 hours (dog shit). All I wanted to do was get a nice shower and have some warm food. Just heading back to Lympstone now.

Day 150 – Saturday 05 November

Woke up to a double period of Bottom Field this morning, and for some unknown bizarre reason, I was so up for it.

Today was Bottom Field Pass Out (BPT) practice session.

A pass on the real test next week means you are physically conditioned and ready for the final stages of training and the 'Commando Tests', but this test is no easy feat:

- 1 × 30ft rope climb with full kit: 21lbs + weapon
- 1 × lap of the Bottom Field assault course (sub 5 mins) with full kit + weapon
- 1 × 200m fireman's carry – carrying another lad both wearing full kit + weapon
- 1 × full regain over the tank with full kit + weapon

I nailed it – so happy. We have the real test next Monday and now my confidence is sky high; it was brutal though!

Day 151 – Sunday 06 November

Chilling out and generally worrying about yet another week in HELL.

LESSON 22

Humility and the facilitation of continual learning are only possible when you embody a willingness to accept your own limitations.

Humbleness or the practice of humility are crucial values that the Royal Marines embed in all their successful recruits. From day one, you are taught, and learn quickly, to refrain from self-indulgence and to value the people around you and the wider community; to respect and value the opinion of others without basking in self-pride or pity.

Demonstrating unconditional humility means refraining from being boastful, displaying arrogance and vanity; it gives those who practise it (without hesitation) the ability to view and treat others as equals from all different social, cultural and economic backgrounds. Thus allowing Royal Marines to extract the very best results available from social interactions, and enabling them to excel in all situations.

For example, possessing the social intelligence and moral grounding to hold attentive talks with tribal leaders in Afghanistan, or interacting with members of the Royal Family and senior government officials. The Royal Marines culture of humility allows them to negotiate these vast, sometimes extremely sensitive and contrasting social encounters.

Remaining humble in relation to your capability is also a fundamental ingredient for learning and acquiring new knowledge. In the Royal Marines, inter-personal communication between all ranks is encouraged. This creates an environment of intersubjectivity where no one person is expected to know all the answers regardless of their seniority. It facilitates a culture of invitation, where all Royal Marines can share their opinions. In the Corps, it is encouraged and perfectly OK to say, 'I don't know how to do something.'

We are taught during training, and once in our units, that nobody expects you or anyone else to know all the answers. This invitation to pronounce our lack of knowledge and understanding breeds humility and thus invites opportunities to learn, develop and grow. It is not thinking less about yourself, but thinking about yourself less.

To learn more and excel in life, we need the support and help of others and that duty must be reciprocated when called upon. Thus, how we do anything, is how we do everything.

Key Points:

- Becoming humble and thus refraining from being boastful, arrogant and vain allows you to practise unconditional humility towards people from different social, cultural and economic groups.
- Humbleness and unconditional humility offer the practitioner the ability to extract the very best results possible from all social interactions, which in turn create opportunities that facilitate the possibility of success in all situations.
- Remaining humble when it comes to your capability is one of the key ingredients for learning and acquiring new knowledge.
- In an organisation, inter-personal communication between all employees cultivates a culture of humility.
- There is an opportunity to learn something from all people. Humility allows us to excel in life by drawing on the help and support of others, and to reciprocate that duty when called upon.

25

NOTHING GROWS IN YOUR COMFORT ZONE

Staying on course despite crippling setbacks

WEEK 21

Day 152 – Monday 07 November 2005

Each morning I wake up, it's like I'm constantly fighting demons. It's awful – anxiety, uncertainty and a general lack of motivation, with a mild state of depression thrown in for good measure. The time spent here is intense and you can never fully relax – there is always someone watching. Monday mornings are especially bad; the depression I feel is unbelievable and hard to snap out of when I'm staring down the barrel of another solid week of training here – and judging by the rest of the lads, I'm not alone!

This morning was spent doing defensive position lectures followed by 2 periods of GPMG training. After, we had lectures from the Assault Engineers (AEs) teaching us about bomb making and finding and disarming land mines – to some basic extent.

After lunch we had phys on Bottom Field, and whilst jumping over the 5ft wall, I twisted my body aggressively to reset myself to run up the hill and my left knee (with the ACL rupture) dislocated, clicking out briefly for the first time during training. Straight away I thought of Hunter Troop. I couldn't get up off the floor – it was like someone had hit me full whack on the knee with a baseball bat, and all the PTIs were standing over me screaming: 'Get the fuck up! Move you fucking cunt! Get going!'

I pulled myself up using the side of the wall and got back to my feet hanging out and in pure agony. My knee immediately filled up like someone was blowing up a balloon, only it was fluid, and I hobbled away trying to mask the injury and keep it secret. My immediate thought was, I'm done here, but then I made my way over to start the 200m fireman's carry – still in full kit – and carried Rob Wills. Luckily, it held out, God knows how.

Wrighty, Rob Wills, and Percival have been back-trooped to 903 Troop in Week 16 – that's 4 weeks back! I'm gutted for Rob, he's a sound lad, but I can see why Wrighty and Percival got back-trooped, they can't seem to get anything right at this stage of training and are falling behind.

Day 153 – Tuesday 08 November

Woke up to a very swollen knee this morning, it's full of fluid and looks like a small football. I was hoping, maybe somewhat naively, that it had sorted itself out with it holding out this long, but obviously not.

Feel proper down today and envious of the lads who aren't carrying an injury like mine. 894 Troop, who passed out last Friday, are on camp at the moment rehearsing for November Ceremony duties this Sunday. They're all wearing their Commando Flashes on their combats now and it makes me feel so threaders to look at them boys . . . I hope that's me in 11 weeks' time.

Just done CBRN training then had a lecture on life in a Commando Unit – good.

Bottom Field done just before dinner. I was flapping about my knee, but it held out. Hopefully the swelling will go down and it will be OK, but I must now start and do isolated strength work on it, in my own time.

P.S., By now if I was in the American military, I would have just completed the Navy Seals course!

Day 154 – Wednesday 09 November

CBRN practical test first 2 periods, which covers enemy chemical attacks and nerve agents. Then it's Bottom Field period 3. My knee feels weak as piss and so unstable – like it is made of jelly and could go again at any moment. I must make sure I never fully lock my leg out or my knee will click/slip out of the joint – it's a disgusting feeling. If it happens with one of the lads on my back during the fireman's carry, it will be completely written off.

This has really knocked my confidence and made my future here uncertain – a horrible feeling and I can't tell anyone, especially the Training Team, or they'll send me to sickbay and on to Hunter Troop.

After dinner we had a mine warfare lecture, which was quality and interesting. It covered how to disarm certain mines and what to look out for in the ground.

Day 155 – Thursday 10 November

It's a chilled day today: CBRN, swimming, and then the rest of the morning with the AEs. They are taking us through actions on finding mines, minefields, and boobytraps. I love this stuff and find it so interesting. The guy was telling us about a certain type of mine that's placed in the ground at a 90-degree angle and connected to a trip wire (that goes across a vehicle access route), which is usually around 5 metres in front or behind it.

On contact with the wire, it counts down five seconds then detonates – firing a slug of molten hot steel at 1000 mph through the side of an armoured vehicle – splintering off on impact and shredding those inside to bits. What's more, the vacuum it creates by the speed of travel literally sucks anything (people) through the hole created, which is usually the size of a tennis ball . . . JUST WOW. To think human bodies are sucked through such a small space is mind-blowing!

This is a poem we were told here a few days ago:

The Green Beret Men
by Rod Spinks

A word in the House, a stroke of a pen,
The country disbanded a body of men
With fighting finesse and fitness supreme –
The creme de la creme wore the Berets of Green.

Their training was tough, it had to be so,
How to fight with a knife, how to kill with one blow.
Salerno, Bardia, Dieppe, St Nazaire,
When impossible odds, the commandos were there.

Their raids so successful that Hitler once said,
'If captured, no prisoners – I want these men dead!'
Too late he discovered his men were not keen
To battle with those wearing Berets of Green.

NOTHING GROWS IN YOUR COMFORT ZONE

On D-Day at Sword beach they were there to the fore
As they jumped from their craft and made for the shore,
Their contempt for the Nazis was plain to be seen
For they wore not steel helmets, but Berets of Green.

When it was all over – the fighting no more
The first they disbanded, the Green Beret 'corps'
Who went back to their shire, their town and their glen,
A body of gentle, self-disciplined men.

Yet, forty years on they still meet, it is said,
To talk, toast their Queen, and remember their dead
Whose memorial stands at the foot of the 'Ben'
Where they trained for the right to be Green Beret men.

For our freedom of movement, our freedom of speech,
To those who come after, this gospel I preach –
A word in the House, a stroke of the pen, cannot
Wipe out our debt to those Green Beret men.

PER MARE PER TERRAM

Day 156 – Friday 11 November

GPMG lessons all day then it's my weapon handling test, which will enable me to live fire on exercises in the weeks to come. Can't wait!

I passed, although I'm not happy with my performance. My knee feels very weak, I don't know whether it's physical or just mental and I'm over-thinking it. Either way, it's wearing me down. We had another Bottom Field mock pass out session today in loose order (*no kit*), which went very well, and I felt

195

physically strong throughout. The real pass out is on Monday and although I'm shitting it, I feel quietly confident. It's a major hurdle and a milestone in training.

After scran we had GPMG live firing; the 'kick back' (*recoil*), power, and sound it produces is absolutely phenomenal and a right buzz – truly immense piece of kit!

Day 157 – Saturday 12 November

Chilling today and as always, worrying anxiously about the week ahead.

Day 158 – Sunday 13 November

We have been to Remembrance Day on camp this morning, then the afternoon was spent worrying myself stupid about BPT pass out in the morning.

LESSON 23

Don't let adversity tempt you into drinking the quitting tonic, it tastes sour and is highly addictive.

The moment my left knee briefly slipped out of the socket, I felt an unbelievable rush of despair and realisation. Over the course of training, I had convinced myself that this significant injury had somehow repaired itself naturally. This was incredibly naive and irrational, but it helped me cope and allowed me not to feel physically disadvantaged compared to the other lads. Telling myself that it was fine and no longer a problem helped me to attack the course with aggression and without the fear of my knee semi-dislocating.

When my knee eventually went that day on Bottom Field, it provided me with the perfect opportunity to get out of that period of Physical Training. More generally, I could have gone into Hunter Company to get it repaired (reconstructed) and thus taken the rest, recovery and reprieve from training that course of action would have afforded.

But what would have been the benefit of taking either of those two options? Both opportunities to step out of training were short-term, excuse-laden responses to adversity, which would have granted me immediate comfort and respite, but would have halted my progression, momentum and long-term aspiration to achieve my end goal. I viewed both options then and I do now as mental weakness.

Taking the easy way out, or withdrawing from a journey towards goal acquisition, brings short-term mental comfort and safeguards oneself from mental and physical (in my case) pain or discomfort. But – and this is crucial – the progression stops. At the absolute best, I would have got out of that period of physical training without any impact on my success on the course, but for me personally, it is the start of a defeatist mentality that can compound into habit – making it easier to quit on other instances of adversity, and to larger extents.

I wanted to remain resilient. I didn't want to use the oppor-tunity to get out of an adverse moment: staying in that period of PT allowed me to uphold my mental strength and resilience – to not perceive my injury as a disadvantage. I did not acknowledge it and walked tentatively towards the start line for the 200m fireman's carry.

What cognitive processes enable the bearer to continue despite setbacks?

It comes down to motivation again (Chapter 7). Intrinsically I couldn't quit on the session, I would not have felt happy with myself knowing that I had taken the 'soft option' when I could still (barely) continue. Extrinsically, I did not want to attract attention and potentially get labelled as someone that wrapped (quit or gave in easily).

What is more, I did not want the PTIs to examine my knee – that could have been catastrophic for my progression with 900 Troop and my career in the Royal Marines. Thus, I quickly came to the realisation that continuing forward was my only option.

When things get tough, the road ahead becomes murky and adversity clouds your reasoning; it becomes so easy to quit, to drop out or go home, in my example. But know this, nothing grows in a 'Comfort Zone'; development and growth cease the second you put on the brakes.

Key Points:

- Quitting is a habit – a response to adversity that provides those who take the option an avenue back to the place they were trying so desperately to get out of.
- Quitting on the small things leads to a defeatist mindset, which paves the way for future excuses and greater extents of personal defeat.
- When faced with dense, crippling adversity, the option to quit becomes a very tempting distraction. Do not do it! Know that adversity is only temporary, and nothing ever grows in a 'Comfort Zone'.

26

ACKNOWLEDGING MISTAKES

The Royal Marines culture of integrity

WEEK 22

Day 159 – Monday 14 November 2005

During training, there is always something to flap about: gym pass out in Week 9, Baptise Run in Week 15, and now Bottom Field pass out. Training has you in a constant state of future uncertainty that creates anxiety amongst us all. The trick is how to manage it, which is difficult with limited sleep.

I've just returned back to the grots having passed my BPT, so happy – I'm over the moon and now moving on to pastures new (*the last 10 weeks of training*). WOW . . . thanks PTI B – legend!

This is such a huge weight off my shoulders, my knee held up and I felt strong. It's unbelievable, when I first got here and dared to look ahead to this week, I would have said this test was physically impossible wearing full kit. It was unimaginable that I could do that and here I am having just completed it – crazy!

Seven of the lads failed, and some are really close mates, which is gutting. Stirzaker being one of them – such a top bloke, but doesn't have the upper body strength to complete the regain . . . I will really miss him. Mendi, another good lad who always flashes and brings morale to the troop, broke his leg jumping off the zigzag wall; the sound of his leg snapping and his scream was horrific – that's his journey here over now for sure.

Day 160 – Tuesday 15 November

Woke up so relieved I passed Bottom Field, given how badly I twisted my knee last week. I can't express how happy I am. Stirzaker and Binksy have got today and tomorrow to retake the BPT and crack the regain or they will get back-trooped.

They both failed again today . . . gutted for them! Just back from having lectures on 'Fighting In Built Up Areas' (*FIBUA*), POWs, and breaking into buildings (*method of entry*) – loved it.

Ex 'Violent Entry' is getting closer. Once again I'm dreading it. I hate being in the field and this Ex is supposed to be nails!

Day 161 – Wednesday 16 November

Binksy and Stirzaker failed again this morning, so that's them gone from the troop. At the start of training, all the fucking idiots and weak bastards leave, and nobody gives a toss, but now if someone goes, they are usually top lads and their absence leaves a void in the troop.

Sgt P – our Dutch Troop Sergeant on exchange from the Netherland Marines – has warned us it's going to be minus 7 degrees on this upcoming exercise and the chances of getting hypothermia or frostbite are extremely high. Buzzing, brilliant!

Really missing my family, can't wait to go home.

Day 162 – Thursday 17 November

Been going through boobytraps and methods of entry into various buildings on camp today, which was very interesting. Some of the SBS lads were on the ranges – absolutely mint them boys! Going on ex 'Violent Entry' after lunch and it's freezing.

We got dropped off on Salisbury Plain by one of the camp buses, then yomped 3 miles to a derelict house, where we were split into 4-man teams and then ordered to start digging trenches. Digging a 4–5ft deep and 2–3ft wide trench with an entrenching tool (_a small foldaway military shovel_) when the ground is 80% small rocks and white stones – with no sleep – is very, very emotional, let me tell you! Plus, it was absolutely freezing cold. That cold, I had to keep stopping and covering my ears with my gloves.

42 Commando were doing Tez-Ex nearby in prep for operations – probs Afghanistan, so they took priority on the training ground. This meant we had to stop digging and yomp back to our harbour location and get our heads down for the night.

Day 163 – Friday 18 November

We all woke up this morning with FROST on our hair and round the tops of our sleeping bags. One of the lads even had frost on his eyelashes! After morning routine, we yomped back to our dig site. 42 Commando are all over – they are doing a mock, large-scale training operation that prepares the Royal Marines for live operations. Mint to see how it all comes together.

Anyway, we started digging again at 12:00 – it's nails and

my right hand is in bits from the shovel handle – each time I dig down and hit rocks or them white stones, it sends a dull thud straight into the base of my hand – it's bruised to hell. All the lads are flashing (*shouting/arguing*) with each other. It's absolutely GOPPING.

We received orders at 17:00 to attack a farm, which is occupied by terrorists: Hunter Troop lads. We are just about to fly to a 'Stop Short' location near the farm via CH-47s (*Chinook Helicopters*). AMAZING! What a buzz this is going to be – really starting to feel like a proper Royal Marine Commando now.

Just before we crossed 'The Line of Departure', I had an ND (*Negligent Discharge*). Basically, I used my weapon to compress and pin down the top section of a barbed-wire fence, so I could jump over it. The wire must have pushed my safety catch in/off and upon getting over it, I pulled on the trigger and released a blank round, which immediately compromised our position. The enemy opened up on us straight away, which completely jeopardised our mission – fucking everything up and all the Training Team's planning.

What a prick I am! I've had my weapon taken off me (*when an ND occurs, the weapon gets sent away for inspection to ascertain whether it was a weapon fault or the firer's fault*) and been given the GPMG with all the bastard link (*belt-fed ammunition*). We are yomping back to the dig site shortly to continue digging and this thing is going to break me – it weighs a ton!

Day 164 – Saturday 19 November

Been digging the trenches out all night – no sleep – I feel absolutely shocking. It's been minus 7 degrees during the night, and I was gen falling asleep stood up at certain points, but would then wake up violently gibbering my tits off . . . it's brutal this! In fact, brutal doesn't even explain how bad it is, nothing does. Just the most emotional night ever – absolute hangout.

Once the trenches were almost dug out around midday – still zero sleep, the Training Team escalated the chemical state to 'medium' and we had to put on our NBC suits and respirators. I felt physically sick, I was that tired.

We've just been gassed with CS! Then ordered to fill in the trenches we have been digging out for 3 whole days. I haven't been to sleep for 35 hrs now and we've been told to prepare our kit for a long yomp out . . . unbelievable, I'm BROKEN. I'm shitting myself about this yomp, the GPMG weighs a ton and that coupled with no sleep and an 80–90lbs bergen makes for a truly horrific experience!

We yomped 8 miles, my bergen must have weighed about 100–120lbs with all the link top-flapped and I had to manhandle the GPMG – moving it from shoulder to shoulder every 30 seconds – it was horrendous. I've never been in as much pain in my entire life. I don't mind saying this, but I was crying during the yomp on a few occasions, I didn't think I could make it to the RV and my lower back and shoulders were rubbed raw from the bergen and gun straps.

Day 165 – Sunday 20 November

Last night we harboured up in a linear harbour and then set off this morning on ANOTHER yomp. I was straight in the 'Hurt Locker' again – this is the hardest ex I have ever done.

We got contacted after 4 miles: the enemy were positioned in a wood block, we returned fire and eventually took control of the wood block and set up another harbour position. Then about 19:00 we got 'bumped' (*compromised/discovered and/or attacked by the enemy*) and had to extract 2k to another harbour position. It's leaping this, absolutely leaping!

Throughout training, everyone talks about how much they look forward to the FIBUA Ex – Fighting In (*mock*) Built Up Areas. Well so far, all the Training Team has done is make us dig for near enough 3 days solid, yomped us all over Salisbury Plain, and kept us constantly on our toes. My feet are covered in blisters and my shoulders and lower back are rubbed raw in places. To top it all off, it's now minus 9 degrees. I am so threaders at the moment.

LESSON 24

If you don't own it and take responsibility for your mistake, you cannot analyse where you went wrong, or crucially learn from it and then correct it. Integrity: aligning your actions with your beliefs.

The moment I heard my rifle go off, ejecting a blank cartridge, my stomach turned upside down. I was shocked, embarrassed, and experiencing a slow-motion state of disbelief. Initially, I did not want anyone to know it was me, but that was irrational, wishful thinking.

From day one of training and throughout our careers, the Royal Marines instil a culture of integrity – to conduct oneself with unwavering moral principles both at work and in society.

Against my basic instincts, I admitted it was me. I put my hand up knowing that I would receive a ferocious backlash from the Training Team. My actions totally ruined the 'training' mission – and all the planning and coordination that had taken place in days prior between my Training Team and the Hunter Clan (*enemy*).

Not to own up would have meant an escalation: we would have been punished physically as a troop, then asked to collectively de-bomb (*unload*) the rounds from our magazines and lay them out for the Training Team to inspect. This process would not only have convicted me of the discharge, but it would have caused my troop to experience an unnecessary thrashing because of my lack of integrity.

Human beings make mistakes, human error is real, unavoidable, and happens on small and large scales. If the above had been a live operation, my actions would have potentially got a lot of my troop members killed or seriously injured. Therefore, coming forward and owning your mistake is a fundamental part of the learning process – of acknowledgement – that often goes against our human instinct. However embarrassing these moments may be, know you are not the first and certainly won't be the last.

Key Points:

- Owning up to mistakes often goes against your initial instinct. Embarrassment, and repercussion fuel these emotions, but it is absolutely essential to own up.
- Owning up prevents escalations. It nips the problem in the bud and begins the process towards resolving the issue.
- We all make mistakes! The process of coming forward and owning your blunder is a critical part of acknowledgement and learning.

27

THE OVERWHELMING POWER OF PRECISION TIMING

Fighting in urban areas

WEEK 23

Day 166 – Monday 21 November 2005

Just woke up, it is that cold (around minus 9 to 10), I can barely write this. My feet feel completely numb. Apart from the few warm hours in my sleeping bag during the night, I have been frozen to my bones since Thursday evening – 4 days ago. One of the lads, who's from South Africa, even woke up this morning and his hair was frozen solid with frost. Ha ha ha. Mental!

Just yomped 1½ miles to a mock village. It's absolutely unreal here; there's a post office, church, Burger King, and a pub – class and slightly bizarre due to this place being totally uninhabited. We started assaulting houses and utilising various methods of gaining entry – essentially breaking into buildings to kill the enemy and rescue hostages. This is without a doubt the highlight of my training so far . . . it has only taken 23 weeks . . . but this is now absolutely worth it.

Later in the afternoon we were given intelligence that 8 insurgents were occupying Imber village – a small uninhabited 'ghost village' around 6 miles away. So, come night-time, my section is going out to CTR (*Close Target Recce*) the enemy location and gather INT on their patterns of life and weapon capabilities etc. Class stuff this!

Day 167 – Tuesday 22 November

During the early hours, we drove to the village location covertly in a blacked-out Transit van – lights off, wearing NVGs, and at times turning off the engine (*whilst driving*) to keep the noise down on our approach. The two lads in the front, the driver and passenger, wore civilian clothing and were armed with 9mm pistols, whilst another 4 of us hid in the back, fully geared up and tooled up ready to jump out . . . proper SF shit!

We got within 100m of the enemy position and started to compile a pattern of life – how they were living, their sleeping arrangements and patterns (the time they went to bed and woke up), and if they had people on watch during the night or if they all went to sleep. We also noted their weapon capabilities – long or short range and what calibre – and the group's morale, as well as assessing viable methods of entry and extraction. This was proper amazing stuff to be doing and made me feel like a real Royal Marines Commando.

On our return to camp this morning, we've been rehearsing constantly for various troop attacks based on the INT we gathered earlier. We then received orders for an attack on Imber Village that will take place in the early hours of tomorrow morning . . . it's going to be epic!

Day 168 – Wednesday 23 November

The attack was brilliant, we cleared the village in 40 mins, and I went through 2,000 rounds of link ammo. The Training

Team were using mortar 'simunition', which was unreal and so loud. We had to use uber high-level and complex tactics to defeat the enemy.

After taking the village, we did a 12-mile extraction yomp carrying full kit – my shoulders and mainly feet were in pure agony! It took us 4½ hours of unbelievable pain to reach our extraction point, which was at some military camp.

Getting on the coach was a brilliant feeling. The exercise has been mentally and physically the hardest thing we have all ever done, and the weather was horrific – freezing temperatures along with zero sleep and gash rations, which makes daily life horrible and such a mental hangout.

Day 169 – Thursday 24 November

Cleaned weapons and de-serviced our kit this morning and then we are going home on leave for the weekend. I can't wait – very homesick!

Day 172 – Sunday 27 November

I've spent Friday and Saturday at home and can't express how depressed I'm feeling whilst travelling back down to Lympstone on the train. Never felt as bad in my life as I do today, I just don't want to go back!

This course and this journey are so hard for me. Yet, although every day is such a huge test of character now, and even at the beginning, I would rather die on this course than quit or make up some bullshit excuse as to why I can't continue. This is a challenge I must finish off in order to reach my goals in life.

LESSON 25

Being strategic in approach to maximise opportunity requires an understanding that, at times, we must harness restraint.

Conducting a 'triumphant' mission relies heavily on the successful manipulation of timing and its precision. Accuracy or misjudgement here is often the difference between life and death in the Royal Marines. This process begins with a comprehensive gathering of all the 'available' intelligence and information, going through a systematic process of analysis, and then executing a course of action (the timings) underpinned by meticulous planning.

Once the preparation phase is complete and the right time to carry out the mission has been established, the only thing left to do is execute the plan. Get this right and the outcome is often remarkable, overwhelming and unstoppable.

Today, the Fighting In Built Up Areas (FIBUA) model for achieving success in urban areas is now outdated, and has since been replaced with more contemporary CQB (Close Quarter Battle) tactics. However, the process of execution and the principle of effect still epitomises, and notably requires, the precision, harmony, and overwhelming power of timing.

Entering buildings to clear them of enemies takes a precise coordinated effort to achieve a mission or goal. When we apply this systematic approach to life and business, it can have significantly positive outcomes.

There are moments in life and business when opportunity presents itself – an outcome of a complex alignment of variables – although it could be argued that acknowledging such an opportunity relies heavily on individual perception. When opportunities do present, however, it is important to seize them without hesitation and systematically begin to 'prepare'.

Exercising restraint in light of new information and/or new preparation requirements

Equally important is the ability to exercise restraint: to manage time effectively by applying self-control and not becoming 'emotionally invested'. Rushing in, unprepared, will not potentially get you killed, like entering buildings prematurely in the military could do; but it will often have negative consequences, which could have been avoided with better planning and whilst controlling impulsivity.

Resisting the urge of impulsivity and thus taking a step back to evaluate the 'ever-changing' available information and then making 'informed' decisions that influence effective actions, will maximise your chance of seizing the outcome you desire. For example, it is seeing an unbelievable job opportunity to which your skillset is aligned and resisting the urge to submit instantly a CV that is not updated and therefore applicable; or rushing to secure an investment without conducting thorough investor/market due diligence.

In short, don't get emotionally invested: the success of job applications, securing deals and investments, relies heavily on the quality of information, its analysis and the manipulation of timing. It can be the difference between success or failure.

Key Points:

- Assessing all the available information and then acting with good timing will produce unbelievable results.
- When opportunities present themselves, seize them with

both hands, but do not rush in unprepared. Take a moment, assess the landscape, and form an effective plan of action.

- 'Informed' decisions underpinned by the collection and evaluation of information, produce effective actions that maximise your chances of success.

28

THE ROYAL MARINES
BUDDY-BUDDY SYSTEM

<u>T</u>ogether <u>E</u>veryone <u>A</u>chieves <u>M</u>ore

WEEK 24

<u>Day 173 – Monday 28 November 2005</u>

Light Machine Gun (*LMG*) 'Minimi' training all morning, which more or less does the same job as the GMPG only it's smaller, more manoeuvrable, but with less power – 5.56mm belt fed ammunition as opposed to 7.62mm. Then a 4-mile run – Fartlek, which was a piece of piss for me. Surprising after the weekend I've had back home . . . constantly on the piss!

Had to go bastard sickbay this afternoon – my toes are still really numb from the exercise last week; they think I may have the early signs of frostbite!

Just been given a piece of paper with our Kings Squad arms (*drill*) routine on it – what a feeling and major boost coming back off leave . . . it's game time again now.

<u>Day 174 – Tuesday 29 November</u>

I don't know what is up with me. I feel like I have zero motivation lately and can't be arsed, like I don't want to be here anymore, and I literally have only 8 weeks left to push. It's a

212

mixture of mental fatigue and the fact that the Commando Tests are fast approaching and must be adding stress, pressure and anxiety. I am not with it at all . . . Been doing LMG Minimi lessons all morning and I kept screwing up.

Just before lunch we were gathered up and hurried, borderline ragged, up to the 'top' field where two Sea King Helicopters were waiting. We were quickly rushed on board and they took off towards Woodbury Common. We flew around the common at low level at times – it was absolutely class. The Training Team were teaching us how to go into 'Arctic Huddles' and 'All-round Defensive' positions upon disembarkation, which was brilliant. I love all this shit. The classroom lectures bore me stiff.

The Training Team are on our backs constantly and seem like they want us to fuck up, so they can fuck us around again. Wish they would just leave us alone.

Day 175 – Wednesday 30 November

For God's sake, I have woken up feeling like utter shit AGAIN – what is up with me? We had bastard drill all morning rehearsing for Kings Squad. Then we had our introduction to the 30ft wall, which is the final obstacle on the 'Tarzan Assault Course' – the 3rd Commando Test. This entails pulling yourself up a 30ft near-vertical wall (ambulance at the bottom) with a rope, after a 1300–1600m absolutely honking assault course – all in under 13 mins whilst wearing 21lbs + weapon.

It feels so good to be at this phase of training now and starting to prep for the Commando Tests, but the pressure is unreal. Everyone's talking about Kings Squad and Commando Units, I hope and pray I'll be there getting my Green Beret on February 10th!

My body, especially my legs and knees, are constantly sore

and although they must be stronger than ever, they feel weak as piss. I hope my body can hold out 8 more weeks, because mentally I am unstoppable now. I will keep going until I die, that's how committed I am to completing this course.

Day 176 – Thursday 01 December

This morning was spent in current affairs lectures, focusing on Ireland, Iraq, Yugoslavia and Afghanistan. During the war between the Mujahideen (*Afghans fighting against the communist government*) and the Russians, the Americans were apparently funding/supplying the Mujahideen with weapons and communication equipment. The Mujahideen senior commanders were also trained by the CIA, all in a bid to defeat the Russians. One of the men trained by the CIA turned out to be Osama Bin Laden. How unbelievable and ironic is that! He's now the most wanted man in the world and, if you believe the Americans, masterminded 9/11.

It's the Endurance Course (*First Commando Test*) acquaint today – I'm that nervous my legs feel like jelly! The course is 2 miles long over Woodbury Common and then a 4-mile run, best effort, back to camp. We are taking the bus up today, but on the next run-through and actual Test, we must speed march up 4 miles and then start the course.

The first 2 miles consists of horrible hill-type gravel and undulating terrain, small winding tunnels, a deep, waist-high pool of water (*Peter's Pool*), which we've encountered before for wet and dry, and the underwater tunnel known as the Sheep Dip, made famous on the advert '99.9% Need Not Apply'.

Then there are the Smartie tubes, which are long, extremely tight and claustrophobic tunnels, half submerged in water, so you must drag yourself through sideways keeping your head and weapon barrel above the water line, biting hold of the weapon sling clasp to protect the integrity of your weapon system (*this ensures you have no stoppages during the shoot at the end of the test*).

It is vile, requiring discipline and focus when you're breathing air through every cavity of your body, while also having to navigate through deep-water/mud pits that go waist/chest deep, known as 'Crocodile Pits' (*You jump into one, climb/ struggle/scramble to get out and then within a matter of steps, jump into the next and repeat the process – wearing full kit, breathless and under time pressure. This is just awful.*) . . . along with other general horribleness.

We did two laps of the Endurance and then ran the 4 miles back to camp. I completed the 2nd lap and the run back in 67 minutes – without kit and weapon. On the actual test, it must be done in full kit: 21lbs + weapon – THEN, on the return to camp you must get 6 out of 10 shots on target at 25-metres – all in under 72 minutes to pass the test . . . crazy shit!

That's why heavy emphasis is placed on you to look after your weapon and keep it above water and free of mud and shit. If you fail to look after your weapon during the Endurance, which is easily done when you're fucked, you can get back after 6–7 horrendous miles and have weapon problems (*stoppages*), causing you to run out of time and fail the test.

I'm having nightmares about this test, it's shocking!

Day 177 – Friday 02 December

Recovering from Endurance – I am aching like hell and feel 60 years old! We had swimming this morning and played Water Polo and then did 'confidence drills' from the diving board. We had to FALL BACK like a pencil and aim to hit the water head first, but that's not always the case . . . ha ha ha.

After swimming I had my weapon handling test on the LMG Minimi. Passed first time and was awarded: Skilled Pass – buzzing!

We got thinned out early for the day. Looking forward to chilling out, but at the same time I am bricking it at the thought of the 12-mile load carry on Monday. We've all been dreading this for the past 2 months, as it's supposed to be absolutely horrific and a fast pace, mainly uphill across Woodbury Common.

Day 178 – Saturday 03 December

Chilling out today, knowing that the 12-miler is looming!

Day 179 – Sunday 04 December

OH MY GOD . . . 4 of us went out last night (last min) to Bristol, and we did not get back onto camp until 09:20. Hanging out and we have a 12-mile load carry in the morning. What a stupid idiot I am!

The 12-mile load carry is done over a proper hard and gruelling route, ¾ of which is uphill carrying 69lbs + weapon, and before I've even started, I've had no sleep, I am hungover, and my feet – mainly toes – are still numb and sore from our last exercise on Salisbury Plain! I cannot believe what I've done . . .

LESSON 26

Together Everyone Achieves More. Learning the value of teamwork.

No other week in training highlights the importance of the Royal Marines 'Buddy-Buddy System' more than pushing each other in – and pulling each other out of – the Sheep Dip (to achieve an 'individual' goal) on the Endurance Course. Although often perceived as an individual test, this specific section of the course requires the help of others in order for its successful completion in the time allowed.

As previously mentioned, the Sheep Dip was brought to public attention during the 2001 Royal Marines advert, which depicted a young recruit running frantically across the Endurance Course: the first Commando Test. During the advert, the young lad can be seen getting pushed down and into a submerged water tunnel, which strikes apprehension in most, if not all, recruits during the initial stages of training. Although in real life the actual tunnel is a fraction of the size, it is still a daunting experience, which requires teamwork to navigate the obstacle successfully when fatigued, gasping for air, and laden with fighting order (webbing + weapon).

Firstly, the notion of the Buddy-Buddy System at the *micro-level* is one that achieves time efficiency and, you could argue, a factor of safety management. For example, the collaborative system allows Royal Marines to maximise commitments, schedules and opportunities, whether that's helping someone put on and fasten up technical kit – like checking-off abseiling and climbing equipment – or the simple act of cooking someone's food, so they can strip and clean their personal weapon.

Secondly, at the *meso-level*, this system emphasises profoundly that no goal or achievement is ever realised without the help of others, and pulling a friend out of the Sheep Dip to achieve 'their' goal demonstrates and highlights the need for this collaboration beautifully.

At a basic level
The buddy-buddy system teaches recruits the value and understanding of teamwork and how working together directly and efficiently manages the use of time effectively.

At an advanced level
When Royal Marines leave CTC and go on operations, their awareness of this system makes them so attentive to the requirements of others and the troop, they become a devastating force to reckon with. It develops and embeds the situational awareness required to remain attentive in incredibly demanding circumstances, which allows the collective to function like a finely tuned machine.

For instance, the act of throwing a fresh magazine of ammunition to a fellow teammate during a fierce firefight, or simply giving them refreshments to keep them going. The buddy-buddy system dispels selfishness – creating seamless cohesion that produces unbelievable feats of 'efficient' human capability.

Key Points:

- No achievement in life can ever be realised without drawing on and acknowledging the help of external influence.
- The Royal Marines buddy-buddy system highlights the need to call on others to achieve things more efficiently in terms of time, whilst emphasising the power of teamwork.
- Leveraging the help of others, therefore, and establishing strategic networks, is the key to success and thus achieving great things in life. It supports decision-making and encourages focus.

29

DETERMINATION

Enduring discomfort and finding your
'happy place'

WEEK 25

Day 180 – Monday 05 December 2005

HELL FIRE, this morning is a killer. As soon as my eyes opened, I would have accepted death 100% over taking this day on. Knowing I have the 12-miler this afternoon makes me feel like killing myself. I have had no sleep over the weekend (*all self-inflicted*) and within a matter of hours, I must crack a 12-miler with 69lbs + weapon in under 4 hours – ¾ of which is uphill . . . pass or fail!

I would have preferred getting up and getting straight on with it, but instead we've had to endure a few lectures, then got fitted for our Peak Caps (*worn with our blues uniform*), ready for Kings Squad. That felt brilliant and temporarily made me (a) forget about the 12-miler and (b) injected a bit of motivation into me to finish training. I do want this, and this test is what I must overcome to reach my Ultimate Goal. It can be so easy to start feeling sorry for yourself down here and it's like a flu that cripples everyone if you're not careful.

We started the 12-miler at 13:30. The pace was relentless. The Training Team thrashed us through the first 6–7 miles and to be honest, I felt fairly comfortable cardio-wise and in the zone mentally – even though my feet were starting to burn and blister, and the constant friction from my bergen had started to rub the skin off my lower back . . . one of those moments when you must bite down hard and focus the mind.

After the 7-mile point, however, it got emotionally dark and that happened really quick! We could see the top point of the hill that we needed to reach and mentally it became nails – an awful period of time spent inside my own head, convincing my body that all was OK, and reminding my mind that it remained in control.

A fine balance that is extremely difficult to master and one that takes unimaginable skill when thrust upon you. At Lympstone, providing you stay the course and endure, you begin to learn your own mind – its utmost capabilities and the absolute limitations of its boundaries. The mental aptitude you have when you arrive here is constantly pushed, warped, broken, and then rebuilt throughout training.

Come this stage, a recruit is becoming an unstoppable force – quickly developing a state of mind that's capable of pushing them beyond their physical boundaries, allowing the recruit to keep going despite little quality sleep, a lack of food, being mildly or significantly injured, and throughout any weather conditions. The mental transformation of a recruit from Week 1 to Week 20–25, is astonishing to say the very least.

We all finished at 18:00. The amount of times I had to go beyond the pain barrier to receive a small period of physical and mental numbness was unreal. Just awful! Once we reached the final checkpoint, walking to the bus was even more of a mission; it felt like I was walking on broken glass.

Sat on my bed now and my feet are completely fucked!

DETERMINATION

Day 181 – Tuesday 06 December

I'm hammered this morning . . . my underpants were stuck to my lower back when I woke up, from where my bergen had rubbed the skin off, and I can't get my bastard boots on, my feet are that swollen and sore! On the bright side, we have amphibious training today at the SBS base in Poole. Been looking forward to this since I started training, and often wondered if I would make it this far; and now this day has come, it feels very weird but amazing.

The Training Team have been taking us through beach attacks in the Ribs and Raiders (_various raiding craft designed for stealth and infiltration_), which was absolutely awesome, despite being wet and bastard cold. THEN – CAPSIZE DRILLS! Oh My God . . . we had to jump off the side of the harbour (_around 10m_) into the water in 'only' our T-shirts and combat bottoms, bearing in mind it's 6th December and the water temp was 1 degree.

This very quickly became the joint winner for all-time worst experience of my life. The water was that cold, none of us could breathe or even attempt to catch a breath – it was so debilitating. I couldn't move at all and hung onto the capsized rib, literally shutting down and clinging onto life. After having a quiet word with ourselves, we somehow managed to flip the rib over successfully and then had to swim ashore, where the fight was on to claim 1 of 3 hot showers!

Funny, as I review Week 25 in a café in Stamford, during the second edit of this book in 2019, the Titanic _soundtrack is playing . . . oh, the irony._

We are conducting a fully amphibious night attack tonight on Portland Port, which is about 100 miles away against an enemy of Army personnel. CAN'T WAIT . . . NOT – it's freezing!

Day 182 – Wednesday 07 December

It's 06:05 and we have arrived back on camp after the attack. We were due to be finished no later than 02:00, but details of the mission kept changing – funny old thing! We were all crammed into a landing craft from 16:30 until 22:30 and it was emotional – no space and on top of each other and the sea state was horrific – everyone felt sick. I couldn't wait to get off the thing, because my morale was in my boots. However, then came the highlight of training, because 6 miles short of the target, 4 Rigid Raiders came alongside us, and we split into 4 'assault teams', cross-decked onto our predesignated Raider, and began our approach in at speed. I was looking at Tom Curry on our Raider and we were both saying, 'This is mint!' And it was. It 100% made up for all the shit we had gone through in previous weeks.

Anyway, regarding today – fuelled on 1 hour's sleep, we have sea survival lectures and I feel like death warmed up. Again, lads are falling asleep standing up and this is not an exaggeration. After this, we are going to the Royal Marines museum for the 2nd time. What's the point?

Day 183 – Thursday 08 December

We have been on the ranges all day live firing with the LMG Minimis – the power and sound these things generate is enormous. But once you have fired one weapon, you've fired them all. Still a massive buzz though, regardless.

The Training Team turned up this morning and started by saying: 'Who the fuck do you lot think you are, you're walking round here like you own the place – you cunts are not fucking there yet – get on the bus and don't say a word, dick-heads.' We had done nothing wrong at all and at 19:30 it made me feel like shit and just want to go home. 30 minutes later, all was OK, and they were completely sound – mind games at their finest!

Day 184 – Friday 09 December

Just completed my Annual Weapons Assessment (AWA) on the LMG. We had to live fire up to 400m. I passed easy, so happy with that. After the shoot, a weapon barrel was left loafing (*Marines slang for something left lying around or behind*), so we got a right thrashing for 20 minutes – stress positions, sprints, Supermans, and fireman's carries uphill. It certainly brought back horrific memories of the early weeks of training.

However, we did get a chuck up from Cpl M for our amphibious attack, which is awesome coming from him. The first ever 'good effort lads' in 25 weeks. I think he needs checking in – I am referring to his mental health!

My RPs (*Restricted Privileges*) start tonight, so my weekend is FUCKED.

Day 185 – Saturday 10 December

My weekend RP routine:

  06:15: full kit inspection
  10:00: full kit muster
  13:30–15:30: fatigues – camp work
  19:00: full kit inspection wearing drill rig
  22:00: full kit muster wearing CS95 (*combats*)

Day 186 – Sunday 11 December

Same old, same old! However, all being well, we get our 'Cap Comforters' tomorrow, which marks the start of the Commando phase of training. To think I will be wearing a Cap Comforter is absolutely mind-blowing . . . how have I got here?

When I joined training, seeing the older recruits wearing them had me mesmerised – I looked at them like superheroes, never thinking that after 25 weeks I would be on the verge of being that lad. WOW. I never knew if I had what it took to get here and tomorrow by 09:30, I will be able to answer that question.

LESSON 27

Identifying past (happy) memories, or envisioning end goal acquisition, and then preparing to lower the anchor to assure emotional stability, in order to prevent drifting into vulnerable, rocky and detrimental mental states.

The 12-miler . . . By this stage of training, I had been through the pain barrier many times and it never got easier. I developed mental coping strategies to get through and overcome them – an acquired ability that is only possible to achieve by enduring hardship. Therefore, giving yourself the benefit of the doubt to learn and adapt to such uncomfortable experiences requires unbelievable mental focus and determination. In turn, this creates a deeper understanding of the inner and higher-most (performance) capabilities of the mind.

Successful goal acquisition cannot be realised without experiencing and withstanding the onslaught of emotional and physical pain, often for sustained periods of time. For example, the stress and anxiety created by a work or study deadline, or (see Chapter 3) compartmentalising pain during a physically demanding event, assessment, or challenge.

The value of venturing through and beyond the pain barrier
Challenges that elicit such discomfort act as a natural filter that deters and discourages the majority from (a) starting or (b) continuing with an endeavour towards success. Therefore, harnessing the 'fortitude' to pursue and reach an elusive career goal will place you in a position of social and employment value. It propels and lifts you above the average, in a position of envy, respect, and credibility – earned qualities that are incredibly desirable and worthwhile commodities, if and when the arm-wrestle is won with adversity.

Other personal examples of winning the arm-wrestle: finding cognitive anchorage
In my own experiences before, during and after training, finding a mental anchor of focus was a fundamental coping mechanism that allowed me to withstand physical pain and discomfort, and ultimately not quit. There were times when my shoulders and arms would go numb from the straps of a 80–100lbs bergen, resulting in a loss of sensation, or pins and needles in my hands during long and gruelling yomps – like the 25-mile Killer Yomp that all recruits do across Dartmoor during Final Ex.

It would mean continuing on whilst crippled with blisters, or dealing with significant abrasions on the base of my back and hips from heavy bergens and webbing, or reluctantly conducting Wet and Dry routine in the middle of a harsh, morale-sapping winter.

To get through these tough times, I harnessed the power of happy memories, visualising places of solace that I enjoyed going to the most, like a warm, comfortable cabin in the Peak District, as well as loved ones; or I would think about the end goal – life as a fully trained Royal Marine Commando, and realising my ambition of being on live operations in Iraq or Afghanistan.

The alternative motivating factor for me, which was even more enduring, was the fear of failure, of validating the negative opinions I had received prior to joining. I would recount people saying I could not do it and that I would be back within a month.

With the benefit of time, experience, and practice, I could recall all those thoughts and emotions at will. I kept them in mind during gruelling training exercises to combat pain and anguish. They kept me mentally focused and thus steady and strong – providing the fuel to get over every significant assessment, during my time at CTC.

Key Points:

- It goes without saying that managing emotional discomfort and sometimes enduring physical pain forms an intricate part of a journey towards acquiring a significant goal.
- Confronting adversity, coming to terms with it and finding the courage, tenacity and determination to meet it head on, are vital mental processes that prepare the mind for what lies ahead, ultimately safeguarding the integrity of the end goal acquisition.
- With experience, you can harness the power of mental

anchors of focus – internal 'happy places' (memories or imaginations) that distract the mind from the 'temporary' discomfort you are experiencing.

- Remember why you are doing something when times get hard; visualise the progression and change that will follow brief adversity, because if you lose it upstairs, you will lose it in your heart, then quitting becomes easy.

30

RESISTING TEMPTATION

*Imposing personal 'sacrifice' to facilitate
great achievements*

WEEK 26

Day 187 – Monday 12 December 2005

The start of the Commando Course (*phase*) of training! We are kicking the week off with our 6-mile speed march – carrying full kit: 21lbs + weapon. It must be completed in under 60 minutes in order to gain our cap comforter. I'm ready to go and won't return without it.

Our kit was individually weighed, then we set off. The first 3 miles were honking – my legs were like two lumps of concrete, filled with lactic acid – and once we started to ascend towards Woodbury Common, it got dark (*mentally*) and emotional very quickly and to distract myself, I retreated into my 'happy place'. There always seems to be a point mentally – shortly before going through the first pain barrier – where I ask, 'What am I doing this to myself for?' However, once I got through the first 3 miles, the last 3 back in were easy.

On our return to camp, we had a talk from the Camp Commander and Company Major about the history surrounding the Cap Comforter. Many years ago, those in the army who wanted to become Commandos had to travel by train to a station in Scotland called Spean Bridge. Once the train stopped, they had 60 minutes to reach Achnacarry House.

This was no easy feat . . . prospective Commandos had to cover 7 miles wearing kit weighing 36 pounds (16kg) + weapon, and in drill boots, of all things! Those who completed this mind-blowing test of endurance were then turned into Commandos – using training methods that would be completely unethical today. Failure, literally by even 1 second over the 60-minute limit and individuals were Returned To Unit (RTU).

Those few who successfully made it under the time allowed were handed a Cap Comforter (*a military green, woolly hat-type headdress*) and began training to become a Commando.

While I was writing this during my time at Lympstone, I didn't know that I would go on to do the Achnacarry Speed March for the annual anniversary, around two years after completing training (albeit in 'standard' boots: Adidas GSG9 to be exact). I wholeheartedly support the fact that this test of both mental and physical endurance was horrific – one of the hardest physical tests I have ever undertaken – in the same realm of the modern day Commando Tests, and to think those men ran it in drill boots is absolutely astonishing to me.

If you have ever had the displeasure of marching in drill boots, even getting them on, then trust me, you know how truly unbelievable this feat was. Drill boots have an iron heel-plate and toe-plate, and an iron-studded leather sole . . . those men were a different breed of mankind back then!

I can't express how proud and in utter disbelief I am, now that I can wear the Cap Comforter around camp. I've taken things week by week and almost before I know it, we have started the Commando Phase – the final part of training that every recruit dreams of reaching. The answer to the question

I've been seeking for 25 weeks, and the 2 years prior to joining, has been answered today. Thankfully, I am the person I thought I was and not some stupid dickhead going out drinking, fighting, taking drugs and destined for nothing!

One final push to FREEDOM and in my mind, the ULTIMATE ACHIEVEMENT and TEST OF CHARACTER anyone can attain and undergo.

Day 188 – Tuesday 13 December

Woke up this morning feeling absolutely brilliant, because I finally have my Cap Comforter. Can't wait to wear it around camp today!

We've had lectures all day in preparation for 'Final Ex' and I am proper dreading it. It's December, the weather is shocking, and it takes place on Dartmoor! The Training Team keep dropping hints about the Exercise: Killer Yomp, a 25-mile yomp carrying 85–110lbs + weapons – SA80s, LSWs, and GPMGs – is done over uneven, hilly, totally gopping terrain. It is all the recruits here talk about throughout training and it sounds disgusting.

It doesn't get any better. It's the Tarzan Assault Course (*3rd Commando Test*) acquaint tomorrow. It is rumoured to be the hardest test: starting with the death slide, it begins with a High Aerial Assault Course, which is very technical and is so high and dangerous that an ambulance is always on site at the bottom. Then you come off that and sprint down to the Bottom Field: do one lap of the Bottom Field Assault Course, then sprint back up to the 30ft wall and climb to the top (*where the time stops*) using a rope. All this while wearing full kit (*21lbs + weapon*) and covering a distance of around 1.5k in under 13 minutes dead.

Day 189 – Wednesday 14 December

Lectures on Final Ex again all morning, THEN the Tarzan Assault Course – after lunch. The mental torture the Commando Tests create is ruthless!

Queuing up in single file, ready to climb the 30–40ft ladders up to the death slide tower exit, is absolutely horrendous. Not helped by the fact that JR was at the top pushing lads out, and all we could hear from the bottom was '3, 2, 1, GO!' in his ultimate and honking alpha-male voice. He is one scary man! Climbing the multitude of ladders to reach the top was minging and my legs were shaking, knowing that in a few minutes I would be heading down the death slide and thrust into the High Aerial section of the Tarzan Assault Course.

The death slide is basically a rope that goes from the top of a tower to the ground, and a recruit must put a small rope with rope handles over the main rope, attach each hand to the loops at either end and then jump out of the tower (with a little help from JR), which takes you down to the ground at some speed. The adrenaline dump at this point is enormous and trying to gather your composure to successfully navigate the remaining High Aerial obstacles is a brutal task in itself. Not to mention having to do this with all the other PTIs screaming abuse at you from below.

The chances of getting injured whilst falling from the high obstacles are massive. One lad has previously fallen and broken his neck, others have broken legs and arms, or been seriously hurt on this course. The presence of paramedics and an ambulance at the bottom of the 30ft wall doesn't help massage your anxieties either. (*Safety nets have since been introduced under the High Aerial stage to prevent horrific injuries such as those mentioned above.*)

The Tarzan is brutal, but not as bad as expected! It was done without kit this time though. Knowing I must attack this test two more times wearing full kit, 21lbs + weapon, makes me want to vomit in my mouth.

Day 190 – Thursday 15 December

The start of 'Final Ex'! We received orders early this morning to conduct two 'daylight' raids; we are to get a Heli extraction from camp to a farm on Bodmin Moor. It's a very tricky mission that, under normal circumstances, would be carried out during darkness. Once we have executed both raids, we are boarding the helicopters again and going to a Naval Base to board the Rigid Raiders. They will take us by sea along the coast to undertake a cliff assault – it doesn't get much more Gucci and Commando than that.

The start of Final Ex is so surreal. I looked at lads going on this exercise in such awe when I arrived, and I hoped and prayed (not to any God) that I had what it took to get there one day. Now that day has arrived . . . unbelievable!

Major M, the Company major, had a talk to us this morning, and one thing he said was: 'This is it men, this is where you aim to be when you arrive here at Lympstone and begin this perilous endeavour. We have nothing left here to teach you: the rest is up to you. At times you will be tested, but it's important to stay focused and remember why you are here – why you embarked on this journey of self-discovery.'

What an amazing speech – it has really hit me like a bomb-shell where I am now and how far I have come!

Day 191 – Friday 16 December

The Helis got cancelled last minute and the sea police put blockers on our coastal route in the Raiders – wankers! So we had to wait at HMS Drake for transport to 42 Commando. When we arrived at 42, it was absolutely freezing; however, an 8-mile yomp into Dartmoor soon warmed us all up . . . and quick.

We harboured up on the edge of Dartmoor. My sentry was 03:30, which is a shocker of a timing (_meaning I wouldn't get much sleep_). Made worse when the temp this morning was minus 6/7 degrees, and having to lay on solid, frozen ground in the 'prone position' for one hour until 04:30 was absolutely brutal.

My section has been sleeping most of the day while 1 and 2 section have been out conducting CTRs (_Close Target Recces_) and OPs (_Observation Posts_), because we have received INT of enemy activity in our area, and word of a possible attack that will more than likely come our way. Really not looking forward to another night on sentry – it is Baltic and all I can think of is Christmas Leave – just the thought of it overwhelms me!

Day 192 – Saturday 17 December

So bastard happy that morning routine has come, the cold last night was unbearable – I could not stop shaking and haven't slept at all. Based on the INT gathered by 1 and 2 section, we've started preparing models of the enemy location: Ditsworthy Warren House, which is suspected to be occupied by 2–4 enemy packs.

We are due to attack the house at 'first light' tomorrow

morning. My section (3) and 4 section will clear and secure the house, while 2 section provide fire support; 1 section will stay in reserve should something go wrong during the mission.

It's 19:00 and we have received orders for the attack. Just prepping weapons, mags, grenades/smoke, then I will try and get some sleep ready for the attack. The Training Team have hinted that tomorrow will be a 'very' long day!

Day 193 – Sunday 18 December

At 03:15 we woke up and disassembled our harbour – all in complete darkness. I have a telescopic night-vision scope on my weapon called a CWS.

We yomped 6 miles with heavy bergens and stopped short of the target location once we got eyes on. My section (3) and 4 section then monkey-crawled 300m along a bush line/dry stone wall that concealed our approach – it was cool and a right buzz, creeping up on the enemy. Around 50m from the house, we broke cover and attacked with stealth and complete surprise; the Hunter enemy lads didn't even have time to pick up their weapons – it was absolutely class. We cleared and secured the house in under 20 mins!

After the attack, we cleaned our weapons, had scran and were told by the Training Team to prepare to move at 09:00 and to make sure our feet were in 'top condition'. Then they said: 'Lads, you will not stop yomping until tomorrow morning.' KILLER YOMP had arrived! (_At this moment I was completely numb and internally flapping._) The day we had all been dreading since we started was upon us. The rumours of this yomp are never good when you first arrive at Lympstone, and even as you progress through training, knowing that you have this in front of you never gets easier.

Killer Yomp is one of the most infamous and gruelling thrashings you receive in training, and I/we will be starting it in around 20 minutes . . .

LESSON 28

Nothing in life worth having is possible without sacrifice . . . lots of self-imposed sacrifice to achieve success.

Becoming a Royal Marines Commando takes incredible sacrifice. I made it a manageable undertaking mentally by drawing on the radical impact and change my life would undergo if I sacrificed my Comfort Zone and autonomy for 9–10 months, and succeeded in getting my Green Beret. As mentioned in Chapter 3, it was not a difficult trade-off once I had processed that.

Achieving our goals means making sacrifices and being ruthlessly efficient with time, in order to prioritise one thing over another. For instance, when my knee went on the Bottom Field (Chapter 25), I was presented with the easy option to take a reprieve from training, but I felt that was only delaying the inevitable and might have risked the chance of attaining my prized goal. Thus, I sacrificed time, my body and mobility to stay on course to completing my training. I was getting ever closer to the finish line, and I wanted to achieve that as quickly as possible, providing I could continue physically. Therefore, keeping the momentum was crucial.

One cannot reach tangible and sought-after goals in life without sacrifice; we all have 24 hours in a day, but how you utilise it makes the difference. It was my choice to give up time spent with family and friends to achieve something. This meant taking on other short-term discomforts, such as sleep deprivation, unimaginable pressure, and physical and mental challenges, which I had to overcome in order to reach the key milestones in training and accomplish my end goal.

All these sacrifices jeopardised my short-term (and perhaps longer-term) physical and mental health and wellbeing, but I accepted that – and acknowledged the risks that I could incur while in pursuit of an unbelievable achievement, an opportunity for greater change.

There are many pivotal moments in our lives, when we need to venture within and make the choice either to stay in the safety of our Comfort Zone, and shy away from adversity, or accept temporary discomfort by putting aside our familiar and comfortable routines to pursue a desired goal, or reach the upper limits of our potential.

Such sacrifice may be nuanced, temporary, or will become a new way of life (as in my case), but having the self-discipline and resilience to enforce personal sacrifice is the necessary and *only* trade-off available, if we want to succeed in this very short window of life.

In short, don't succumb to 'immediate' desire, comfort or temptation – nothing worth having in life is ever attainable without some form of self-imposed sacrifice. When you are sitting on top of the mountain having reached your goal(s) in life, look down, see how far you have climbed, and know it was all worthwhile.

Key Points:

- We are evolutionarily pre-programmed to forget hard times.

- We all have the same amount of time in one day, but how you utilise it and the sacrifices you impose on your immediate comfort will determine the opportunities you can create.

- You simply cannot achieve anything worthwhile in life without sacrifices to your time, health, comforts, and social relationships. Acknowledge that this is often only temporary in relation to the rest of your life. In that sense, it is not a difficult trade-off.

- There is nothing more tragic in life (for me personally), than wasted talent and ability.

- As human beings, we soon forget hard times; our brains have a way of softening the pain and discomfort once suffered. Life is short, yes, but the window of peak health, fitness and physical performance is even shorter. Why wait?

31

MAKING EFFECTIVE DECISIONS

Cultivating the 'Thinking Soldier'

WEEK 27

Day 194 – Monday 19 December 2005

I survived Killer Yomp! It's 05:00 and we are currently laying low in a ravine at the edge of a barren, moorland-type field, around 1500m from a farm, which is in the middle of Dartmoor. We could not find our preferred RV as it was clagged (*fogged*) in. It was so bad, we couldn't see our hands in front of our faces and had to hold onto the back of each other's daysacks (*small rucksacks*), and even then, we lost two lads in the process.

I cannot walk at all this morning – my feet are covered in deep blisters; however, some of the lads have got shocking trench foot, because they failed to look after their feet properly.

We started the yomp with full kit yesterday at 09:03 and finished, well, reached our RV at 23:05 the same day. In all, we covered 21 miles – 15 of which with full kit – around 85–100lbs bergens + weapons. Then, when we reached a checkpoint 6 miles out, the Training Team said we could continue with just our daysacks.

This meant one of two choices: take our sleeping bags, or ditch them and take our 'warmers kit'. (*We couldn't take both*

238

due to the size/litre capacity of a military 'daysack'/backpack. Notably, either option meant you were cold during the night or cold during the day – a classic zero-sum game.) Well, we all chose to take warmers kit (apart from 1 lad), which turned out to be the very worst decision ever.

What the majority decision failed to realise back then was that their (my) decision came at the detriment of sleep, because our warm kit wasn't warm enough to counter the elements. Therefore, in hindsight, the benefit of experience, and in this case a very valuable lesson learned, we should have taken sleeping bags. It is far better to be rested and cold, than sleep deprived and cold.

It was raining on and off, and so cold last night that none of us slept and we all had to spoon each other physically to keep warm – it was awful. You would pass out through exhaustion, then wake up gibbering your tits off – a disgusting 10 hours. So from around 04:00, me and Tom Curry kept getting up and doing press-ups and burpees to keep warm, or more importantly, stay alive. Looking around now, all of us are completely broken – I cannot wait for whatever sun may come up, simply to take the edge off.

Today, me and a few of the lads have been out and laid trip flares and dummy Claymore mines to secure the harbour against enemy attack. After, we received orders to attack the farm that is situated 1500m away. This will take place at first light tomorrow morning. Reveille time is 02:00 – so I will stay up AGAIN and take the hit on sleeping, because trying to sleep in this weather takes more energy than staying awake. It is currently minus 6 degrees!

Day 195 – Tuesday 20 December

We infiltrated the farm at 05:30 and secured it by 06:15. My section was fire support, which is a shit task – I wanted to get in there first with the other sections and confront the enemy. Last night was the first time in my life I thought I was going to die; it was that cold, my legs and arms were jumping and thrashing around uncontrollably!

After securing the farm complex, the Troop Captain said: 'Pack bergens ready for yomping!' By this point our bergens had been returned. Everyone looked broken and in utter disbelief that we had another yomp to crack – bearing in mind that most of us couldn't walk from Killer Yomp. The distance we had to cover to reach our new RV was around 15k (9 miles), which to me and the others felt almost impossible – we had already covered around 30 miles in 3 days with little to no sleep.

We set off and walked down a dirt track leading away from the farm. Our bergens were heavy with fresh rations, water, ammunition and batteries for our radios, which weigh a fucking ton! Lads were grunting and weeping in pain and swaying from side to side – we were totally exhausted. I was point man and for some reason felt strong (_mentally_), so I pretty much left the lads and kept pace with Cpl Rikards. Literally, as I turned a corner, the 4-tonners were there waiting to extract us – my morale went from 0 to 100 in seconds. Cpl Rikards said, 'Timmins, do not look or go back and tell the lads!'

Even at this stage of training, they did this to see who would break and potentially give up upon hearing the 'sudden' and 'unexpected' news of another 15k extraction yomp. Two lads had already wrapped their tits in just before Killer Yomp – one of them was given the GPMG at the very start of it and he pretended to fake an injury and collapsed. Wrapping and calling it quits at Week 27 . . . zero respect for that.

What a mental test that was – and nobody wrapped. Seeing the lads' faces as they came around the corner and saw the transport was brilliant. We were all so happy and relieved – amazing times that!

We were now en route to a secure location to receive another set of orders to attack a famous (*in Royal Marines training*) fort in Plymouth. Orders revealed that 1 section would abseil down from the roof and enter through the windows, while 2 section would provide fire support from the fort walls. My section (3) would infiltrate the fort through an underground tunnel system – all of which would happen simultaneously at 05:30 – just after first light.

Hell fire, the tunnel system under the fort was unreal and freaky. We had NVGs on and you could see all the old dungeons and cells from back in the day; this place was not where you wanted to be left behind – it was eerie, especially going in with no sleep – 100% haunted.

The Hunter enemy had boobytrapped the tunnels with trip flares and grenades. The attack went to plan, and we managed to secure the fort in around 1 hour. Then we all went into a room that was pitch-black and were ordered to get into a circle and hold hands. No shit, the Troop SGT hit a button and Christmas lights came on – along with music from a stereo that was playing Christmas songs. We were exhausted, cold, wet and broken, but when those lights and that music came on, we all started singing and everything went away. What the Training Team did for us there was absolutely magical!

To this day, this remains one of, if not the best adult Christmas experiences I have ever had.

The transport came at 00:00. Prior to boarding and heading

back to camp, the Training Team lined up the original troop members (11 of us) and said something that was not only spine-chilling and remarkable, but which gave me a sober reality check. They said, 'Lads, statistics say that two or three of you here will get killed or seriously injured within your first year of completing training.' Wow! Mind games?

Just arrived back at Lympstone and we have all been woken on the bus from a coma of deep sleep. Cannot believe I have finished and passed Final Ex. The sense of achievement and the feeling I have of that exercise and experience being over is quite overwhelming. Again, no words can ever capture the emotions and hardship we have all faced. You have to do this to understand, it's that simple.

I mean what do you say: 'Yeah, it was minus six degrees, we had no sleep, little food and walked over thirty-five miles – with kit weighing up to one hundred pounds, including water, rations, ammunition, radio batteries and weapons – over Dartmoor in December.' Gen, who can relate to that?

Day 196 – Wednesday 21 December

My feet are on fire and the open blisters have stuck to my bed sheets all night. My body is generally in bits, however, the relief and comfort of waking up in a warm bed overrides any of that.

De-servicing kit this morning, returning stores, and cleaning weapons and sigs (*communications*) equipment ready to hand back in, so we can go home!

All I can think about is going home, nothing else matters at this moment in time. It feels like a dream come true that I will be on the train heading up north tomorrow. Unbelievable feelings!

Day 197 – Thursday 22 December

HOME TODAY!

It was supposed to be a 13:00 cut away home today, but the Training Team have fucked us around again, for nothing at all. They said it's because 'we are walking round like Commandos' and they wanted to bring us back down to earth!

Going home . . .

Upon finishing Final Ex, I went home for Christmas. This should have been a time for relaxation and recovery, given the fact I was going back to the infamous 'Cheeky Week' – an intense and extremely brutal week of Commando test run-throughs – which included on the Wednesday of that week the Tarzan Assault Course in the morning, and the Endurance Course after lunch. An unbelievable and terrifying feat of physical and mental requirement and a day that instilled fear and anxiety throughout training.

Looking back, I have zero rationale for what I did during my leave periods – it's as if I'm looking through binoculars at a person I once knew, and I'm so thankful that I left this reckless part of me behind. However, that twenty-one-year-old lad went home (somewhat influenced by a heavy Royal Marines drinking culture at that time) and consumed more alcohol than a raving alcoholic.

During Christmas leave, I literally drank myself into the ground, with poor sleep, lack of good quality food, and a complete lack of general care for myself; given that at this point in Royal Marines training, I was considered to be amongst the fittest one per cent in the world, on a level with an Olympic Athlete.

That behaviour absolutely baffles me now, given how I conduct my life today. I can even remember on the train *journey back to start 'Cheeky Week' the following day, I spewed up three times, having been with friends that morning snorting Tramadol – a strong, opioid-based pain-relief medication – for something to do. Astonishing behaviour and completely irresponsible.*

Day 198 – Sunday 08 January 2006

Going back . . .

LESSON 29

Negotiating the frontier between benefit and disaster when making strategic or impulsive decisions about our future – often when confronted with limited information and/or unequal power dynamics.

Throughout the military, when discussions take place regarding the distinction between Royal Marines and the other elements that make up the UK Armed Forces, the term 'thinking soldier' (as a generalisation) is never far away. Recruit training and the culture within the Royal Marines invite their future and serving Commandos to 'think outside the box' – to be creative, display ingenuity and make informed decisions. What is often not obvious is that these decisions come with consequences – a trade-off where success and undesirable outcome(s) are produced.

The warmers kit and sleeping bag dilemma
As with the example above (Day 194), when we were asked to decide what to take with us into the final phase of the exercise – warmers kit or sleeping bags. However, this choice was based on both limited information and inexperience. Here's why the

benefit of hindsight and experience (after completing Final Ex) taught us that sleep and the quality of that natural process MUST be prioritised at all costs, where possible.

Whilst tired, fatigued and exhausted, we chose (apart from one recruit) to take warmers kit, thinking it would (a) guarantee warmth throughout the day and (b) as a result of this understanding, it would by default enable us to sleep . . . big mistake! Yes, we were warm (barely) during the day, but COULD NOT sleep at night, which then made the following day incredibly more excruciating.

The smart play would have been to ditch the warmers kit and opt for our sleeping bags, in order to afford good quality sleep and then endure the cold weather the following day – rested rather than raw with sleep deprivation, which was considerably worse.

Reflections and learning points
In hindsight and with experience, we should have analysed the available information more thoroughly before executing a course of action. This arguably would have minimised our levels of what became quite severe fatigue, and further safeguarded us against what could have been potentially catastrophic outcomes, such as individually going down with cold weather injuries or hypothermia.

Psychologically, self-confidence played a huge factor here and so did the influence of unequal power distribution created by the authority that the Training Team had over us. For example, we couldn't really ask what was the best course of action, nor challenge it. Consequently, we fell naturally into the majority vote, which was void of any form of effective debate or analysis.

This collective group sway manipulated our individual decision-making; a psychological phenomenon called 'group-think'. We did all manage to reach the end goal of completing the Final Exercise, yet we did so despite our poor decision-making, causing it to be considerably more arduous than it needed to be.

Conclusion

The key point of analysing the available information is to acknowledge what your decision is based upon. In many cases, decisions must be made without a comprehensive level of information, sometimes none. Therefore, time spent evaluating the right course of action (if at all needed) is fundamental, if we want to assure our chances of success when formulating and acting on the right course of action.

To assist this process and assure the chances of success, draw on past experiences of similar decisions that did or did not lead to the desired outcome. Play devil's advocate and make clear the drawbacks to each course of action. Crucially, consider your own bias in the assessment of this process, and constantly reassess the source of information – as well as the dilemma you are trying to mitigate – whilst remaining adaptive to change.

Key points:

- Maximise the time you have to make your decision fulfil the 'desired' outcome. Remember, all decisions come with consequences.
- If a bad decision is made – reassess the information you had at the time. Based on the 'available' information, it may not have been a bad idea inherently.
- It is important to acknowledge the detrimental effect unequal power dynamics can have on your ability to make the right decision, if the balance is not in your favour.

32

THE PERCEPTION OF ADVERSITY

Re-conceptualising failure

WEEK 28

Day 199 – Monday 09 January 2006

First day back after Christmas Leave! I drank heavily every day and partied constantly. The Training Team's advice before we left – to undertake 6–10 mile runs (best effort) – hasn't been done, and not one bit of bastard phys has been cracked in 2½ weeks! What a dickhead I am!

That said, this is the best I have ever felt coming back from leave. I think it's because in my mind I have 3½ weeks left to push – to reach my goal and end this nightmare. This excites me and gives me some comfort. Yet mixed emotions keep flooding in, because these next 3½ weeks are going to be horrific and the uncertainty of whether I can pass the Commando Tests fills me with pure anxiety. It's an awful feeling, living with this 'daily burden of failure'.

What will I do if I get injured at this stage now or fail a Commando Test? The pressure is overwhelming to say the very least. I must look after and stay aware of my ruptured left ACL (*knee*) and its limitations, and also stay conscious of my right Achilles, which is partially torn – both of which have hampered me for months now.

The Commando Tests consume my every thought. Mentally, I am certain I will pass, but one slip-up and it will all go wrong for me. I keep running through each one and visualising them at every crucial stage, where possible, but how does anyone visualise doing the 30-miler? Just praying to whoever is out there for my body to hold up for another 4 more weeks – my mental state is not concerning me at all, it's my broken body.

Been to college today, which was boring. Then after, we had a specialisation brief this evening from the SBS. The SB guy was saying that after passing selection for UKSF, you are sent straight to Washington DC to learn how to deal with gunshot wounds – working alongside US paramedics in real-world gunshot trauma callouts – WOW!

Day 200 – Tuesday 10 January

Been at college again all day. I've passed two exams but I find it so boring. It's been a good laugh with the lads though. Can't stop thinking about 'Cheeky Wednesday' . . . this is notorious from Day 1, Week 1 of starting here; a brutal and ruthless day that tortures you mentally in the weeks before and during, and destroys the body after.

The day starts with the Tarzan Assault Course, then straight after lunch, you do the Endurance Course. HONKING! That's two Commando Tests in one day, both of which are widely considered to be the hardest 2 of 4 physically demanding tests of endurance and stamina in the world.

Come 'Test Week', the Endurance is done on the Saturday then the 9-mile Speed March on Monday, followed by the Tarzan Assault Course on Tuesday. Then it's straight off to Okehampton Camp on Dartmoor ready to start the 30-miler in the early hours of Wednesday morning. Waking up tomorrow morning will be like waking up in hell!

The Tarzan is around 1500m of honking High-Aerial and Bottom Field Assault Courses in under 13mins. The Endurance starts with a 4-mile speed march up to Woodbury Common. For me, this is the toughest Commando Test yet, and it's absolutely horrific. Once at Woodbury, the course then starts with 2 miles of tunnels, water crossings, the Sheep Dip, steep inclines, Crocodile Pits – all of which are done with your weapon's operational capability in mind.

Then it's a 4-mile run (best effort) back to camp, where I have to load my weapon with 10 live rounds and hit a target at 25m with 6 of the 10 rounds to pass successfully in under 72 minutes. If I don't look after my weapon and it gets wet and caked in mud and shit, it could be the difference between a pass or a fail – progress towards my Green Beret or a train ticket home! All this, like the rest of the Tests, is done with 21lbs of kit + weapon.

Day 201 – Wednesday 11 January

Cheeky Wednesday! I am writing this after both Tests, here goes . . . well, this is undoubtedly the hardest day in training and my life ever . . . oh my God!

I did the Tarzan in 12:14 minutes, which was pure frantic pain with an element of emotional disbelief and a huge dump of adrenaline to deal with, which made my legs go weak as I was transitioning from obstacle to obstacle on the High-Aerial section of the course.

However, down on Bottom Field, I couldn't get over the 6ft wall with kit on and had to (embarrassingly) run around it, which 'luckily' went unnoticed by the PTIs, but NOT by 2 of the lads! My upper body strength just wasn't there to 'bridge my core up' – put my left boot on top of the wall and pull myself over. This has now made me flap, because on the actual test day, if I can't get over the 6ft wall, I will fail 100%.

What is more alarming is that I nearly passed out doing the half-regain, but managed to hold it together, complete it and move on to the next obstacle. Gen, if I screw up on both the 6ft wall and half-regain on the day, it will mean I would be outside of the 13 min time limit and fail the bastard. Every obstacle must be executed with technical perfection and at speed to get under the 13 min set time.

I cannot believe how much I underestimated the Endurance Course . . . those weeks on Christmas Leave pissing up and generally not looking after myself have fucked me over big time. I was well and truly in the Hurt Locker for 74 minutes, which meant I failed the run-through by 2 minutes. I have now technically failed both the Endurance and Tarzan run-through acquaints and my confidence is completely shot to shit!

The Endurance was really uncomfortable and a mental onslaught. In fact, I felt like I was going to die – like I wanted to quit – and thought, what am I doing here? I also nearly lost all my teeth biting hold of my weapon sling clasp, trying to keep the barrel and working parts of my weapon out of the drink (*water*) as I shimmied through the partially submerged Smartie tube on my side.

For anyone watching my run back to camp, it must have been like watching the scene from the film 'Full Metal Jacket', when Private Pile is getting dragged along by the lads on their troop run. GOPPING! I did get 9/10 shots on target safely though; but at 74 minutes, I am 2 mins over the limit. Some of the lads came in at 62 minutes and above – I'm just broken mentally now. The 6-months conditioning regime I put myself through prior to joining training must have made me peak too early and now I am playing catch-up. There's nothing there in the tank – my upper-body strength is non-existent.

Day 202 – Thursday 12 January

Mentally struggling today; I feel low and hugely disappointed in myself that I failed the Endurance run-through. Oh, and I couldn't get over the 6ft wall on the Tarzan, so I failed that too! I was below standard – my standard, to which I hold myself to account. I should be passing these all day long. I do them both for real in two weeks. I am sure I will be OK – I will have to be for fuck's sake!

My feet are troubling me a bit – I keep having to soak them in warm water, because I am still experiencing temp numbness in my toes from dig ex some weeks back. Had drill all morning, shit. We were watching Kings Squad pass out . . . it's us next. Just hope all goes well and I am stood there in 4 weeks!

After lunch we had a swim, then weapon lectures on anti-tank/heavy weapons. The Cpl taking the lecture was saying that a bloke wearing a CBA (*a shitty old-school body armour with only a front and back plate that covered your heart*) was hit in the chest area by a .50 cal round/bullet. Get this, the plate stopped the round, but projected the plate through his chest and it came to rest on his spine, crushing him to death. That's just mad! The .50 cal Browning is a devastating weapon.

Day 203 – Friday 13 January

Tarzan Assault Course again this morning! I was nervous as hell and lacked the motivation if I'm honest. Queuing up at the bottom of the death slide tower, seeing lads getting pushed out and hearing Sgt R's deep voice shouting, '3, 2, 1, GO,' is GOPPING. Of all the PTIs you want at the top of the tower, he is the very last one.

I was dangling (*hanging out*) AGAIN. However, during the past few days, I have been putting my kit on during the evenings and jumping up onto the top of my cupboard and bridging my body up to simulate the 6ft wall. I am trying to get my technique better and hopefully build some last-minute core and upper-body 'panic' strength. The lads thought I was crazy!

Anyway, as I came off the Tarzan and ran down to Bottom Field, I could see the 6ft wall in the distance. The negative side of me (*which very rarely emerges*) emerged and started to talk me out of it – my confidence was rock bottom. As I jumped over the water ditch and made my approach to attack and get over the 6ft wall, I jumped up and put the tip (*toe section*) of my left boot into the wall to propel myself up, but my foot slipped off the mid-section of the wall (*because my boots were wet*) and I failed to get over with my first attempt . . . AGAIN.

Welcome back the demons. At that point I was so angry that I ran back and took another run up, biting down hard with my teeth, and somehow nailed it technically and managed to pull myself up and over – and then continued to execute all the other remaining obstacles with ease. I passed with a time of 12:39 (*21 seconds to spare*). On the day I reckon I can shave 1½ to 2 minutes off that. Thank fuck, I am so happy and relieved!

After, we had Combat Battle Stress lectures on PTSD. We watched a video of soldiers who were 'shell shocked' after fighting in the First World War (*to this day, the video footage still holds a vivid place in my mind*). It was truly gut-wrenching to see those poor men in such a state, and nobody knew anything about PTSD then or spoke about it.

Then we had CQC (*Close Quarter Combat*) learning how to throw kicks, knees, various body throws, and disarming techniques with knives and guns, etc. I love this side of it all and would happily do it all day long if I could.

Finally, we had an interview regarding which unit we wanted to go to after completing training, which is very surreal. I chose: 40, FPGRM (to hopefully get on FSRT), 42, and then 45 Commando!

Day 204 – Saturday 14 January

Final Endurance run-through! I really need to pass this one for my confidence. They say everyone has a demon at some point here – a brick wall that must be penetrated to succeed – and without a doubt the Endurance is mine.

Failed at 73 mins – 1 min over! The extra water weight you take on after going through Peter's Pool and through the Sheep Dip is filling my webbing pouches, pockets and boots up with water and absolutely killing me. The gravelly incline up through the woods after the Sheep Dip is honking to get up with full kit and the extra water, and I feel completely fucked by this point; but that's only the start of the course, more or less – there's still a good 1½ miles to do, plus the 4-mile run back to camp. Gopsville!

The 4-mile run back to camp is nails and to get the time I need to pass, I cannot seem to generate the energy to make it happen. It's not a mental block, there's just nothing in the tank. I had to walk at times and on the day, IN TWO WEEKS, I cannot afford to do that. It is making me fail by 1 to 1½ minutes.

That is all my Endurance run-throughs now failed, which is my first official fail in training. I must get over this quickly and pull myself together mentally, ready for the real test, a week on Saturday. Deep down though, I know I will do it. It's weird, like a quiet voice of comfort that's whispering to me, don't worry Gareth, you will be OK.

Day 205 – Sunday 15 January

I am waking up now to the sheer realisation of how close I am to the end, and that's really overwhelming in the best way ever. We are going away now for two weeks' live field firing: FX 1 and FX 2. When we return to camp, it's TEST WEEK.

Hopefully the last 5 days of brutal training are now banked. When we arrive back on camp, we move into St Carlos block – it is where you go in your final stages of training – Kings Squad. The pressure now to pass is unlike anything I have ever experienced – I want this so bad; I am prepared to die!

My fitness seems to be in a sorry state compared to the rest of the lads – bearing in mind, I was a PT Superior in Week 9. It's all gone wrong at the most crucial part of training. For the first time, I feel a sense of paranoia – like the lads know I am struggling and probably think I'm a 'Phys Biff' (*someone who is terrible at physical exercise*) – even I think I'm a Phys Biff! I have no answers at all.

LESSON 30

Adversity facilitates the introduction between the self and the 'true' self. Whether goal acquisition is eventually realised depends on one's ability to withstand setbacks, whilst acknowledging that beneath the façade of failure lies perseverance.

Following my return from that disastrous Christmas Leave period, this week of training delivered the second most significant taste of failure that I had experienced in my young life. Today, with the benefit of wisdom and hindsight, those moments of despair and uncertainty enabled me to learn so much about myself, and discover how stubborn and resilient I was in the face of adversity.

In general, we are raised in a society that influences us to avoid failure at all costs. It is a term that evokes fear and operates to shackle people from attempting to achieve great things. However, failure and all it embodies is a misused and misrepresented label – it is a very generic concept, and only describes an outcome where those that have tried, and fallen short, are not good enough. It does not highlight the different avenues (such as perseverance) a person can take to learn, get better, and make a successful attempt.

Because of this misrepresentation, people become (a) afraid of experiencing failure and (b) deterred from trying, based on what they perceive will be the negative perception or representation of opinion cast on them by 'others'.

Therefore it strikes deep into our subconscious like a sharp-bladed instrument, creating feelings and thoughts of incompetence when we fall short, which in turn, shatter self-confidence and inhibit our propensity to reload and go again – or even step out of our comfort zones to make an attempt in most cases.

Success and realising achievement(s) are not possible without experiencing a degree of failure along the way. Thus, as painful as failure may appear, know that each and every exposure to it comes with rich opportunities to explore and investigate the previously 'hidden' pattern embroidered into its fabric. In this sense, the confrontation of failure, when harnessed and put to good use, can be reframed as a key opportunity to acquire new knowledge. It allows the privilege of insight, of learning the often unforeseen requirements needed to acquire, pass, or succeed at something.

For me personally, someone only fails when they make no further attempt after the initial disappointment or rejection. Therefore, learning to overcome failure is an absolute necessity and a key ingredient in one's endeavour to become successful.

Take Michael Jordan, for example, the most successful basketball player in history, a pioneer, a needle pusher, and a sporting icon, who transcended the sport to become widely regarded as one of the greatest athletes ever. He once famously said: 'I've missed more than nine thousand shots in my career. I've been trusted to take the game-winning shot and missed. I've failed over and over and over again in my life. And that is why I succeed.'

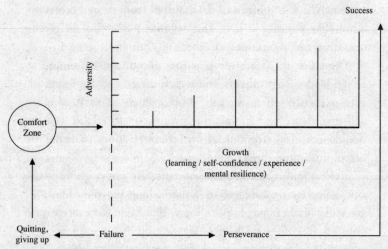

In this sense, failure is a process of learning, a matter of perspective only. In its wake, ask yourself: What went right – and at what point did things go wrong? What actions or factors contributed to the unwanted outcome? What can you do differently next time to improve your performance, and achieve the desired outcome? Indeed, harnessing the ability to adapt and keep going whilst displaying 'cheerfulness in adversity' is one of the five Royal Marines Commando maxims.

Key Points:

- Adversity and 'perceived' failure, however difficult to come to terms with, give you an opportunity to refocus and grow.
- Failure is like the underrated best friend of success – the grey man that never receives the right acknowledgement! Although lurking in the shadows, his impact on success is everything.
- You can only conceptualise failure as it is defined in the dictionary if after your first unsuccessful attempt, you never try again; if you lick your wounds, learn, readjust, and go again . . . that is not failure, it is 'perseverance'.
- The confrontation of failure provides an indicator that you have ventured outside of your comfort zone. Something that most, will never experience.
- Learn to view and approach failure like Michael Jordan.

33

TRUST

Selecting the right team

WEEK 29

Day 206 – Monday 16 January 2006

It is the start of FX 1 (Live Field Firing Exercise) today and it's cold, wet, and I cannot be arsed! Been zeroing weapons all day, which means aligning the scope/sight with the weapon barrel to aim accurately and then hit the specific area of a target you want to hit, which is usually the 'centre' of mass (*chest*). We then had to run back to our accommodation, which is a converted barn, with bunk beds and zero heating. It's Ice Bats! (*Royal Marines slang for extremely cold.*)

Really anxious about the Commando Tests; they are occupying my every thought and affecting my performance. It's like I'm obsessed by them, and I find myself switching back and forth constantly on whether I will pass or fail. It is a minging day-to-day existence.

Been talking to the Training Team about the Tests to extract some form of comfort. Their experience of doing them, coupled with their advice on how to approach them from a mental perspective, has helped me to cope better with the stress and pressure I'm feeling at the moment. This past year of pure hell and discomfort, along with the huge risk and personal sacrifice I have put myself through, relies solely now on the successful completion of the Commando Tests. That is pressure!

Self-Reflection (in 2006)

What I find strange is that I visualised a lad at this stage of training being so mentally nails that he wouldn't feel stressed about anything now, including the Tests; he would be completely void of emotion. Yet, being here myself, it is totally different to how I thought it would be. Yes, I have learnt who I am and my capabilities – I have discovered I will never quit and would rather die trying – but I didn't expect to feel so much self-doubt and uncertainty at this stage of training. I guess some emotions are so deeply embedded in our genetic make-up that nearly 32 weeks of training cannot override them.

Day 207 – Tuesday 17 January

We have been on a live firing range all day, doing fire and manoeuvre drills with live ammunition! We work in teams – one team will lay down fire, while another team manoeuvres back (*breaking contact*) or forward into/towards contact (*enemy fire*). Then the firing teams swap over and repeat the process – breaking contact (*under heavy enemy fire*) or advancing to kill the enemy.

I must say, breaking contact when ambushed or over-whelmed by enemy fire is a right buzz using live rounds, and experiencing them winging past and over your head, or around your general location, is the most unbelievable adrenaline buzz ever.

After today's live drills, we moved on to a night attack – again firing and manoeuvring, but this time using tracer rounds (*bullets with red glowing tips, known as 'Red Wasps'*), often used to indicate to your oppos the location of enemy attackers, or locations of interest while under the cloak of darkness. Watching them flying over at lightning speed and ricocheting off pop-up targets was amazing. I watched those tracers in sheer awe and fascination.

The speed with which a bullet travels is absolutely mind-boggling, and it reminds me of the fascination I saw in my son's eyes, the first time he saw fireworks explode in the sky.

They say you can be hit by a bullet and if it doesn't kill you instantly, you can then hear it leave the weapon barrel, or hear the bang after. That is how fast they travel – faster than the speed of sound. Regardless of this, I still cannot get the tests out my head! They start in just over one week.

Day 208 – Wednesday 18 January

Troop phys this morning: 5-mile run with hill sprints, fireman's carries, and interval training thrown in. Pretty intense but enjoyable and a good feeling, because it all adds up and goes in the bank ready for the Commando Tests.

We have been in the accommodation all day, the clag (*fog*) was too bad, and the Training Team said we were doing a night nav, which is a bit out the blue and random. Come the evening, we were told to prepare a route card, pack kit, and get ready to move. Me and some of the lads were suspicious. The feeling was that they couldn't bear us just laying around, so they got bored and made up some bullshit task to keep us busy and to see who would wrap their tits in.

17:30 came and we all had our kit on and had a briefing.

Then suddenly one of the lads received a text saying, 'Get in the fucking showers, you cunts.' Thank God for that, ha ha . . . Wankers!

Day 209 – Thursday 19 January

Today has been all about section attacks. These attacks using live rounds take so much concentration, especially when you are covering large amounts of uneven ground at speed, wearing full kit, and whilst staying conscious of your every movement and the positioning of your section members. Absolute hangout!

You must control your rate of fire, while being aware of your tactical positioning in relation to your section – coupled with the fact that you have a specific mission to achieve. However, the adrenaline is pumping throughout to the max – especially with 'Red Wasps' flying around – it's class!

Finally arrived back at the accommodation and we are now relaxing; these are long, arduous days, but very enjoyable. We are apparently moving to a better camp tomorrow, which should be good. The Test demons have arrived again though.

Day 210 – Friday 20 January

Yet another day of section attacks! It's been really good, but it's so mentally and physically taxing. We then tested the new Underslung Grenade Launcher (UGL), which attaches to the undercarriage of the SA80: awesome bit of kit this. It fires grenade cartridges up to 300m – SF style!

Well, we returned back to our accommodation thinking the day was over, until the Troop SGT turned up in his webbing and carrying a weapon. SPEED MARCH TIME. We speed marched 4 miles with weapon, webbing, and our daysacks. It was a dangle, but good phys in the bank ready for next weekend . . . Test Week!

Just arrived at Okehampton Camp, what a weird shit place this is – reminds me of how an old Butlins resort looked on my mum and dad's pictures in the 1970s, but still nice to be in a warm bed, chilling out.

Day 211 – Saturday 21 January

Weekend off.

LESSON 31

Your network, and the people around you, can either make or break you. Therefore, surround yourself with those on the same mission as you.

No other period of training epitomises and highlights the essential requirement to 'trust' the people around you more than 'live' Field Firing Exercises 1 and 2 (FX1 and FX2). From a training perspective, the live field firing exercises cement a recruit's seniority as a trained soldier, soon to be elite Commando. When you arrive at this stage, you are trusted by the Training Team and your fellow oppos to fire live ammunition in and around one another; to harness the awareness of others' positions, whilst knowing your unique role in the firefight.

It is also about displaying absolute self-control and composure whilst navigating undulating terrain when fatigued, and laden down with personal fighting equipment. To be effective in these situations demands cohesive trust, an understanding that trust and competency are assured and unquestioned. The Royal Marines produce this bond, this team understanding and cohesion, like no other.

From an operational perspective, trusting those around you provides the backbone of comfort and safety when contact is made with the enemy, and during moments of stark realisation and vulnerability, when a mission has not gone according to plan. Quite frankly, a Royal Marine Commando is nothing without their trusted companions, and the wider tactical assets in support.

To achieve goals and great achievements in life, you must harness the power of others (as discussed in Chapter 28). Know that your selection of the 'right' people is crucial to how successful you will become and whether your end goal will come to fruition. To succeed, be bold enough to cut away the bad; those that you question, the ones with questionable in-tegrity and motives.

For us, come FX1, the Royal Marines had discouraged those misplaced individuals and what remained were colleagues whom you trusted with your life.

Key Points:

- Surround yourself with people who have your very best interests at heart and who will make you thrive – cut away the bad energy and influence.
- To achieve greats things in life both individually and as a team, the make-up of its people must be unques-tionable, and trust should provide the backbone of its culture.

34

NO CUFF TOO TOUGH

Being entrepreneurial

WEEK 30

Day 212 – Monday 23 January 2006

Monday morning blues once again. Cannot be bothered and find myself in a shocker of a mood – I want to be left alone and not socialise with anyone at all, which is impossible living with lads. Just had to complete a questionnaire on our experiences of training, as we are now at the end – it bored me to tears. I wanted to say: 'It's long, hard, you are always cold, wet and in a general shit state . . . end of questionnaire.' We have a troop attack at 13:15 and can't be arsed with that either – bad day this for me!

Just had Tactical Radio Communications training, which was so good – and that has boosted my morale. After completion of our Troop Attack, we were talking to the Training Team about our Pass Out Parade . . . CANNOT honestly believe it – that we are talking about the end of training and I am on the verge of getting my Green Beret. This has been around two and a half years in the making (*including failing my first maths test at eighteen years old, to passing the second test a year later, then the six months build-up/conditioning training regime prior to going down for my PRMC, and then starting training, to where I am now).*

However, I still feel reluctant to let my emotions get too far ahead of themselves – getting through the Commando Tests is a huge hurdle I must navigate successfully to reach my goal. Nonetheless, if all goes well, in 1 week and 2 days I will have my Green Beret and get my Commando Flashes . . . and be a Royal Marines Commando.

AWESOME, JUST FUCKING AWESOME!

<u>Day 213 – Tuesday 24 January</u>

The reward of finishing training is overwhelming, and it still fills me with disbelief. I never thought I could do this. You see the programme of training and your mind tells you that this course is beyond human capability, honestly. The emotional journey that I and the remaining lads have been on to get here has been unbelievable, and so mentally gruelling.

What I do find strange is that this way of life now feels like it is all I have ever known, as if my previous life and existence has died, and I've adopted a completely new identity and lifestyle. Hopefully, come next week, it will change 100% for the better and provide me with a solid foundation for the rest of my life.

I want this so bad; I am prepared with every part of my being to cross that bridge at the end of the 30-miler and receive my Green Beret. Doubt is always there, though, like a parrot on my shoulder, tormenting the hell out of me – it just won't shut up. Why do I feel this way? I've earned this moment, I took a HUGE risk, against massive odds and injuries, and with 98% of people laughing at me when I told them of my intention to join the Royal Marines.

I'm hoping and praying to whoever or whatever is out there, that I stay strong and finally finish what I started here!

Day 214 – Wednesday 25 January

My eyes have opened, I am one step closer. This time next week I will be on the 30-miler, more than likely hanging out my hoop. I feel ready though.

We should have had a section/troop attack today, but it got cancelled due to the clag (*fog*) . . . FOG, I love you! We did Troop phys this evening – a 3 to 4-mile interval booted run. I felt strong and not depleted. This has reinforced my confidence for Saturday: the Endurance Course and the start of Test Week.

Major M was talking to us and said (in his ever so charismatic way): 'One week today, men, and you are all elite Commandos!'

Day 215 – Thursday 26 January

We did a troop attack today, which was really good but taxing; the concentration and fitness required to operate at the very highest level under contact is incredible.

I'm really anxious about Saturday, this is it now – everything I have done up to this point in training has come down to this next 6 days.

Cpl Rikards came into my grot and said to 3 section (his/my section): 'This is it. I've taught you lads everything I know within the realms of Lympstone. You are six days off being Commandos and you will learn even more once you get to your units, but for now, the Tests are all up to you – good luck, fellas.'

Day 216 – Friday 27 January

Well, hell fire, it's the eve of the Commando Tests! I am so sick and mentally exhausted of feeling this anxiety, I just want this nightmare to be over now.

We've been lashed up with 5 periods of drill ready for our pass out parade. Cpl C called us 'Kings Squad'. Not going to lie, it was a brilliant feeling, but indirectly applies maximum pressure to get there! The emotional strain is relentless; the waiting game and the uncertainty is just gopping.

At scran time in the evening we all went to the front of the galley queue – passing all the other lads behind us in training – what a buzz. Nearly a year ago, I was looking at lads like me now with such awe and admiration, and here I'm the one walking to the front of the queue to get my food, it's mint!

I know in the morning when I wake up at 03:00, I will feel like dogshit, but I'm going to do it for me and the man upstairs – RM (_Roger Monks: my Grandad_) xxx

Day 217 – Saturday 28 January

Start of the Commando Tests! All up this morning at 03:00 to get ready for the 4-mile Speed March up to the Endurance Course.

My kit has just been weighed and weapons are slung. The day has arrived and surprisingly, I sit here moments away feeling relaxed and pretty confident, even though my body is broken – knee fucked, and Achilles torn. I just want this bastard finished now. I am so pumped up this morning, focused and aggressive, and ready to go!

Whilst walking the 4 miles up to the Endurance, I went through so many emotions, reflecting on what I was about to go through. I must admit, it was at times a 40/60 split in favour of the negative side of my confidence – bearing in mind that I hadn't passed this Test on both of my run-throughs. I kept talking to myself and getting angry.

Once we reached the start point on Woodbury Common, we were split into teams of 3 or 4 and then lined up in order of who would go first. I was fourth to go and hearing the words from the PTI: '3, 2, 1, GO!' and watching the first 3 lads depart made my stomach turn upside down. We then progressed forward . . . closer to the biggest physical and mental thrashing anyone can imagine!

All of a sudden, we were next to go . . . 3, 2, 1, GO! It was now the run of my life and it felt partially surreal, mixed with sheer terror. My legs felt like jelly from the massive adrenaline dump that had just landed in my stomach as I ran like a headless chicken towards the first tunnel. Upon exiting the tunnel, I felt really strong – the nerves had gone, and I waded through Peter's Pool with my weapon raised at shoulder height (*to protect the barrel and working parts*) and departed at speed up a gradual incline leading towards the famous Sheep Dip.

I went first, took a huge deep breath and was then pushed straight under and through the water tunnel, came up gasping for air, and then pushed one of the lads in and dragged the other out. We then all headed up a steep incline weighing a stone heavier from all the extra water in our webbing pouches and boots.

However, something was different! Whereas before I had to walk up this incline, this time I ran up . . . and smashed it, and with that my confidence grew and grew. I knew at this very moment the gas tank was there and I felt unstoppable. I knew I had it in the bag and would get the time I needed to pass the Test, providing I didn't get injured and protected my weapon for the shoot at the end. My training nemesis was being defeated!

For the 4-mile run back to camp, I'd asked my good friend Dane Binks (*Binksy*) to meet me at the last obstacle on the Endurance and run back with me. (*He had been back-trooped through injury in the earlier stages of training and luckily wasn't engaged in training that morning.*) Binksy was there waiting for me, and with him in my ear, the 4-mile run back to camp was comfortable – by no means enjoyable, but I was not mentally or physically stressed like on previous attempts.

I will never forget what Dane did for me that morning and how he supported me to the end. I am forever indebted to you, Royal!

I came in at 67 minutes, shaving 6 minutes off my previously (best) failed run-through time and got all 10 shots on target. Absolutely over the moon! This is unreal – I'm a quarter of the way there. Next, the 9-mile Speed March on Monday.

Day 218 – Sunday 29 January

Rest day.

I went for pizza and to the cinema with Tom (*Curry*) and Ben (*Whatley*) and then chilled!

LESSON 32

How the challenge of the Royal Marines attracts, cultivates, and goes on to produce unbelievable entrepreneurial talent through their cultural mantra: 'No Cuff Too Tough'.

Deeply engrained into the psychology of all Royal Marines (throughout the training process), is an ability and determination to overcome obstacles. They are encouraged to think 'outside the box' and come through adverse situations to achieve an objective, despite (at times) not having the adequate kit, equipment, or first-hand experience – or when confronted with an unfamiliar task.

For example, imagine being asked to do something technical that you know nothing about, or having to achieve an aim with limited or no equipment. Royal Marines are not only entrusted to make an attempt at completing the task, but are expected to excel and produce winning results, by thinking creatively and being innovative. This 'find a way, any way attitude' is called 'Cuffing It' in the Royal Marines.

Notably, when this concept is mentioned in the working environment, it acts as a stimulus reinforcing a culture of fluidity, which does not get deterred by sudden, unexpected changes in 'expectation', yet by no means encourages anyone to cut corners. It is about quickly coming to terms with change (Chapter 11), being flexible in approach, and possessing the confidence to back yourself to produce the goods in moments of uncertainty.

It is about achieving the mission or aim despite any foreseen or unforeseen setbacks. For example, if a Royal Marine is given a task that is beyond his remit or expertise, or something he has not had any training for, he will get on with it without a second thought, make no excuses, and work it out for himself or enlist the help of others. He will, in effect, 'Cuff It' – hence the term, 'No Cuff Too Tough' – and get that excellent result.

Billionaire Richard Branson emphasised this kind of mindset brilliantly, by saying, 'If somebody offers you an amazing opportunity, but you are not sure you can do it, say yes – then learn how to do it later.'

That embodies cuffing it! It is about controlling emotions and not becoming overwhelmed by new things; backing your capability through self-confidence; and applying yourself in a creative way until something is understandable, coherent, and then brought to fruition.

In a wider business sense, this culture is the embodiment of entrepreneurialism; instilling the confidence, resilience and tenacity to start new ventures by devising fresh, original, and ingenious ways to achieve excellence, despite the negative odds applied by adversity.

Key Points:

- In essence, Cuffing It is adapting to change and expectation instantly and finding new and creative ways to succeed, with often limited understanding and insight.
- It is about being entrepreneurial, and demonstrating the ability to realise the end goal, while confronting problems and solving them effectively.
- When we apply ourselves, we can do anything life throws at us. Stay responsive, adaptable and be confident in your ability.

35

COMMANDO TEST WEEK

Acquiring an unstoppable mindset

WEEK 31

Day 219 – Monday 30 January 2006

2nd Commando Test: The 9-mile Speed March! Just got back. We had 90 minutes to complete 9 miles with full kit and weapon. Apart from the first 3 miles, which were a hangout, the rest was easy. However, two lads failed who had only just joined our troop from Hunter to complete the 9-Miler, Tarzan and 30-miler. This appears to be a common occurrence, as some lads who joined us for the Endurance also failed it. It's like they are not fit enough, or don't want it bad enough.

I mean, how do you just give in at this stage of training? You go until you drop – fucking madness and weak-minded, if you ask me!

Once we arrived back at camp and in line with tradition, we were drummed into and escorted/paraded around camp by the Royal Marines Band. Those who are out and about in camp line the road and clap as you pass by, it's brilliant. This marks the transition from 'Troop' to 'Kings Squad'. I have always been the one stood on the sidelines clapping, now lads are clapping me. Amazing, by far the highlight of training and my life!

Day 220 – Tuesday 31 January

3rd Commando Test: The Tarzan Assault Course! Never in my life have I been as nervous as I am this morning – I have spewed up twice and can't even eat my breakfast, which is a major problem given the fact I am due on the Tarzan in 90 mins. This is the third and, in my opinion, second-hardest Commando Test and a huge hangout – 13 minutes of pure balls-out self-thrashing . . . best effort to pass the Test. ABSOLUTELY GOPPING!

Your time starts when you begin your descent down from the Death Slide. This is the worst part, as you feel like you're sliding down to your death, and such is true. As soon as your feet touch the ground, it is best effort as you start to navigate all the High Aerial Obstacles – ambulance ready at the bottom. It is pure Hurt Locker time – literally verging on exhaustion and all you can do is keep going.

I passed the bastard in 11:15 minutes! My best time ever, and in less than 24 hours, fingers crossed, I will be awarded the coveted Green Beret. All the lads around camp are wishing us luck. They stop us daily and ask us questions about various points in training; the same questions I once asked when I first arrived here – it really is unbelievable, and I would be lying if I said I didn't enjoy it and the attention.

Just had scran and we are now travelling by bus from Lympstone, straight to Okehampton Camp on Dartmoor in preparation to start the 30-miler tomorrow morning.

Day 221 – Wednesday 01 February

4th and final Commando Test: The 30-miler! I have just woken up at 04:30, well, if you can call it that – I managed to get around 2½ hours' sleep/rest from 02:00, but now have to be up to prep and weigh my kit and get breakfast, so I feel absolutely shocking and so fatigued. My legs are stiff and my right Achilles is fucked. However, I am in good spirits – positive, focused and aggressive – this is a big day.

It is still pitch-black outside, and my kit weighs around 51lbs + weapon, and I feel physically but not mentally broken. My thought process is this: keep moving, that's all it is, in its simplest terms. I just need to keep my left foot in front of my right and vice-versa, and that gets me there. Mentally, I have broken it down to that simple process and shut out the fact that I'm about to embark on 30 miles of pure hardship across the most horrendous undulating terrain in the UK.

Allow me to stress this: I underestimated the 30-miler . . . ABSOLUTELY MASSIVELY! After a final kit weighing and an amazingly motivational speech by a Colour Sgt, we set off at 07:30. I said to myself: 'Gareth, you are prepared to die.' The initial pace up a steep hill that veered off to the right was absolutely honking – my lower legs were solid with lactic acid. The awareness of what was now my reality hit me like a sledgehammer and my step-by-step coping strategy left my head faster than a fat kid chasing an ice-cream van!

Shit got real very quickly and I was blowing and inhaling air through every hole in my body, and we hadn't even done 1 mile! It was now purely 'hang in there, hang on, do not stop, or even contemplate quitting' – a matter of out-and-out survival mode.

We reached the 12-mile checkpoint (2) and I felt like I'd been running all night and day, and we weren't even halfway! Immediately upon stopping and quickly refuelling (sausage rolls, pasties, and gels, etc.) – the pain coming from my feet and the skin rubbed raw from my webbing (around my hips) was unbearable. I wanted to keep moving to make the pain go away, but at the same time, I wanted to lay down on a comfy bed and go to sleep. I was also really dehydrated from the other 3 Tests. Not good – a proper sorry, shit state!

At checkpoint 3, we had done 18 miles in roughly 4 hours and I was completely shattered – broken both mentally and physically. Cpl Rikards said, 'There will be a time during this next twelve miles where you will individually hit a wall, a black spot – resulting in a mental block. Your wall will have to be broken and knocked down if you're going to finish this test. Lads . . . hang onto your mental strength, your end goal, and that will guide you to the finish line. If you lose it upstairs, you'll lose it in your heart, and then quitting will become easy. Lads, in four hours' time, you'll have Green Berets on your heads.'

At the final checkpoint we had completed 24 miles . . . and I was about to meet MY WALL. Just prior, I was so exhausted that I had to pull myself up the side of a farmer's field by a partially downed, old and rusty barbed-wire fence – using it like a rope. The barbed-wire cut my hands to bits, but by that point I had gone past caring!

Anyway, at the 24-mile checkpoint, I was seriously exhausted and once again underestimated how far 6 miles was – well, in the state I was in anyway. This turned out to be a huge mistake. After refreshments and warm pasties, we cracked on to the finish. I was only 1 mile in and started to fall behind my section and then started hallucinating. The lads and Cpl Rikards had no option but to leave me behind, or the whole section would fail, coming in over the 8-hour limit.

Luckily, I had my troop PTI hang back and he kept talking to me and pushing me (not physically) along, but I was going down rapidly and getting slower and slower . . . basically, I was on the verge of piling in and therefore going to fail the Test. This was the worst I had ever felt in my life by a mile – my feet were numb, knee fucked, and my hands cut and bleeding all over – my body was failing, but mentally I couldn't let go. I was never going to quit – only death would take care of that in my mind. This was MY WALL, and it was an absolute epic to get through!

Probably around 2 miles from the bridge (*finish*), I remembered I had a tube of 16 Jaffa Cakes in my left day-sack pouch. I asked the PTI to take them out for me and he replied, 'Who the fuck has 16 Jaffa Cakes on them?' and laughed hysterically. Let me tell you, those 16 Jaffa Cakes earned me my Green Beret and ended the year-long nightmare I had been through.

I smashed all 16 down with a swill of water while still running (if you could call it that) and then set off like a mad man and unbelievably caught up with my section just as they were being formed into two singular ranks (*files*) to cross the bridge of dreams. The Troop Commander was there and said, 'Recruit Timmins, everything you have just done there and the adversity you have overcome is the epitome of the Commando Spirit and ethos – I am exceptionally proud of you, young man.'

I was now about to walk over the bridge that marks the end of training, the bridge I had dreamed about, obsessively visualised daily, and often wondered if I would ever cross. I could see it now and it was within touching distance.

My section crossed the bridge at 15:20, with 10 minutes to spare and all our other oppos who had set off before us, and arrived first, now lining the bridge and clapping us in. It was so emotional, I started crying – the best feeling ever!

Shortly after, we got presented first with our Commando Flashes – I looked at Tom (*Curry*) and he said, 'Look at them, mate.' After, I was handed my Green Beret. I was told to remove my Cap Comforter and replace it with my new Green Lid! It was a moment of sheer disbelief and amazement, and the sense of achievement I felt in that moment was so raw and overwhelming. After 34 weeks (*2 extra holding weeks*) of living with the oppressive and daily burden of failure – I am now, finally, a Royal Marines Commando!

I can genuinely say, hand on heart, I don't know how I have got through this. But I now stand here today as an elite fighter, widely regarded as one of the best soldiers in the world!

Day 222 – Thursday 02 February

First day as a Royal Marines Commando! Woke up with an horrific hangover after going to Jollies, the camp pub, with a few lads and getting absolutely steaming. Although I have a hangover from hell, I feel totally amazing – the best I have ever felt in my life. What an unbelievable feeling of achievement and relief. IT'S FINALLY OVER. That past year has been horrific!

I called my mum last night and said, 'I am now one of Her Majesty's Royal Marines Commandos,' and she started crying. She hasn't slept all week during my Tests.

I can't walk at all and my body is written off. I really don't care though, I am just so, so happy. We are going to Amsterdam tomorrow for a few days for our Kings Squad Piss Up. Can't wait, it will be complete carnage!

Day 223 – Sunday 05 February

Just back on camp from Amsterdam. We drank solid for 48 hours. We were all fighting on the bus there and I now have a black eye. Once we arrived, I fell asleep and Tom (*Curry*) shaved off my right eyebrow. The Training Team said absolutely no eyebrows to be shaved off with it being our Kings Squad pass out next week. I look a right twat.

I also got arrested in Amsterdam for having a piss in the street and had to pay 300 euros to get out of jail. Now I can't afford my troop photos and video.

LESSON 33

The distinction between the old and new me; coming to terms with what hadn't changed and discovering my 'Secret Weapon', which was always underlying.

By this week of training, I was so mentally exhausted and physically broken, I didn't have much more left in me. Reflecting on how significantly the course had changed me at the end of training was incomprehensible, as I was crippled with injury, fatigue, and still coming to terms with the end of what had been a living nightmare. However, one thing was absolutely certain, my connection to my previous life had been severed.

When I started my journey to join the Royal Marines, my perception of what mental strength meant to me was a Commando training that would ultimately strip me of all emotion: no fear of anything, no feelings of anxiety, no perceived vulnerabilities, and absolutely no understanding of personal uncertainty or lack of capability.

However, in reality, as we made our way up to start the Endurance Course, I felt anything but that – all those thoughts, feelings and emotions were raw, vivid and unrelentingly crippling. To my surprise and you could say horror, I still felt human, not superhuman.

The benefit of time has taught me that all the above 'natural' responses to the challenges of adversity, fear and uncertainty are so deep-rooted in our genetic make-up that no amount of training can rewire them. The skill – and what the Royal Marines taught me – was how to identify and manage them, and that is only possible when you undertake something large enough that it allows you the opportunity to explore the innermost workings of your being, and to find resolve.

It has taken me time, reflection, and intensive study to understand and analyse this distinction. At twenty-one years old, my expectation of mental strength was at odds with how I was feeling, going into the Commando Tests. I was, quite frankly, confused. However, I failed to acknowledge my *secret weapon* – one that had been under cultivation for the past thirty-three weeks and acquired arguably before – from birth; a reliable mental attribute that I took for granted.

My secret weapon was the '0.1% Mindset', which I had developed through exposure to a raw and extreme experience; a newly founded belief-system of inner strength, resolve and resilience. It was the ability to know that no matter how difficult times got, I would never give up – never quit; and the resolve to travel forward at all costs and meet adversity head on, despite the often self-defeating urge to stop when the emotional alarm bells would start ringing.

In terms of values
Come the end of training, the Royal Marines had ingrained in me the value and influence of *excellence*; to endeavour to learn something new each day, and to strive to do better than the previous day. They taught me the value of *integrity*; to

tell the truth, to be honest with my self-evaluations and live with an unwavering moral code. The value and power of *self-discipline and self-control*; to uphold standards and never opt for the easy option. Finally, to exercise *humility* in all situations and towards all people around the world, regardless of their social or cultural norms, and socio-economic standing.

In terms of spirit, mental strength, capability, and maturity
The Royal Marines gave me the *courage* to undertake any future challenges in my life and solidified within me the *self-confidence* to know, without a glimmer of uncertainty, that I could achieve whatever I set my 0.1% mindset to. They reinforced my *determination* to succeed in life and to demonstrate *selfless compassion* to all the people I continue to meet. Finally, the Royal Marines taught me to *smile in adversity* and that such periods of hardship are not only temporary, but should be welcomed as key opportunities to grow.

Key Points:

- When you decide to step outside the confines of your convenience and safety, you embark on a journey of self-discovery.
- As human beings, we all experience the same emotions; *exposure* to life *experiences* provides the tools we need to manage them in a way that can make us realise unbelievable feats of human capability, success and achievement.
- When all the lessons and insights come together, when

you align behaviour and apply yourself with consistency, the emergence of a 0.1% Mindset is produced. Once it is embedded, you will become unstoppable in your pursuit of success.

36

THE PSYCHOLOGY OF A ROYAL MARINES COMMANDO

A personal perspective

WEEK 32

Day 224 – Monday 06 February 2006

I never wrote another entry in my diary after Sunday. The following days up until my pass-out parade were tediously boring, with endless drill rehearsals consuming each day in preparation for our Kings Squad Pass-out Parade.

LESSON 34

A personal analysis into the make-up of a Royal Marines Commando Recruit Transformation.

The way in which CTCRM produce the end product, a Royal Marines Commando, is nothing short of a genius feat of humanistic engineering. The meticulous design of the course's structure and how it operates to instil self-belief and resilience to adversity in young people – and witnessing and experiencing that change in others and oneself – is absolutely mind-blowing.

Week 1 to Week 32

The distinction and transformation that occurs between Week 1 and Week 32 is astonishing. For example, at Week 1, a typical recruit is weary, disorientated, and incredibly vulnerable; their senses are under direct and persistent attack. However, come Week 30, that same recruit has become battle-hardened: a steely-eyed individual who can be witnessed running into camp at the very end of the Endurance Course, on the cusp of becoming a fully trained Commando.

It is the same kid, yet that nine to ten months' journey of intensive training and self-discovery has reinforced his belief-system; transforming the way in which he carries himself, physically resonating a posture of supreme confidence, ability and relentless focus and commitment. The young, naive-looking boy, who looked out of place wearing 'military fancy dress' in Week 1, nine months later resembles every inch the embodiment of a Royal Marines Commando.

A soldier's psychology of war

The general public are often perplexed as to how a man or woman can be willing to go to war, or into an intense hostile environment. It's not that fully trained Royal Marines and other military personal do not fear the potential consequences of war – the risk of serious injury and the possibility of death. These are outcomes that are impossible to resist contemplating.

Rather, the fascination and draw towards conflict comes from an irresistible sense of adventure and freedom; of conducting yourself and your daily responsibilities with purpose, in order to ensure survival. It could arguably be the rawest and most archaic form of life experience obtainable – one that affords the bearer the most vibrant form of sensual optimisation, which only ignites when navigating the boundary between life or death. It is this innate calling that draws recruits in and entices trained soldiers to go and experience war.

The threat and fear of getting injured, or killed, elicits the same emotional response for soldiers as it would civilians. However, here lies another distinction: throughout the training process to become a Royal Marines Commando, each recruit is trained to understand war and conflict – its tactical and strategic opportunities, the boundaries and limitations of weaponry, the shortcomings of the enemy, and so on. In that sense, it is no different from any other job in which you have no prior experience.

For instance, a new job may seem daunting at first, and elicit feelings of anxiety about the unknown. Yet, once you have been exposed to the culture, and undergone an element of training, which in turn creates working relationships and an understanding of role requirements, you begin to relax and settle in. Before you know it, going to work is no longer a process filled with apprehension, it becomes a subconscious daily process – the norm. That is exactly what happens with soldiers and their relationship with war and conflict.

What is a Royal Marine?
Royal Marines are transient creatures. Their behaviour can at times be completely at odds with the public perception and persona of a Royal Marines Commando – like the behaviour I witnessed being surrounded by the rugby lads as a small child. Yet, when it is time to stand up and perform the role for which Royal Marines are trained, no other bunch of people can turn it on and perform at a moment's notice with such rigour, seamless collaboration and intensity. It could be argued

that the process of training embeds a subconscious under-standing, a form of sixth sense that allows Royal Marines to instigate action through a form of instruction, as if connected subconsciously.

Training appears to forge a subtle cognitive bond between Royal Marines; an understanding that emerges when con-fronted with responsibility on complex training exercises and, more so, during hostile operations. For example, Royal Marines become intricately and emotionally aware of each other and appear to know, without hesitation, where to go, what to do and how to maintain the 'collective effort' to achieve an outcome that assures victory (life) over defeat (serious injury and/or death).

Remarkably, Royal Marines are publicly reserved in nature (minus alcohol). This demeanour is the physical representation afforded to someone who has arguably earned the ultimate prize and thus has nothing left to prove to themselves, or in a military context (barring UKSF). The completion of training provides a rite of passage that gives them all the answers about the self they require, and this erects an internal structure of self-confidence that endures timelessly.

Royal Marines, in general, persist in seeking goals and objec-tives (both collectively and personally) despite overwhelming adversity, setbacks and unequal odds distribution. They endeavour to succeed at all costs . . . and more often than not, they do.

Reflections on training

Some fifteen years on, and with every year that now passes, I find myself reflecting on the time I spent at Commando Training Centre Royal Marines. This always elicits the most amazing memories of a truly pivotal moment in my life – mixed with a sense of sheer disbelief at what I experienced there and, more importantly, how I managed to pull it off.

Although I am still tormented with periodic semi-nightmares of not completing training due to the Endurance Course – the same recurring dream of starting with 'heavy legs', only to be running out of time as I approach the end – I am so incredibly thankful for that brief nine- to ten-month period of what was undoubtedly the greatest experience of my life to date.

During the years after leaving Lympstone, the mere thought of training would conjure up traumatic emotions that didn't resemble what it actually felt like to be in that highly stressful training environment. Whereas now, such memories have been replaced with the greatest sense of adventure and emotional accomplishment I could ever have wished for, and shortly after leaving the Marines, I did resume my thirst for arduous challenges, achievements, and the pursuit of success.

For us recruits in 2005, our training created uncomfortable and raw emotions of uncertainty, which cultivated fear with an element of crippling doubt; but also excitement and idolisation, which flowed through us all to varying degrees. Back then, I was searching for answers and at the tender age of twenty, I managed to select a path that would turn into a long and treacherous road, eventually answering all my questions, and slaying the demons acquired during my rugby years. This journey was filled with adversity, often misery, and packed with young men trying desperately to attain what was perceived to be an impossible dream.

I remember vividly during the first few weeks at Lympstone, the shock of capture, the instant lack of control, and the realisation of what was in front of us, transcended our subconscious. It was physically manifested in every man's body language and facial expressions: we were like a herd of sheep, startled and scared, frightened and unsure of which way to run, who to speak to, or what to say.

That adventure was, and is, the most amazingly raw and uncertain, harrowing, and exhilarating quest of self-discovery I believe any man or woman can (with free-will) undertake in their lifetime. Now, aged thirty-six, to think I'll never have the opportunity to experience such a mental and physical test again – due to my age – can often make me feel incredibly sad.

I recall being crippled in pain at the 12-mile checkpoint during the 30-miler; carrying a left ACL rupture, a tear in my right Achilles, and deprived of sleep, whilst lame with blisters and webbing abrasions. I thought that nobody would ever realise the magnitude of what we had gone through there. The tears were streaming down my face and I was suffering from a state of emotional despair – but like all the obstacles and adversity that training had thrown at us, I suppose myself and the other lads who passed valued the 'end goal' more than the often overwhelming urge to stop or to quit.

Out of the fifty-one hopefuls, only eleven originals finished training together – earning the coveted Green Beret.

The anti-climax
The gradual adaptation to the environment, the culture and the lifestyle changed me beyond belief. At the end of training, like in many positions of privilege, I didn't realise the magnitude of what I had achieved and therefore I didn't appreciate it, nor fully acknowledge it.

The progression from a civilian to a Royal Marines Commando felt like a lifetime, yet despite all the ups and downs – the exhilarating highs and the depths of despondency – I was about to get my Green Beret and Commando Flashes.

However, all too soon, the sense of euphoria dispersed as the novelty of my title cascaded away.

It is only with the benefit of hindsight and maturity that I have been able to acknowledge fully the enormity of what was achieved by marching off the parade square in February 2006, and how that moment and the Royal Marines in general not only changed me, but also saved my life.

What attracted me and others to the Royal Marines?
In one sense, our world is socially constructed in a way (through combative pastimes and pursuits) that facilitates our innate human urges to fight, protect and bear arms. However, such activities clash with a modern society that upholds the morally acceptable notion of peace and harmony, over the morally toxic reality of war and conflict. Yet, we still can't resist them.

The eleven originals who passed training were all drawn to war and conflict in some form, and arguably wanted to take part, not for Queen or Country, but to experience life's ultimate adventure. A purpose to being alive that is undiluted, and attempts to preserve life while defeating another faction of humanity in the most ruthless of ways.

In my opinion, and that of many of the lads I have worked with, this is the fatal attraction – the potential experience of being engaged in war. The fine line where one mitigates the boundary between life and death is what entices young people to elite military units, like a fly to a luminescent lamp.

It is in these moments when you feel the most alive and attuned to your environment. However, this poison is highly addictive and too often costs people their lives, and often their physical and mental health to varying degrees.

In loving memory

Sadly, the Training Team's casualty briefing we received upon the completion of Final Ex came true (Day 195). Within three years of leaving the Commando Training Centre, Tom Curry, Ben Whatley, and Ben Reddy were tragically killed in Afghanistan.

Some years after, once I had left the Royal Marines, I bumped into another former troop member, Craig Wilson, at an hotel in Cairo. He was a member of the point section who went into Jugroom Fort, in Afghanistan, and was hit three times in his vest (which saved his life), but took a round through his wrist. This was during the infamous Royal Marines attack in Helmand Province in 2007, which resulted in lads flying back into a Taliban compound strapped on the wings of Apache Gunships, to rescue the body of a fallen Royal Marine, Lance Cpl Mathew Ford.

Being honest with you now, my nerve went, especially when shortly after Tom was killed, Ben Whatley and Ben Reddy were both fatally injured. We were dropping like flies and I was convinced my number was up. I realised that if Tom Curry – the Commando Medallist – could get killed, then anyone could.

Memories

When I was desperately trying to join the Royal Marines, with a ruptured left Anterior Cruciate Ligament, asthma and eczema, I never imagined I would have lived the life I have today. The Royal Marines were crucial for me at that point in my life.

When I left training and the Royal Marines for life outside, it came with a huge anti-climax for me; I felt extremely negative about the experience, but now I have unreserved respect for what they did for me and the positive influence it continues to play in everything I do.

The Royal Marines, I hope, would be proud of the man I am today and how I live my life, which is defined by internal discipline and self-sacrifice – an embodiment of what constitutes the qualities of the Commando Spirit.

That experience in 2005, going through such hardship, adversity, and uncertainty has turned me into a self-assured man with a determination to explore the world and a desire to have no regrets. I welcome a challenge, knowing I can rely on the traits instilled by the Royal Marines to face all difficult tasks with the mental ability and confidence to succeed.

I still yearn for opportunities to grow and better understand myself, whether physical, mental or educational, and often find myself inviting mental discomfort in the form of arduous challenges, fully acknowledging that emotional adversity is not only momentary, but a notable part of the journey. With sacrifice comes success and achievement, and I find these two outcomes very addictive. It is what makes reaching the finish line so worthwhile – and that is the take-home message from this book.

Finally, as hard as it was training to be a Royal Marines Commando, I will never regret becoming a member of the 0.1 per cent.

SELECT BIBLIOGRAPHY

Bringslimark, T., Hartig, T., & Grindal Patil, G., (2007). 'Psychological benefits of Indoor Plants in Workspaces: Putting Experimental Results into Context' in *HortScience*, Vol. 42: Issue 3, pp. 518–87. Available at: https://doi.org/10.21273/HORTSCI.42.3.581 (accessed 18 May 2019).

Ericsson, K.A., Krampe, R.T., & Tesch-Römer, C. (1993). 'The role of deliberate practice in the acquisition of expert performance', *Psychological Review*, 3, pp. 363–406. Exercise 11, pp. 212–22.

Ericsson, K.A., & Harwell, K. (2019). 'Deliberate practice and proposed limits on the effects of practice on the acquisition of expert performance: Why the original definition matters and recommendations for future research', *Frontiers in Psychology*, 10, 2396.

Gladwell, M. (2008). *Outliers. The Story of Success*, Little, Brown and Company, New York.

Hardy, D. (2012). *The Compound Effect*, CDS Books, New York.

Kaplan, R., & Kaplan, S. (1989). *The Experience of Nature: A Psychological Perspective*, Cambridge University Press, New York.

Kaplan, S. (1995). 'The restorative benefits of nature: Toward an integrative framework', *Journal of Environmental Psychology*, 15:169–82. DOI: 10.1016/0272-4944(95)90001-2.

Kubler-Ross, E. (1969). *On Death and Dying*, Macmillan Publishing Company, New York.

Tajfel, H., & Turner, J. (2001). 'An integrative theory of intergroup conflict' in M.A. Hogg & D. Abrams (eds.), *Key Readings in Social Psychology. Intergroup Relations: Essential Readings*, Psychology Press, pp. 94–109.

Maslow, A.H. (1970). *Motivation and Personality* (2nd ed.), Harper and Row, New York.

McClure, B.A. (1987). 'Metaphoric illumination in groups', *Small Group Behavior*, 18(2): pp. 179–87.

Ulrich, R.S. (1983). 'Aesthetic and Affective Response to Natural Environment' in Chambers University of Technology. Available at: DOI: 10.1007/978-1-4613-3539-9_4 (accessed 10 September 2020).

Wilson, Edward O. (1984). *Biophilia*, Harvard University Press, Cambridge, MA.

Zhang, Z., & Zypnur, M.J. (2015). 'Physiological functioning and employee health in organizations' in: Colarelli, S.M., & Arvey, R.D. (eds.), 'The biological foundations of organizational behaviour', University of Chicago Press, Chicago, pp. 139–67. Available at http://press.uchicago.edu/ucp/books/book/chicago/B/bo18990975.html (accessed 18 May 2019).

GLOSSARY

Military terms

4-tonner A military truck used to transport military personnel and large amounts of kit stores.

Admin or Administration Basically, becoming fully independent. For example, washing clothes, ironing, cleaning, and polishing boots. As well as maintaining weapon effectiveness, field kit, and so on.

Amphibious A vehicle that is suited for both land and sea. Also, a term used to describe military forces arriving on land from the sea. For example, an amphibious cliff assault.

APWT Annual Personal Weapon Test.

Ashore A term used when leaving camp, or going out drinking: 'Are we going ashore (out)?'

AT Adventure Training.

Back bearing A compass bearing taken pointing to the exact opposite of the direction of travel.

Beasting Military slang for a physically demanding fitness session. It is a term that is interchangeable, but is often attached to moments when recruits have messed up and have thus received a harsh punishment in the form of physical exertion.

Bergen A high capacity military backpack/rucksack that allows military personal the ability to carry substantial amounts of personal and team kit.

Boresighting A process by which the axis of a gun bore and the line of a gunsight are made parallel, or are made to converge on a point.

Bottom Field (Assault Course) is a harsh and rugged area of grassland littered with obstacles, gradual inclines, high obstacle apparatus and 30ft ropes. It is at the bottom/south end of camp and adjacent to the railway track (that brings recruits to Commando Training Centre) and the notorious 'Mud Flats' of the river Exe.

CBA Combat Body Armour.

CBRN Chemical, Biological, Radiological and Nuclear.

Chit A short official note. For example, a sick/doctor's note.

CIA Central Intelligence Agency (USA).

Close Target Recce (CTR) is conducted to identify means of access, exfiltration, enemy living arrangements, morale, transport, weapon capabilities and residential and/or commercial constructions and potential structural vulnerabilities.

Concealment Protection from observation (only).

Cpl Corporal.

Creamed in Slang for hypothetically 'collapsing' due to excessive exercise, alcohol, or illness.

CWS Common Weapon Sight – an image-intensification night vision scope.

Drill A fundamental part of military training regimes worldwide. It enables senior military personnel to move troops from one place to another in an orderly fashion. It also aids disciplinary training by instilling behavioural habits of precision and response to orders.

Exfil Exfiltration – extracting/removing military personal from an area when operating in hostile environments.

Flap Slang for worry and/or panic.

Flash/Flashes Slang for outbursts of anger, rage and/or frustration.

Foundation Block The first accommodation space that recruits reside in during the first two weeks of training. Here, recruits begin to transition into military life at Lympstone; it is an open dormitory with over 50 single beds and lockers. During this period recruits are stripped back and taught how to hand wash and iron their clothing and bedding, as well as how to shower, clean the accommodation, make their beds, and prepare for inspection.

FPGRM Fleet Protection Group Royal Marines, now called 43 Commando.

FRV Final Rendezvous (point).

FSRT Fleet Standby Rifle Troop.

Funny old thing Slang for 'Surprise, Surprise . . .'

Galley A cooking/eating area aboard a ship. However, in the Royal Marines, this terminology is used to describe all military establishment kitchen/eating places, regardless of whether they are sea or land based.

Gash Slang for rubbish/poor quality.

Gen Genuine, it's a term used to establish if someone is being serious, telling the truth – like using the term 'honestly'.

Gipping/Gopping/Honking/Leaping Slang for horrible, disgusting – something to be avoided. For example, food, exercise, or a person based on looks.

Grots Slang for accommodation.

(Shot) Grouping The closer the shots are on target to each other measures the combination of a person's skill when applying all the marksmanship principles – the smaller the grouping, and the less erratic the shots on target, the better the marksman.

Gucci Usually refers to an item of kit. It means something is of quality, desirable and/or looks very good/the best.

Hanging out Slang for exhaustion through physical exercise. It is, however, used to label yourself or someone who is hungover, ill or in poor physical 'aesthetic' condition, as well as someone not particularly pleasing on the eye.

Harbour (patrol/triangular) This allows military personnel to establish an All-round Defensive Position when deployed in the field. Other benefits include Mutual Support, Interlocking Arcs of Fire, ease of Command and Control and ease of Admin Support – personal hygiene, cooking, maintaining operational kit and equipment, and sleeping.

Heartbreak Lane An infamous country lane – the base of which is situated across the road to the north of camp. It is the main thoroughfare up to Woodbury Common, and marks the start or finish of many arduous physical tests during training, including the Endurance Course, where all Royal Marines recruits take note of the iconic tree-mounted sign: 'It's Only Pain . . . 500M To Go.'

Heli/Helo Helicopter.

H-Hour The hour an attack is to be launched, an assault wave is to land, or a movement is to begin.

Hoofing Slang for brilliant, good, amazing, etc.

Hoop Slang for arse.

Hurt Locker A desperate state of physical and mental discomfort.

IMF/C A collective and synchronised form of exercise circuit that improves fitness, motor skills, and demands fast and technically efficient body movements at the sound of orders.

Infil Infiltration – a point/area where troops pass through an opening in the enemy's defensive position(s).

Instinct A natural or inherent aptitude (genetic/from birth), impulse or tendency that is mediated at a subconscious level.

Insurgent(s) A person fighting against a government, or an invading force.

INT Intelligence.

Iron Sight Fixed iron sights are non-telescopic and typically composed of two component sights, formed by metal blades: a rear sight mounted perpendicular to the line of sight and consisting of some form of *notch* (open sight) or *aperture* (closed sight); and a front sight that is a *post, bead or ring*. When aligned, they assist in the accurate aiming of a firearm.

Jack Military slang for someone who only thinks of themselves; a label nobody wants to have.

Jerry Can A robust, pressed-steel liquid container, typically painted Olive Green.

Kings Squad is the culmination of 32 weeks' Royal Marines Commando training. This transition and title has been given to troops at Lympstone since 1918, and marks a transitional period from recruit to trained Royal Marine.

Kit Muster A key element of a recruit's field 'morning routine', which ensures that they maintain the highest possible standards of personal administration whilst deployed. They must lay out (in a particular way) every single piece of their equipment (including rifle stripped down) in a clean and maintained condition, ready for inspection by their section commander. Failure here results in the 'Flank', which in diplomatic terms means corrective advice followed by corrective action – such as stress positions, press-ups, burpees and other forms of 'undesirable' physical exercise.

Lashed up Slang for 'given'.

Line bearing means 'As the crow flies'.

Line of Departure is the starting position for an attack on enemy positions.

Magazine In a military context, a magazine or mag is an ammunition storage and feeding device that attaches to and from a Firearm.

Map to Grid (get rid), Grid to Map (add) is a simple mnemonic to help you remember how to make the correct adjustment after either taking a bearing using a magnetic compass, or taking a grid bearing from a map.

Mission A specific task or duty assigned to an individual, team, troop or unit, and so on.

NAAFI Navy, Army and Air Force Institutes.

Nails Slang for hard or tough.

NBC Nuclear, Biological, Chemical.

Nod(s) Slang for recruit(s), because their heads are always nodding due to sleep deprivation.

Oggin Naval slang for the sea/water.

Oppo A fellow soldier, work partner, colleague or friend.

PO Number A personal service number used to identify a soldier within a large group.

Pays To Be a Winner A competitive and feared fitness scenario created by the Training Team, where recruits must set off from a starting point towards an object in the distance, and return as fast as possible. The winner can drop out of the following round . . . and on it goes until you are successful, or there is no one left to compete against.

Phys Biff Someone who is terrible at physical exercise – struggles, is always at the rear, or must get in the safety wagon (during training).

Piling In Slang for hypothetically 'collapsing' due to excessive exercise, alcohol, or illness.

Poncho (Tent) A tactical waterproof shelter that attaches to the base of trees using paracord via two points, and which is then attached to the ground by inserting tent pegs into grommets along the sides. This method of shelter houses two military personnel whilst deployed in the field.

Prone Position is a body position in which a person lies flat on the ground (chest down).

PRR Personal Role Radio.

GLOSSARY

PT Physical Training.

Radio Voice Procedure Techniques used to clarify, simplify, and standardise spoken communications over two-way radios.

Raid An operation, generally small scale, involving a swift penetration of hostile territory to secure information, confuse the enemy, or destroy their installations. The operation ends with a tactical withdrawal upon completion of the assigned mission.

Rats Military slang for someone who is undesirable to look at . . . ugly.

Recce Reconnaissance.

(Rope) Regain encompasses the execution of six key technical positions, which need to be performed from a hanging position in order to 'regain' the traverse position on top of a rope.

Reveille Wake-up time for personnel in the Armed Forces.

Ridge Raider Fast raiding assault craft.

Rig Slang for clothing.

Round (the bullet casing) refers to the unfired cartridge, because the bullet is only the projectile tip that is released when the round is ignited.

Route Card is a document that is created to aid navigation and route planning.

RV Rendezvous – a position/location where people are to meet.

SAS Special Air Service: UK Special Forces.

SBS Special Boat Service: UK Special Forces.

Sea State The general condition of the surface of a large body of water, which is measured on a scale of 1–9, with 1 being 'Calm' and 9 being 'Phenomenal'.

Section Attack An attack/raid utilising the strategic collaboration of different sections (6–12 soldiers).

Sentry A position, most often strategic, where a soldier is stationed to keep guard, control access, and/or provide an early warning capability when confronted by enemy forces.

SF Special Forces.

Sgt Sergeant.

Sickbay Medical Centre.

Simunition Ammunition that if fired through modified military weapons is characterised as having a 'non-lethal' paintball tip (bullet).

Speed March A combination of marching and running that enables the efficient and controlled movement of troops over specific distances. This method of movement allows soldiers to cover significant distances with kit, permitting them to arrive at their destination in a physical state to fight and defeat the enemy.

Stop Short Location A predesignated location that is selected 'short' of an intended target location. A stop short location is factored into each mission to allow troops to conduct a soak period, as well as carry out reconnaissance of an intended site, to ensure it is safe before committing more troops or to engagement.

SUSAT Sight Unit Small Arms Trilux – a 4 × telescopic sight, with tritium-powered illumination.

Thinned/Thin Out Slang for cut away, finished early, asked to leave, or left.

Thrashing Like beasting, punishment inflicted by another person by means of physical exhaustion. For example, press-ups, sprints, stress-positions and so on. Can also be used to express one's ability to push themselves to their limits physically. For instance, I've just beasted/thrashed myself in the gym.

Threaders Slang for gutted, angry and upset – a phase used when mourning.

Top-flapped The process of opening the top part (flap) of a bergen or daysack and adding more kit or equipment before re-covering (closing) and ratcheting down securely with the 'top flap', in preparation to move via foot (commonly), or transport (less-commonly).

Tracer (rounds) Bullets that are built with a pyrotechnic charge in the base allowing the bullet to light up in the dark. It is used to provide essential information to soldiers in contact during dark hours, by highlighting the location of enemy positions, and thus coordinating collective and strategic suppressive return fire.

Trench Foot A condition affecting the feet, which is caused by prolonged exposure to wet, unsanitary, and cold conditions. For example, keeping feet submerged in water, like wearing wet boots. A condition clinically known as Immersion Foot Syndrome.

Troop A group of recruits up to on average 50–60 people.

Uber Slang for 'very'.

Weapon Bore Sighting A method of visually pre-aligning a firearm barrel's bore axis with the target, in order to more easily zero the gunsight (optical or iron sights).

Woodbury Common is in East Devon, England, and is a vast area of common land adjacent to the village of Woodbury. It forms a massive part of the outdoor field exercise training area for the Royal Marines during training.

Yomp Your Own Marching Pace – a term used by the Royal Marines that describes long-distance marches carrying full and often heavy amounts of kit.

Zeroing a firearm The process of adjusting the sights to the weapon barrel, so the bullet may be placed at the exact point of the sight picture.

Psychological and other terms

ACL Anterior Cruciate Ligament – one of the key ligaments that stabilises the knee joint.

Attentional Resources The amount of attention available to perform cognitive tasks that require effort, where the ability to distribute attention is under an individual's control.

Bias Cause to feel or show inclination or prejudice for or against someone or something.

Biophilia According to biologist E.O. Wilson, humans possess an innate and genetically determined affinity to connect with the natural world.

Cognitive Cognition (mental processing) of the brain, responsible for perception, memory, judgement, and reasoning.

Disillusionment The feeling of disappointment one experiences when discovering that something is not as good or accurately represented as initially believed or perceived.

Executive Function A set of cognitive processes that are necessary for the cognitive control of behaviour: selecting and successfully monitoring behaviours that facilitate the attainment of chosen goals. For example, planning and executing a degree at university. Human beings are the only living organisms that possess this ability.

Extrinsic Motivation Reward-driven behaviour. For example, doing something for praise, fame or financial gain.

Extrovert An outgoing, socially confident person.

Fortitude Courage in pain or adversity.

Gene(s) A unit of heredity that is transferred from parent to offspring.

Heuristics Simple efficient rules, learned or inculcated by the evolutionary process that explain how people make decisions, form judgements, and solve complex problems and/or with incomplete information.

(Cognitive) Impulse A sudden urge or desire to do something.

Innate A characteristic existing in an organism from birth.

Interpersonal Relationships or communication between people.

Intersubjectivity The interchange (common agreement) of thoughts and feelings – both conscious and unconscious, between two people or more.

Intrinsic Motivation Doing something that brings enjoyment and relaxation, rather than something that offers any obvious external reward.

Introvert A reserved, quiet person who is often considered to be socially shy.

Masculinity Qualities or attributes regarded as characteristic of men.

Mental Resilience The ability to cope with crisis and discomfort, or return to a pre-existing state of functioning, during a crisis both mentally and emotionally. In essence, it is one's ability to protect the self against the negative effects of stressors.

Meso-level Research/observations that focus on people who make up communities or organisations.

Micro-level Research/observations that typically focus on an individual in their social setting, or a small group of individuals in a particular social context.

Nuanced Subtle shades of meaning or expression.

OCD Obsessive Compulsive Disorder.

Pain Barrier A state of pain elicited through physical exertion. By pushing through this threshold, pain begins to diminish – more commonly known as the 'second wind'.

Perception The way in which something – for example, external information – is regarded, understood, and/or interpreted (subjectively).

Philosophy A theory or attitude that acts as a guiding principle for behaviour.

Prejudice Preconceived opinion that is not based on reason or actual experience/evidence.

Proximal Learning The zone of the closest, most immediate psychological development for learners.

PTSD Post Traumatic Stress Disorder.

Reality The state of things as they actually exist – how we perceive them to be, as opposed to an idealistic or notional (theory) idea of them.

Reinforcement In 'Behavioural Psychology' reinforcement is a consequence applied to a scenario that will strengthen an organism's future behaviour. In short, positive reinforcement is the process of encouraging or establishing a belief or desirable pattern of behaviour.

Savannah-type Environment A mixed woodland–grassland ecosystem characterised by the sufficient separation of trees, allowing light to reach the ground.

Self-adulation Displaying an excessively high opinion of oneself or one's importance.

Self-discipline The ability to control one's feelings and overcome one's weaknesses.

Self-esteem Confidence in one's own worth or abilities.

Self-regulate Emotional self-regulation is the ability to respond to the ongoing demands of experience with a range of emotions in a manner that is socially tolerable and sufficiently flexible to permit spontaneous reactions, as well as the ability to delay spontaneous reactions when needed.

Socially Constructed A theory that people develop knowledge of the world in a social context, and that most of what we come to believe and perceive about reality is based on shared assumptions. In this notion, as society changes, so too can our perception and belief-system about things like masculinity, gender identity and gender equality, for example.

Social Intelligence The perceptual capacity to know oneself and to know others. It develops through experience and interactions with others, as well as by learning from success and failure in social (communication) settings – also known as 'tact'.

Social Structures The distinctive, stable arrangement of institutions whereby human beings in a society interact and live together.

Solace Comfort or consolation in times of distress or sadness.

Stereotype A widely held, fixed and oversimplified image or idea of a particular type of person or thing.

Stimuli A thing or event that evokes a specific functional reaction in an organ or tissue. For example, like your ears responding to sound.

Stress Reduction Theory (SRT) The theory of how exposure to natural environments can reduce psychological stress.

Subconscious A part of the mind that is active, influencing one's actions and feelings, but which is not in focal awareness.

Theory A system of belief or ideas intended to explain the outcome of something, or justify a course of action.

Traits Specific characteristics of an organism. Traits can be determined by our genes or the environment, or the interaction between the two.

Visualisation The mental formulation of an image or future outcome.

ACKNOWLEDGEMENTS

To my son, Jax. Thank you for being my driving force during the past six years and holding me to account. I love you dearly and I hope this book both inspires you as you grow and makes you eternally proud of your dad, as I am of you.

To my mum, without you giving me the diary, this book would not have been possible – a snapshot in history unrecorded. What I thought initially was a truly bizarre gift turned into my proudest and most fulfilling achievement to date; thank you Mum – I love you lots.

To my dad, thank you for all your support, guidance and investment during my rugby years. Your mentorship and that exposure to those high-level environments nurtured and reinforced my mindset in preparation for the challenges I encountered in the Royal Marines.

To my beloved Grandma, I have the fondest memories of a wonderful loving, safe and secure childhood, and that is due to both you and Grandad. Thank you for always seeing the best in me and loving me unconditionally. I have no doubt that you are significantly responsible for the person who has written this full account of the past thirty-six years.

To my Grandad, my hero. You were in my thoughts every step of the way throughout training and ever since. I wish you could have stayed around a little longer to witness me going on to do what you had proposed I should.

To my family, I may not always show it, but I am deeply

enriched by your care and attention. I would not be the person I have become without your support over the years, your patience, and enduring belief in my capabilities. Thank you for being you.

To my dear and best friend, Chris Snowden. The best of friends – brothers for almost thirty years – thank you for always believing in me, mate, and for supporting my every venture with my best intentions at heart. You fulfil everything (unreservedly) that one could wish for in a friend. Thank you.

To Ann Hopton, my academic mentor, the most special person I have ever met. A person who gives unconditionally without the expectation of anything in return. Your mentorship, advice, patience and concern undoubtedly guided me through my studies and helped me unpick the diary into thirty-four lessons that I cannot believe I have written. Thank you, Ann – you have no idea how much I appreciate everything you have done for me during the past eight years.

To my literary agent, Nick Walters. I cannot thank you enough for reviewing my work and taking it on. This book is solely down to your foresight and vision; the idea of adding the thirty-four lessons was your brainchild. It not only made immediate sense, but it transformed the book comprehensively into something that I will be forever proud of having done. Nick, you are an incredible talent and have emerged as a fantastic friend.

To my editor, Cameron Myers, and the publishing team at Hodder & Stoughton. Thank you for believing in the concept and seeing the value in my work. I could not have wished for a better publishing house, editor, and team to take on my life's work. Thank you dearly for all you have done and continue to do for my book.

To my copyeditor, Barry Johnston, thank you for treating my

manuscript with such care and attention to detail. Your input on the finished product has been truly remarkable and greatly appreciated.

To Ben Williams. Royal, you unlocked the door to an industry that is inherently fickle for an emerging new author trying to make progress and bring a book to publication. The selflessness and humility that you offered by connecting me to Nick embody the values that run deep in the Royal Marines, and make the bond so special. I wish you every success with your book *Commando Mindset* and all that comes after. An enduring friendship forged.

To Gareth Vause, the guy that lurks in the shadows, yet whose impact is everything. Thank you, Gareth, for your unique quality of care and attention to my work and businesses. You are an incredible talent, a graphic designer and friend with an unbelievable eye for detail. I appreciate everything you do and look forward to what the future holds.

To Ed Stirzaker, I am so eternally grateful that our paths crossed whilst soul-searching together in 2005. Although we eventually took separate paths, I knew then I had stumbled across someone incredibly special. Thank you for your unconditional support and for the care, interest and input you put into this project.

To Dr Caroline Henderson – the absolute best tutor a final year student could wish for. Thank you for being an integral part of this journey. Your support in my final year of university was incredible. More importantly, your expert and honest review of my lessons has not only added crucial value to this book, but has given me the confidence to explore further education.

Finally, to all the original members of 900TP and our Training Team of 2005/06. Thank you for giving me my greatest and most fulfilling memories. Much love and respect!